M&A in the Middle East

A Practical Regional Guide

Consulting Editor **Michael Kortbawi**

Consulting editor
Michael Kortbawi

Managing director
Sian O'Neill

Commissioning editor
Katherine Cowdrey

Editorial services director
Carolyn Boyle

Production manager
Paul Stoneham

Group publishing director
Tony Harriss

M&A in the Middle East: A Practical Regional Guide
is published by
Globe Law and Business
Globe Business Publishing Ltd
New Hibernia House
Winchester Walk
London SE1 9AG
United Kingdom
Tel +44 20 7234 0606
Fax +44 20 7234 0808
Web www.globelawandbusiness.com

Printed and bound by Gomer Press

ISBN 9781905783632

Table of contents

Introduction

Michael Kortbawi
Bin Shabib & Associates (BSA) LLP

1. Introduction

The Middle East and North Africa (MENA) has been a hub for trade and commerce throughout history, originally comprising an integral part of the spice trading routes and serving as a link to the West for the Silk Road. The overland routes through the MENA region were eventually exhausted due to the efficiency of water routes, and the region remained relatively quiet on the commercial front until the discovery of oil in the early 20th century. Over the past three decades the corporate market has re-emerged to become once again one of the most lucrative places to conduct business worldwide.

The MENA region's flourishing financial environment attracts a diverse customer base from every jurisdiction, providing businesses with expansive opportunities and profits unlikely to be achieved elsewhere in the world. The wide variety of corporate infrastructure options, the growing availability of business facilities and advantageous cost and tax structures have all made the MENA region desirable for multinational companies looking to expand into emerging markets.

The traditional structure of family businesses in the region is also evolving. Family businesses have begun expanding their infrastructure and goals to become sophisticated global players, where once they were only local entities surviving for just two or three generations. Family businesses are now attracting customers and business from around the world. Corporate governance standards in family businesses are also being developed and implemented at a feverish pace, boosting companies' profiles to compete with their international counterparts.

However, rapid regional growth also brings many challenges, particularly since legislation has not kept up with the fast-moving economic changes. Both foreign and local M&A practitioners have called for the implementation of stronger, more consistent corporate laws. There is also a need for the application of international best standards and practices in corporate transactions and corporate governance. From the outside, the MENA region appears to be rife with corruption and unpredictable regime changes. The perception is that the rule of law is applied inconsistently, and that there is little to no transparency. The region's growth has also created a steep learning curve for companies and practitioners who wish to enter and thrive in the emerging MENA marketplace. This book provides a comparative guide to M&A in 11 countries across the MENA region: Bahrain, Egypt, Jordan, Kuwait, Lebanon, Morocco, Oman, Qatar, Saudi Arabia, Tunisia and the United Arab Emirates. Each country must be viewed not only as a separate jurisdiction, but also as a dynamic part of the region as a whole.

This book is intended to be used as a comprehensive reference tool for both lawyers and non-lawyers. It has been written to target seasoned M&A practitioners, as well as directors, shareholders and other parties who are approaching M&A transactions in the MENA region for the first time. It introduces readers to each jurisdiction's business practices and provides country-specific tips for navigating a variety of M&A options. An outline of each jurisdiction's legal system and laws ensures that both practitioners and parties to M&A transactions are made aware of compliance issues, due diligence practices and limitations on foreign ownership in every jurisdiction. The information contained herein will assist readers to make informed decisions and develop effective strategies regarding business deals in the region.

Each chapter focuses on a single jurisdiction's approach to M&A, including the legal and governmental limitations of merging or acquiring companies. The chapters are written by legal practitioners with local M&A knowledge in their respective jurisdictions. These experts have worked extensively in M&A transactions and bring a rich background that cannot be matched by practitioners who merely research local M&A transactions without having experienced the language, practical situations and cultural nuances of each jurisdiction.

The official language of each jurisdiction in this book is modern standard Arabic, which is also the official language of the regulatory and legal systems in each jurisdiction. The authors are well versed in civil law and have practised in the region for a number of years. The insider approach to each chapter allows for not only a comprehensive overview of M&A practices, but also invaluable experiences and case studies on how M&A activity is carried out in each jurisdiction. Readers can be confident that using this book will enable them to navigate the basics of each jurisdiction's specific systems in regards to M&A procedures.

The structure of each chapter includes a detailed evaluation of due diligence, merger agreements, pre-merger agreements, the scope of M&A agreements, important clauses in M&A agreements, choice-of-law clauses and dispute resolution clauses. Each chapter also includes an analysis of post-merger issues that may arise and individual case studies from past M&A transactions.

2. Legal structures in the region

Most countries in the MENA region operate under civil law systems. A civil law legal system is codified and is therefore somewhat easier to negotiate for outsiders than a common law legal system, which is based mainly on precedents. The civil law legal system in the MENA region is an amalgamation of the French legal tradition and Islamic *Sharia* laws derived from the *Quran* and the *Sunnah*. *Sharia* law is developed by Islamic scholars and leaders who make decisions by consensus regarding legal issues that are not directly addressed by the *Quran* or the *Sunnah*. The *Sharia* laws in the MENA jurisdictions are generally codified as part of the main legislative body.

This union of different judicial cultures is manifested as a dual legal structure of secular civil law courts and religious courts based on Islamic traditions. Naturally, there are nuances particular to each jurisdiction's legal system. For instance, Morocco's hybrid structure is also influenced by Jewish traditions. The legal system in Jordan contains some areas of law that still reflect the early Ottoman traditions in the region. Similarly, Bahrain's legal system also includes some traditional tribal laws specific to that jurisdiction. Tunisia distinguishes itself in that *Sharia* law was abolished in 1956 – the *Sharia* courts were dismantled at that time, but *Sharia* law still influences some personal status areas of Tunisian law.

Saudi Arabia is the only country represented in this book that has a vastly different legal system from the others. *Sharia* law is used in Saudi Arabia, but it is not memorialised in any formal code. This can lead to uncertainty in the application and content of Saudi Arabian laws, and the lack of judicial precedent also makes legal interpretation problematic. Recognising these challenges, in 2010 the Saudi Arabian government announced its intention to codify *Sharia* law in order to provide more consistency and clarity to the rule of law.

The differences among the laws of the MENA countries make it imperative to consult with local legal advisers at all stages of a business transaction. Legal advisers should not advise on transactions in the overall region due to the specificities present in each jurisdiction.

3. Evolution of family businesses in the region

Much of the growth in the Gulf Cooperation Council (GCC) over the past 50 years has been thanks to family businesses. Today, family businesses comprise between 75% and 80% of the GCC market, fostering a healthy commercial environment.[1] Family-owned companies in the region have traditionally enjoyed limited international competition and access to vast amounts of capital and information from the surrounding area.[2] In particular, the cultural specificities of inheritance law within the GCC have allowed some companies to flourish and avoid succession disputes over the short to medium term. The typical structure of a family business allows it to circumvent many of the challenges posed by traditional models of corporate governance. However, without the continuing diligence of management, adaptation to generational changes and an adequate management succession model, many of these businesses fail to survive past the third generation.

The causes of the deterioration of a family business over time are not dependent on common factors. They are generally based on family dynamics, succession disputes, conflicting individual interests and a lack of corporate sophistication and financial planning. The two most frequent problems are the difficulties of balancing business objectives with family interests and working with the regulations in place within MENA jurisdictions.

Long-term management plans must be implemented by family businesses in order to move the company into the hands of third-generation owners. This involves not only a change in corporate governance, but also a change in the management's mindset. Most managers of family businesses are balancing business efficacy decisions against their underlying loyalty to the greater family goal. Often, these decision makers are in conflict and only a strong corporate governance model can help a business to overcome this disparity.

---

1 See www.arabianbusiness.com/family-business-focus-at-doha-conference-85044.html and www.pwc.com/m1/en/advisory/family-business.jhtml.

2 Booz&Company online report at www.booz.com/media/uploads/GCC_Family_Businesses_Face_New_Challenges.pdf.

The interaction between members of a family business is dominated by a loose relational model whereby employment contracts are vague, if they exist at all. This is completely different from the strict contractual models found in normal businesses and multinational corporations, which must be governed by such a model. Increasingly, family companies are finding that they must incorporate a hybrid model which uses elements of both relational and contractual models. This focuses on keeping the core aspects of relational interaction, but includes the safeguards of contractual relations to foster a more efficient means of dispute resolution.[3]

Despite the dominant presence of family businesses in the region, there is no legal platform that promotes the growth of such companies. Within the United Arab Emirates, the main legal framework relating to business activities is the Commercial Companies Law – a rigid body of law that lends no service to the specificities of family business. The law creates conflict for the management of family companies as they try to balance the rules of generational succession and the restrictions placed on company shareholders and owners.

4. Growth in the region

The investment of both capital and infrastructure within the MENA region has seen a significant increase over the past 50 years. With the region's population growing by almost 500% over this period, there has been a huge push for political, economic and social development. This development has primarily been fuelled by oil and has been incredibly successful at maintaining a significant level of mid-term expansion. Public spending by many jurisdictions within the region has been another driving force behind their prosperity. This level of capitalism creates an attractive climate for mergers and acquisitions.

Public sector-driven and protected industries can no longer sustain the economic growth or the job creation seen in recent years. This has led the more progressive governments, such as that of the United Arab Emirates, to stress the importance of diversifying public and private investment. The MENA governments are calling for trade and investment reforms, which historically have yielded higher growth rates than governmental funding, and moreover, trade and investment reforms also generate employment.

In order to foster investment, countries must focus on certain areas of regulation and authority, such as providing strong legal platforms, political stability, government transparency, reputable economic and financial institutions and favourable corporate tax structures. If these areas are weak, prospective investors will either demand higher returns on investment or refrain from investing entirely. Thus, it is crucial that governments cooperate with other federal institutions and business leaders to develop their economies to bring down the costs of foreign investment.

The region experienced a drop of around 35% in foreign investment in 2011, which was attributable largely to worldwide economic stagnation, but also to uncertainties created by political and social changes.

Over the past 50 years the region has seen considerable growth in infrastructure

---

3 Online report at www.nrf.ae/bulletin/january-2013-v1-iss4-en.pdf.

and real estate. Multinational corporations have swarmed to the region to take advantage of tax structures and, within some sectors, relaxed labour laws. Although there has been growth, there must be a continued effort to invest in areas that create jobs and to alert the rest of the world that the MENA region is an attractive investment.

5. Country particulars

5.1 Saudi Arabia

The kingdom of Saudi Arabia is an oil-rich country which attracts the business of multinational companies from all over the world.

Legal due diligence can be time consuming and difficult when conducting M&A transactions in Saudi Arabia. Little public information is available on corporate entities, and therefore the buyer must mostly rely on the seller's disclosure of corporate documents. The availability of information for due diligence depends on the target's standard of corporate governance, the management structure and the seller's willingness to cooperate with the due diligence exercise.

The typical forms of business merger in Saudi Arabia are:

- the private acquisition of shares in the target;
- the private acquisition of the target's assets and business; and
- the acquisition of shares in a joint stock company.

In Saudi Arabia, tax primarily consists of corporate income tax, withholding tax and *Zakat*, the religious levy. For local companies, tax is assessed on the share of profit of the foreign partner in the local company. Companies owned solely by Saudi and GCC nationals are subject to *Zakat*. A foreign acquirer should seek the advice of a chartered accountancy firm regarding the withholding tax implications of the payment of dividends to non-resident shareholders in a Saudi company.

Sharia is the fundamental law of Saudi Arabia and governs all contractual interactions between the parties. As stated above, the broad nature of *Sharia* law means that Saudi courts can apply broad discretionary powers in the review and interpretation of business documents. This makes the transaction process largely unpredictable in Saudi Arabia.

There is also a Saudisation policy in place which requires that in a business with 20 or more employees, at least 30% of those employees must be Saudi nationals. Foreign companies must comply with Saudisation practices in order to remain registered to conduct business in Saudi Arabia.

Foreign investment is allowed in every sector in Saudi Arabia except the following:

- exploration, drilling and production of oil and gas;
- manufacturing of military equipment;
- road transportation;
- real estate investment in Mecca and Medina;
- real estate brokerage;
- printing and publishing services;

- audiovisual and media services;
- recruitment services;
- commercial agencies and franchises; and
- fisheries.

Regarding alternative dispute resolution, Saudi Arabia has acceded to the United Nations Convention on Recognition and Enforcement of Foreign Arbitral Awards (the New York Convention).

5.2 Egypt

The Egyptian courts and other government agencies do not use electronic or online databases and search capabilities. As a result, due diligence and information disclosure can be extremely time consuming. Certain searches require an application by the target itself or a party with power of attorney for the target. Under Egyptian banking law, the secrecy of a client's accounts and information may not be disclosed without the client's prior written approval.

Due to the leniencies of Egyptian law, the laws governing M&A agreements can be non-Egyptian if the parties so desire. However, this is valid only to the extent that such laws do not contravene Egyptian federal law or other moral and cultural rules. Usually, Egyptian law is chosen to govern such transactions to avoid any unnecessary difficulties that may arise during the proceedings.

Tax matters are generally handled by specialised tax accountants, rather than by lawyers. However, there is no capital gains tax or withholding tax on dividends for non-Egyptian tax-resident shareholders. The purchaser will not be liable for any previous unpaid taxes or tax evasion, but may be subject to the payment of sales tax.

In general, the purchaser will not be required to obtain new governmental permits, approvals or licences for the target to continue as a going concern or for the performance of its activities as conducted before the closing date. The seller will also generally continue to be responsible for all or part of the vast majority of the target's pre-closing liabilities.

There are generally no foreign ownership restrictions in Egypt, and companies can be up to 100% owned by foreigners. This allows many more avenues for foreign direct investment than other Gulf countries provide. This gives Egypt the potential to attract significant amounts of investment; however, to facilitate this, more political and economic stability will be needed.

Egyptian law regards the intentions of parties entering into contractual obligations as important in ascertaining the actions to which parties are bound. Memoranda of understanding are an integral part of the acquisition process in Egypt and are usually non-binding. That notwithstanding, there are obvious implications for engaging in activity that runs contrary to such documents. To make the process more efficient and avoid ambiguity over parties' obligations, such memoranda must specify the date on which each company is free to pursue other transactions.

The documentation involved in M&A transactions is fairly complex and will include regional and company specificities. According to general business practices, documents are usually prepared in English. However, if a government agency is in any way involved. documents are submitted to this agency in Arabic and then translated into English. Due to the problems that arise during this process, many companies believe that a standardisation procedure should be incorporated into the M&A process. This would make Egypt more attractive for businesses wanting to engage in the process, but which are discouraged because of the lack of rigid procedural standards.

Share purchase agreements operate fairly efficiently within Egypt, with title to shares transferring automatically from the seller to the purchaser, if desired. The purchase price can be transferred to the seller in whichever currency it prefers, as there is no currency control in place.

M&A contracts will often include dispute resolution clauses. As a party to the New York Convention, Egypt recognises foreign arbitral awards as valid and binding. The only exception to a New York Convention award would be in cases where the Egyptian courts have exclusive jurisdiction. Documents that must accompany an application for enforcement of a foreign award include:

- original and authenticated copies of the agreement and the award;
- an Arabic translation of the award;
- a copy of the minutes of the issuing court; and
- a copy of notification of the award to the party against which the award was made.

The Egyptian courts also have non-exclusive jurisdiction in relation to entities or assets situated in Egypt and in respect of obligations that were, or were to be, performed within Egypt.

5.3 United Arab Emirates

The United Arab Emirates provides a unique option for companies seeking to do business within the region. All seven emirates are subject to UAE federal law, with each emirate having its own specific rules and regulations. Within Abu Dhabi and Dubai, a number of business areas are designated as free trade zones. These pockets of land are considered to be separate corporate states with respect to the laws that govern them. The free trade zones aim to provide special legal and economic platforms that the UAE federal law cannot offer at present.

With the advent of these free-trade zones, there has been an influx of multinational companies into the United Arab Emirates. Along with this influx, the legal system has had to adapt rapidly to the jurisdictional and contractual problems that have arisen.

The United Arab Emirates has developed objective market indicators which acquirers can use to value targets. This makes the valuation process efficient and helps companies through early stages of M&A deals, which often prove difficult. Confidentiality and non-disclosure agreements have also become standard practice in connection with M&A transactions.

Valuing a company can be difficult when both parties have to agree on the fair market price of the seller's goodwill. This has become more difficult in jurisdictions such as the United Arab Emirates, where there is no objective market price for the shares of a company. In such cases, the parties must engage in a considerable amount of empirical assessment and communication to reach mutually acceptable share prices.

The most common business vehicle within the United Arab Emirates is the limited liability company (LLC). Although companies that attract the interest of acquirers are generally well managed in the United Arab Emirates, the internal records of these companies are rarely well maintained. No independent body of information in the United Arab Emirates allows acquirers to cross-reference any information provided to them. This presents a particular problem for M&A deals, where the acquirer must rely on the target for disclosure of material information. Thus, an acquirer needs a mindful and thorough due diligence team that can continually check for inconsistencies in the information provided.

When a conglomerate wishes to acquire a UAE-based company, problems often arise due to a lack of knowledge of both reporting standards and cultural specificities of the country. Often, the due diligence process is hampered by acquirers failing to incorporate such specificities into their initial requests for information. It is essential for the success of an M&A transaction in the United Arab Emirates that acquirers gain a firm understanding of the key aspects of UAE law that are relevant to them, and also of hurdles that are likely to impede the due diligence process. There have been recent attempts by the government to foster disclosure and transparency to encourage investment and stability within the United Arab Emirates.

The most common M&A activity in the United Arab Emirates involves the purchaser buying either the shares of a company or the assets of the business. The tax structure of the United Arab Emirates is particularly lax with respect to commercial activity. The free trade zones are given complete tax immunity for a certain period (generally 50 years). This means that no fees or taxes are imposed on the acquisition of shares and assets. However, notary public and governmental administrative fees are associated with formalising the M&A process, which are calculated on the value of the transaction in question.

UAE law requires all companies incorporated within the United Arab Emirates, with minor exceptions, to have at least 51% local ownership. This presents a unique legal challenge to M&A transactions. In addition to these foreign ownership restrictions, the majority of board members in any joint stock company incorporated in the United Arab Emirates must be UAE or GCC nationals.

In case of any failure to perform contractual obligations, the Civil Code allows for recourse for actual and direct damages suffered. Civil actions can be brought up to three years after such damages are incurred, although parties can contract for a shorter limitation period if desired.

5.4 Oman

A number of issues need careful consideration before entering into M&A transactions in Oman. Historically, M&A has not been commonplace in Oman compared to the other GCC countries. Recent global economic developments have propelled Omani companies into the M&A world, since they have had to consider consolidation to survive.

The most common corporate vehicle in Oman is the LLC. The LLC allows for the operation of small businesses without cumbersome regulatory capital and disclosure requirements. The requirements imposed on these companies reduce the information that they disseminate, making the due diligence process much more difficult.

Structural issues often present themselves to companies wishing to undertake M&A activity in Oman. One of the major problems for acquiring companies is the transfer of employment visas from a foreign company to an acquirer. Omani labour law prohibits any foreign (non-Omani) person from working within the sultanate without first obtaining the correct labour certification. This certification is subject to certain conditions and can cause issues for companies with foreign employees which are considering M&A leads.

All profits earned from the sale of assets, including the goodwill of the company, are subject to income taxation within the sultanate. This requirement excludes the disposal of securities listed on the domestic capital market. Companies in certain industries (eg, banking, insurance, electricity and water providers) must also adhere to certain regulations.

Foreign investment laws state that non-Omanis are prohibited from conducting commercial activities at any level without the appropriate licence. For instance, any potential investors in an Omani company must obtain a foreign capital investment licence from the relevant authority. Foreign ownership can be up to 70%, or more if the owner obtains special approval. This is a departure from the more stringent ownership rules enforced in the United Arab Emirates.

Disputes that arise through M&A transactions in Oman are traditionally dealt with through arbitration. Oman is a party to the New York Convention and thus participates in the mutual enforcement of foreign arbitral awards with other jurisdictions. M&A agreements in Oman are likely to include an arbitration clause stating which jurisdiction will hear any disputes.

Of particular note is the introduction of the Ministry of Manpower, which has the sole purpose of promoting the employment of Omani citizens. The ministry requires that a certain percentage of any company's employees be Omanis. This will be an important consideration for any M&A transaction regarding future company endeavours.

5.5 Kuwait

The current financial climate has produced difficulties for Kuwaiti companies which lack the liquidity to complete pending M&A transactions. Three types of company can be involved in M&A activity within Kuwait: LLCs, unlisted joint stock companies and listed joint stock companies.

Kuwait is one of the MENA jurisdictions that imposes income tax. A flat tax of 15% is imposed on net taxable income within Kuwait. Any foreign company wishing to acquire a stake in a Kuwaiti company will be subject to income tax unless the profits are derived from dealings on the Kuwaiti Stock Exchange.

The acquisition of listed joint stock companies is governed by the Capital Markets Authority, which has the power to decline share purchases. The authority also provides minority shareholders with the right to challenge any acquisition if they make a compelling case against the prospective acquisition.

Kuwait operates a rule requiring that the majority shareholder of any company be a Kuwaiti national. Of course, there are some exceptions to this rule. In certain circumstances, the majority shareholder of a company can be a GCC incorporated company. However, the enforcement of such rules has been *ad hoc* in recent years and, as such, there are no clear guidelines as to how and when they will be applied.

Kuwaiti conflict law outlines the procedures for dealing with contractual breaches should a party wish to seek damages. Dispute resolution clauses are often stipulated in M&A contracts so that parties may avoid the costly formalities associated with traditional litigation. Kuwait is a party to the New York Convention, and thus arbitration agreements are popular within M&A contracts involving Kuwaiti companies.

As in many other countries in the region, the residency of foreign nationals in Kuwait must be sponsored by their respective employers. Residency documentation is kept at the Ministry of Social Affairs and is thus easily found by companies wishing to access such information. Kuwait has also enacted laws requiring companies incorporated in Kuwait to have a minimum percentage of Kuwaiti employees.

5.6 Tunisia

Tunisia has embraced M&A transactions and is in the process of developing its legislation to handle the complexities of the process. With the advent of new statutory provisions, there is growing demand for the requisite business and legal acumen to deal with these changes. The ability of companies to mitigate the risks to which they are exposed while staying informed of financial developments is a key aspect of the M&A market in Tunisia.

There are many regulatory procedures in Tunisian M&A transactions. Clearance must be obtained from both the minister of trade and the Competition Council. Issues that both the buyer and seller should consider are the social and economic repercussions of such a transaction and whether it complements Tunisian M&A policy.

Tunisia has strong antitrust laws to ensure that M&A transactions do not change the market structure or discourage competition. Tunisian law states that companies involved in mergers must satisfy certain criteria if they are to complete the transaction successfully. These criteria require the companies' combined market share, sales and turnover within local markets to be scrutinised, to ensure that a monopoly will not be created.

Tunisia also has foreign investment rules that are stipulated in the Investment Incentives Code. At present, foreign ownership in Tunisia's industries and services is unrestricted, which affords foreign companies a freedom not currently enjoyed in other countries in the region. Only LLCs in Tunisia require a majority stake to be held by Tunisian persons or entities.

In general, Tunisian law will apply to any M&A transaction that involves Tunisian nationals. Arbitration clauses are often drafted into M&A contracts and this is becoming a popular means of dispute resolution.

An important aspect provided for by the Tunisian Employment Code is the effect of future obligations in the form of pensions. Pension liabilities can have a major impact on the value of a company and increase the need for due diligence by the acquirer.

Most M&A activity in Tunisia involves family-owned businesses and thus does not involve many of the pitfalls associated with corporate bureaucracy. These transactions operate more efficiently, since the parties base their relations more on trust and less on contractual terms.

Tunisian employment law makes for smooth transitions with regard to the transfer of employees to a new company following M&A activity. Employee work permits are automatically sent to a new or existing company and remain effective until their original expiry date. This significantly reduces the costs associated not only with visas, but also with the due diligence process.

5.7 Lebanon

Companies in Lebanon take four distinct forms;

- general partnerships;
- limited partnerships;
- LLCs; and
- joint stock companies, whose activities are governed by the Lebanese Code of Commerce.

No body of law within the code deals specifically with M&A activities. Instead, these activities are addressed by laws governing joint stock companies and their respective dealings. Since the code does not explicitly mention the three other forms of company, rules relating to joint stock companies can be applied to all four company types in M&A transactions.

Lebanese law does not require each of the contracting companies to have the same form or nationality, which means that there are no foreign ownership issues.

When Lebanese companies are dissolved, they must undertake certain actions regarding shareholders' rights. Three-quarters of a company's shareholders must be present at a meeting to pass a motion regarding the company's dissolution. The resolution must then be ratified by no less than two-thirds of the attendees.

Approved M&A transactions must be offered to public subscription in Lebanon. Publication of the transaction must be registered in the Commercial Register. It must also be published in the *Official Gazette*, in a business newspaper and in a local daily newspaper with all relevant information pertaining to the transaction. The information includes the new/acquiring company's name, address, object, capital, share price and value of in-kind contributions. Parties should exercise proper due diligence regarding tax concerns, since some transactions may produce double taxation for the company and its shareholders.

5.8 Bahrain

Bahrain is a developing country and has not yet seen much M&A activity. Its economy is mainly comprised of governmental/quasi-governmental bodies. Foreign direct investment in Bahrain has increased in recent years as the country has taken a more relaxed approach to foreign ownership rules. The increase in investment has prompted the introduction of tighter rules and regulations. The tightened regulations allow the finance industry to develop in mitigation of the risks that are involved with M&A activity.

The Bahrain Commercial Companies Law is the defining piece of legislation governing commercial transactions. The Central Bank of Bahrain (CBB) has recently issued a set of regulations which complement the existing law. The effectiveness of the CBB's new regulations has yet to be tested, but they have a wide scope and are subject to revision at the bank's will. The CBB has restricted the actions of parties to M&A activities before and during their dealings to prevent the disclosure of sensitive information. This allows for a more efficient and effective transaction process.

A number of activities within Bahrain are restricted to Bahraini and GCC nationals, depending on the industry and the business activities performed by the company in question. Any company operating within Bahrain must be duly incorporated and registered with the Ministry of Industry and Commerce. Foreigners wishing to form a company in Bahrain must incorporate as an LLC, a closed Bahrain joint stock company or an open Bahrain joint stock company. Each type of company has different operating capabilities and procedures which it must follow.

Bahrain has no specific antitrust laws, although the Commercial Companies Law prohibits M&A activities from resulting in monopolisation of any market or industry. The tax structure of Bahrain, save for in the oil and gas industries, is incredibly attractive: there are no corporate tax contributions and no rules on the repatriation of capital and profit. However, companies must pay municipality tax, currently set at a rate of 10% of the rent payable on the company's leased premises.

Bahrainisation is an important aspect of M&A dealings that needs to be considered. This legislation requires that a certain percentage of each company's workforce comprise Bahraini nationals. All foreign and local staff must be registered with the General Organisation for Social Insurance, which is responsible for social security taxes.

5.9 Jordan

Jordanian law does not specify a procedure or mechanism to be followed for the request or disclosure of relevant company files. Each party must adhere to previously agreed mutual terms and contractual obligations. The law provides no evaluation system for defining the price of the target's assets. The law instead requires that an evaluation committee be formed to determine the net equity of the relevant parties. A valuation mechanism is usually agreed on before such evaluations commence and is imperative to the success of the deal.

Jordanian law provides for a tax exemption for the companies and shareholders involved in a merger. Grouping structures are an alternative means of connecting companies together if they wish to enjoy the tax benefits of merging without being subject to the liabilities of the other company. This is generally a swifter process that requires fewer governmental approvals. However, the resulting companies will be subject to taxes that arise from such activities that parties to M&A transactions are not subject to. Under grouping structures, any company that legally ceases to exist post-grouping must be officially liquidated. This process can be time consuming and costly.

Once a merger or acquisition has been confirmed by all relevant parties, the controller of companies will register the successor company. Subsequently, the transaction must be published in the *Official Gazette* and two local newspapers. Shareholders of the merging companies have the right to object to any takeover within 30 days of publication in the *Official Gazette*.

Any parties to an M&A transaction that contravene any public order or violate Jordanian law will be subject to legal proceedings. It is thus extremely important that due diligence teams do their utmost to ensure that the respective parties have fulfilled their obligations and have observed all relevant laws. The Jordanian Companies Law recognises the liability of directors and management of companies in order to discourage the use of M&A activity for illegal purposes.

Antitrust laws in Jordan are strict and apply to all commercial activities that are conducted within Jordan. This extends to offshore activities that have a direct material impact on commercial activities within Jordan. Where a merger or acquisition would result in one company obtaining a market share of more than 40%, special approval must be sought from the Ministry of Trade.

Jordanian law limits foreign direct investment to no more than 50% of the total value of the company or project, depending on the activities and industry. Non-Jordanians are completely prohibited from engaging in certain areas of commerce (eg, investigative services). Due to the lengthy procedural requirements, it is difficult to determine the precise point at which an M&A transaction is considered to be completed under Jordanian law. This poses numerous problems for companies and requires substantial measures to mitigate the risk associated with this uncertainty.

5.10 Morocco

Takeover bids in Morocco are governed by the Law of Public Offerings under a number of different categories. The most relevant for M&A transactions are those governing share purchases, tender offers, public exchange offers and combined offers. The *Conseil Deontologique des Valuers Mobilieres* stipulates that a draft takeover bid must be filed with its offices when the takeover would result in one company owning more than 40% of the target's voting rights. This is required only insofar as there is a change in control of the company.

Draft takeover bids generally include the relevant party information, the objectives of the merger, an appropriate valuation of each company's assets and liabilities, the terms and conditions of share delivery, the effective date, relevant financial statements, the projected merger premium and any special rights afforded to any parties.

Most companies operating out of Morocco are either limited liability companies or joint stock companies. The shares of a limited liability company can be purchased by a third party only if all relevant parties associated with the target approve the transaction. This approval is generally sought through an extraordinary shareholders' meeting. Existing shareholders may exercise their pre-emption rights on shares to prevent any form of takeover.

There are few online databases in Morocco, and thus the due diligence process is often protracted and expensive. This has a major impact on the projected timings and the ability of each party to rely on information available to it.

Although the French language has no official status in Morocco, most important documents involving the courts, politics and administration are written in French. The official language of Morocco is Arabic, but documents may be drafted in either language. This presents problems for foreign companies wishing to perform commercial activities within Morocco and can hinder the M&A process.

Morocco encourages foreign direct investment. With the promulgation of the Investment Charter, capital restrictions have been relaxed and the cost of investment has decreased. Most sectors are open to foreign investment, with minor restrictions imposed on the banking, farmland, shareholdings and telecommunications sectors.

Michael Kortbawi has gained hands-on experience in the Middle East and North Africa region, having practised in the United Arab Emirates for over 10 years and having supervised the organic growth of Bin Shabib and Associates (BSA) LLP into the five jurisdictions in which it now operates.

His specific areas of expertise include mergers and acquisitions in the insurance and energy sectors, directors' and officers' duties under UAE and DIFC laws, setting up insurance and reinsurance companies in the GCC, and deregistration of commercial agencies.

Mr Kortbawi heads a team of eight corporate lawyers who are involved in corporate and regulatory advice in relation to all aspects of corporate law, including cross-border business transactions and mergers and acquisitions in the United Arab Emirates, Iraq, Oman and Lebanon.

Bahrain

Bill Jefferies
Abdullah Mutawi
Trowers & Hamlins LLP

1. Introduction

Bahrain is a leading banking and financial centre in the Gulf region whose government has, for a number of years, adopted a policy designed to diversify its economy and encourage inward and pass-through investment. Institutions in Bahrain take a fairly liberal approach to foreign investment, although certain restrictions still exist in relation to foreign ownership in the petroleum, retail and property sectors. Bahrain is a relatively young and developing economy, dominated by governmental and quasi-governmental entities, and does not have the same volume of mature enterprise as drives strategic M&A markets elsewhere. While recent research suggests that mergers and acquisitions in the Gulf region are expected to increase, it remains to be seen how activity in Bahrain will be affected by economic and socio-political challenges, although it is likely that moves towards consolidation and diversification will see the regional trend replicated in Bahrain. In recent years foreign investors have been increasingly looking to invest in this offshore jurisdiction by acquiring stakes in local companies or entering into joint ventures in order to develop new enterprises. This influx of international investment, as well as the increased capabilities of local investment funds, has led to the greater development and tightening of M&A rules in Bahrain.

The Commercial Companies Law 2001 is the key piece of legislation regulating corporate entities in Bahrain. The legal framework governing mergers and acquisitions is established in the law, which sets out a basic structure, and in detailed regulations and guidelines issued by the Central Bank of Bahrain (CBB) in respect of mergers and acquisitions in the capital markets. However, the CBB regulations have not yet been heavily tested, particularly in light of the recent economic crisis, and therefore a degree of uncertainty remains around their implementation and interpretation.

2. Due diligence

The basic objective of a due diligence exercise in relation to a merger or acquisition in Bahrain is generally no different from that in other markets. The due diligence exercise includes an investigation into the business of the relevant entities. This allows directors and shareholders of the relevant company to access all material information in order to make an informed decision. This will generally require the review of pertinent service or sales contracts, corporate governance documents, licences and registration certificates, employment contracts and any documents showing proprietorship in real assets.

Bahrain, in line with the rest of the Gulf region, may require a company to hold more approvals, consents or licences, depending on the activities undertaken by the entity, than would be required in Europe or North America. It is important that these be reviewed when undertaking due diligence, as they may be vital to the company in carrying out its business.

Financial records should also be reviewed. Public listed companies are required to publish their annual accounts each year; however, other information that may be available in mature M&A markets may be unavailable in Bahrain.

As stated above, restrictions may be placed on foreign ownership depending on the company's activities, and therefore attention should be paid to the nationality of the shareholders of a company to ensure that a merger or acquisition will not be hindered by such restrictions.

2.1 Due diligence under the CBB regulations

Offers that are subject to the CBB regulations are tightly controlled by the CBB, and an offer may not be withdrawn or reduced unless the CBB consents or a CBB-approved condition is not fulfilled.[1] Due to the rigidity of offers made under the CBB regulations, an offeror must have a basic understanding of the circumstances of the target and have undertaken a certain level of due diligence. Therefore, the CBB regulations provide certain requirements in respect of due diligence.

The directors of the target are obliged to make available certain documents, such as constitutional documents and profit forecasts. The directors will be responsible for ensuring that all such information is compiled to the highest standards. Obligations also exist to update any relevant information as appropriate during the offer period. All information, documents, advertisements or statements issued during the offer period must not be misleading and must be of the highest standard and accuracy. The documents issued must contain certain prescribed statements as set out in the appendices to the CBB regulations.[2]

The disclosed information may be required by the CBB at short notice, and therefore both the acquirer and the target should be in a position to disclose documents quickly.

3. Legal structure of mergers and acquisitions

3.1 Commercial Companies Law

(a) Corporate entities

The laws of Bahrain require that any entity carrying out business activities in the country have a legal presence.[3] Corporate entities must be incorporated and registered with the Ministry of Industry and Commerce,[4] which will specifically determine and approve the commercial activities that may be undertaken.

1 Takeovers, Mergers and Acquisitions (TMA)-2.5.1 of the CBB regulations, Volume 6 – Capital Markets.
2 Appendix C, CBB regulations, Volume 6 – Capital Markets.
3 Article 4 of Legislative Decree 21/2001 promulgating the Commercial Companies Law.
4 Article 72 of Legislative Decree 21/2001.

Consideration should be given to the nature of activities that may be undertaken following a merger or acquisition and whether, in the case of an acquisition, the existing commercial registration of the acquirer will sufficiently cover those activities.

The Commercial Companies Law prescribes the types of company that may be incorporated in Bahrain. Foreign investors incorporating a company must use a limited liability company, a Bahraini closed stock-holding company or a single person company. The most common corporate entities are as follows:

- A limited liability company is a private company with no more than 50 shareholders in which the liability of the shareholders is limited to the value of their unpaid shares.[5] The minimum share capital requirement is Bd20,000 and the minimum value of each share is less than Bd50.[6]
- A Bahraini closed joint stock company is a private limited liability company with a minimum share capital of Bd250,000. The shares may have a minimum value of between Bd0.10 and Bd100 each.[7] For the first three years of incorporation, the shares shall be non-negotiable, except between the original founders of the company.[8]
- A Bahraini open joint stock company is the structure used for a company which lists its shares on a public exchange. The minimum share capital is Bd1 million.[9]

To a large extent, the differences between the types of corporate entity are administrative in nature, with both closed and open joint stock companies facing greater administrative burdens. If foreign corporate entities or individuals are to be shareholders of a Bahrain entity, then additional documents must be provided, such as the constitutional documents of the foreign entity or copies of passports and residence permits, as well as shareholders' CVs and bank references.

A number of activities are restricted to Bahraini and Gulf Cooperation Council (GCC) citizens and companies. Depending on the activities undertaken by a target or merging company, consideration must be given as to whether any of the foreign ownership restrictions will apply. Restricted activities are listed in section 5 below.

(b) *Mergers and acquisitions*

The Commercial Companies Law sets out the primary legislation governing the merger and acquisition of companies in Bahrain. The law sets down a far less detailed framework than may be found in Europe or North America. However, the nature of incorporating a company in Bahrain and the rules governing each form of company are more burdensome than would be expected in an offshore jurisdiction. The rules of incorporation and governance of corporate entities (eg, the restriction of foreign ownership, the time-consuming procedures to amend constitutional documents and

5 Article 261 of Legislative Decree 21/2001.
6 Article 264 of Legislative Decree 21/2001.
7 Implementing Regulations of Legislative Decree 21/2001.
8 Article 234 of Legislative Decree 21/2001.
9 Implementing Regulations of Legislative Decree 21/2001.

the non-negotiability of shares) will also have an effect on the structure or outcome of mergers and acquisitions in Bahrain.

Part 11 (Merger of companies) of the Commercial Companies Law sets out the structure of mergers and acquisitions. This part of the law deals jointly with the traditionally separate concepts of mergers and acquisitions as different methods of merger. Article 312 states that a merger can be effected by one of two methods:

- acquisition, which involves the winding up of a company and the transfer of its assets to an existing company; or
- consolidation, in which two or more companies are wound up and incorporated in a new company (traditionally known as a 'merger').

In order to effect an acquisition, the target must pass a resolution to dissolve itself in accordance with its articles of association. The target's shares shall be evaluated in accordance with the Commercial Companies Law. The acquirer must also pass a resolution to amend its capital in accordance with the evaluation results of the shares of the target.[10] It is unclear whether local authorities would also expect a foreign company to comply with this requirement. The capital increase due to the acquisition is distributed among the shareholders of the acquirer in proportion to each shareholder's original respective stake.

In order to effect a merger, each company shall pass a resolution dissolving itself and a new company must be incorporated in accordance with the Commercial Companies Law. In addition, if the company is a closed or open joint stock company under Bahraini law, an expert report will be required to value the in-kind shares. Each merged company is then allotted a number of shares or stakes equal to its shareholding in the company's new capital.[11]

Article 315 requires that notification of any proposed merger or acquisition be published in the *Official Gazette* (issued by the government) and in a local daily newspaper, in addition to being recorded in the Commercial Register maintained by the Ministry of Industry and Commerce. Objections to a merger or acquisition may be made by creditors within 60 days of publication of the merger or acquisition by registered letter with a delivery note. In such cases, the transaction is binding only if:

- the creditor withdraws the objection;
- the court, on reviewing the claim at the company's request, rejects the objection; or
- the company pays the creditor's debt or provides the creditor with adequate guarantees for its settlement.

If no objection is made within the 60-day period, the merger or acquisition shall be effective towards all creditors and the newly merged or acquiring company shall subrogate the merged companies or the acquired company in all of their rights and obligations.

---

10 Article 313(c) of Legislative Decree 21/2001.
11 Article 314 of Legislative Decree 21/2001.

Where a company has borrowed by issuing bonds, the board of bond holders must approve the resolution to merge or acquire by a majority of those representing two-thirds of the loan bonds; alternatively, the company may settle the debt in a way that is accepted by the same majority. If the board of bond holders does not approve the merger, acquisition or subsequent offered settlement, then a representative of the board of bondholders must object to the resolution by registered letter with a delivery note. In such case the merger or acquisition results will not be binding on the bond holders until they have withdrawn their objection, a court has dismissed the objection or the company has paid the debts due.[12]

The Commercial Companies Law imposes restrictions on the negotiability of shares of an acquired or merged company. Upon an acquisition, any new shares or stakes that are obtained by the partners or shareholders of the acquirer may be traded only if one year has lapsed since incorporation of the acquired company. In the case of a merger, the shares of the newly merged company may be traded only if one year has lapsed since the incorporation of each merged company.[13]

(c) *Dissolution of a company*

Upon a merger or acquisition, a company (or companies) will be dissolved according to the Commercial Companies Law. The law states that on dissolution, a company shall be in a state of liquidation and the powers of the board of directors will terminate, although managers can continue to manage the company.[14] A liquidator will be appointed to manage the company's assets and will lead the transfer of assets to the offeror company or newly formed company. On distribution of the dissolved company's assets, the liquidator must apply to have the company struck off the Commercial Register.[15]

3.2 Mergers and acquisitions in the capital markets

(a) *CBB regulations*

The increased activity and development of the capital markets led the CBB to introduce new regulations and guidelines regulating the capital markets sector in December 2008, including a module in respect of takeovers, mergers and acquisitions in Bahrain. The Bahrain Stock Exchange was created in 1987 and commenced operations in 1989. The CBB regulations are the first attempt at rules to regulate all aspects of the capital markets in Bahrain. The CBB has the power to modify or ease the application of the CBB regulations where, on the facts of the transaction, a regulation would be too restrictive or burdensome.

The CBB regulations apply to relevant persons that are engaged in, or may engage in, a merger or acquisition of a controlling interest in a Bahrain-based or international company whose primary listing is on the Bahrain Stock Exchange. A 'controlling interest' is defined as a holding of 30% or more of the voting rights of a

12 Article 317 of Legislative Decree 21/2001.
13 Article 316 of Legislative Decree 21/2001.
14 Article 325 of Legislative Decree 21/2001.
15 Article 343 of Legislative Decree 21/2001.

company.[16] However, the CBB regulations are generally drafted in such a way that contemplates only a complete acquisition of a listed company, rather than the acquisition of a block of majority shares from certain vendors. Nevertheless, a partial acquisition would fall within the CBB regulations.

The CBB regulations apply to listed and unlisted companies where such an offeror or offeree company makes an offer for any listed company or is an associate, affiliate, subsidiary or holding company of any listed company. An 'offer' is defined as including both acquisition and merger transactions, however effected.[17] The CBB regulations generally will not apply to offers for non-voting, non-equity capital entities, where the equity securities do not confer a voting right on the holder of such securities or where the transaction is an exempted share repurchase.

The CBB regulations provide details on the requirements for the timing and method of any offers, announcements and documents, as well as the disclosure of adequate information to shareholders in respect of any proposed merger or acquisition.[18] The purpose of the CBB regulations is to facilitate the fair treatment of shareholders of public listed companies. The regulations are not concerned with the financial or commercial advantages or disadvantages of a merger or acquisition. The Capital Market Supervision Directorate is the body of the CBB that undertakes a direct supervisory role under the regulations.

(b) Duties under CBB regulations

The CBB regulations require that all relevant persons follow the principles embodied by the regulations, as well as the letter.[19] Where the specific provisions provide insufficient guidance on a matter, these principles may be applied by the CBB in order to provide extra clarification to companies. The CBB regulations require any person engaging in or intending to engage in a merger or acquisition to treat all holders of each class of securities in a fair and equitable manner, demonstrating no bias to a single group or class of shareholders.[20] The CBB regulations attempt to protect the interest of minority shareholders and require that rights of control be exercised in good faith. In order to ensure compliance with the CBB regulations, a duty is imposed on the directors and financial advisers of a company involved in a merger or acquisition to ensure that the requirements of the regulations are complied with in the conduct of such transactions.[21]

(c) Making an offer

The CBB regulations require the offeror to carry out careful and responsible consideration before making an offer.[22] The offeror and its advisers should be satisfied that the offeror can, and will continue to be able to, implement the offer in full.[23] All

---

16 'Control', Glossary, CBB regulations, Volume 6 – Capital Markets.
17 'Offer', Glossary, CBB regulations, Volume 6 – Capital Markets.
18 TMA-3.2.7 of the CBB regulations, Volume 6 – Capital Markets.
19 TMA-1.1 of the CBB regulations, Volume 6 – Capital Markets.
20 TMA-1.2 of the CBB regulations, Volume 6 – Capital Markets.
21 TMA-1.12 of the CBB regulations, Volume 6 – Capital Markets.
22 TMA-1.7 of the CBB regulations, Volume 6 – Capital Markets.
23 TMA-2.2.1 of the CBB regulations, Volume 6 – Capital Markets.

offers must be made to the board of the offeree company, even where the acquisition of a block of shares is contemplated. Once an offer has been communicated to the board of an offeree, it may not be withdrawn or the price lowered without the CBB's consent. An offeror must continue to implement the offer unless it was subject to the fulfilment of a specified condition and such condition has not been met or a higher offer was posted, in which case the CBB may allow the offeror to withdraw the offer. An offer must initially be open for acceptance for at least 15 calendar days.[24]

Due to the inflexibility facing an offeror in respect of its offer and any variation thereof, careful consideration must be given to any conditions that may be appropriate to ensure that the offeror is required to proceed with the proposed transaction only on commercially acceptable terms. However, the CBB will require notification of any conditions in the offer and has the discretion to disregard them.[25] Therefore, any conditions should be drafted in a manner that is consistent with the guiding principles of the CBB regulations.[26]

In the first instance, an offer is put forward to the board of directors of the offeree in writing. The identity of the offeror or potential offeror must be disclosed at the outset to the board. The board of the offeree is entitled to be satisfied that the offeror is in a position to implement the offer in full and the offeror must provide reasonable information to verify that this is the case.[27]

Upon receipt of the offer, the board should appoint a professional independent adviser to determine whether the offer is fair and reasonable. Such advice should be in writing and shared with the shareholders. The board can then make a recommendation as to whether the shareholders accept such offer.[28]

Once an offer has been communicated to the board of the offeree, no action should be taken by that board which may frustrate the offer or deny the shareholders of the offeree the opportunity to decide on the offer's merits. In particular, the board may not, without approval:

- issue any shares;
- create, issue or grant securities or options, warrant in respect of shares or sell, dispose of or require assets of the material amounts;
- enter into contracts other than in the ordinary course of business; or
- cause the offeree company to purchase or redeem any shares in the offeree company.

Where an offeree is under prior contractual obligations to undertake any of these actions the CBB must be consulted.[29]

(d) *Mandatory, voluntary, partial and forced offers*

The CBB regulations set out when mandatory and voluntary offers are required.[30] A

---

24 TMA-2.14 of the CBB regulations, Volume 6 – Capital Markets.
25 TMA-2.3.18 of the CBB regulations, Volume 6 – Capital Markets.
26 TMA-1 of the CBB regulations, Volume 6 – Capital Markets.
27 TMA-2.1.2 of the CBB regulations, Volume 6 – Capital Markets.
28 TMA-2.2.1 of the CBB regulations, Volume 6 – Capital Markets.
29 TMA-2.20 of the CBB regulations, Volume 6 – Capital Markets.
30 TMA-3 of the CBB regulations, Volume 6 – Capital Markets.

'mandatory offer' is an offer for the remaining outstanding shares of an offeree company made by a shareholder where the shareholder increases its voting rights to the extent that:

- where it initially held less than 30%, it would hold more than 30%; or
- where it initially held 30% to 50% of the voting rights, it would increase this by more than 1% in six months.

In such case the shareholder is required to make an offer to acquire the shares of all holders of each class of equity share of the company.[31] The offer price must be higher than the highest price paid during the offer period or the period three months before the offer, and must be accepted by at least 50% of the shareholders.

A mandatory offer is not required if control of the offeree is acquired as a result of a voluntary offer to all holders of the shares and other securities carrying voting rights.[32] A 'voluntary offer' is a takeover offer for the voting shares of an offeree where the person is not obligated to make a mandatory offer.

The CBB may waive the obligation to make a mandatory offer if there is an independent vote at a shareholders' meeting of the offeree (referred to as a 'whitewash' resolution) approving the proposed transaction.[33] The shareholders which are involved or interested in the transaction may not vote on such resolution. Certain requirements are set out in relation to the whitewash resolution, including:

- seeking independent advice;
- obtaining CBB approval in advance; and
- sending out a shareholder circular in advance.

In addition, an announcement must be made to the market.[34]

Consent is required from the CBB for any partial offer, which means an offer to all shareholders to acquire a portion of the remaining outstanding shares of the offeree. The CBB regulations state that CBB consent is normally granted if the offer would not result in the offeror owning more than 30% of the company; therefore, it could be inferred that CBB consent would not be granted routinely for the proposed transaction.[35]

Where a shareholder holds or controls more than 95% of the company, it must offer to acquire the remaining shares within three months of acquiring 95% or more. Upon acquisition of the remaining shares, the offeree company must then apply to delist.[36]

(e) *Announcements*

If the offeror has made or is seriously considering making an offer, the offeree, after obtaining permission from the CBB, must make a brief announcement that a

---

31 TMA-3.1.1 of the CBB regulations, Volume 6 – Capital Markets.
32 TMA-3.3.1 of the CBB regulations, Volume 6 – Capital Markets.
33 TMA-3.1.15 of the CBB regulations, Volume 6 – Capital Markets.
34 TMA-3.1.17 of the CBB regulations, Volume 6 – Capital Markets.
35 TMA-3.2.1 of the CBB regulations, Volume 6 – Capital Markets.
36 TMA-3.4.1 of the CBB regulations, Volume 6 – Capital Markets.

potential offeror is considering making an offer.[37] The CBB also requires that serious consideration be given to the idea of whether there should be a suspension in trading of such shares pending publication of the announcement. The potential offeror must not attempt to prevent the board of the offeree from making the announcement or requesting a temporary suspension. Irrespective of any requests, the CBB itself may suspend temporarily shares of the offeree if it deems fit.

There is also an obligation to make an announcement when there are negotiations between a potential offeror and shareholders holding more than 20% of the shares in the company, and the company is subject to rumour or speculation about a possible offer or there is unusual movement in its share price or volume of share turnover due to shareholder actions.[38] The obligation to make such announcement rests with the selling shareholders.

The announcement must be sent to the Bahrain Stock Exchange Licence Exchange and published in two local daily Arabic or Arabic/English newspapers.[39] Any language used in such announcements must be clear and concise, and statements giving the impression that commitments have been made if they have not should be avoided.[40] Where the offer is for cash or includes an element of cash, the announcement of the offer must include a statement that the professional adviser has taken reasonable steps to confirm that sufficient resources are available to fulfil the offer.

(f) *Confidentiality*

The CBB considers all details related to mergers and acquisitions to be inside information; therefore, before an announcement the confidentiality of an offer must be maintained. In addition, once an offer has been made, the offeree is not required to provide information in respect of the company's trade and business secrets.[41]

(g) *Documentation and disclosure*

Once an offer has been made, an offer document must be sent to the board of the offeree within 21 days of the announcement of the terms of the offer in dual text.[42]

The offeree should then send to its shareholders (within 21 calendar days of receiving the offer document) a circular containing information specified in the CBB regulations and any other information that the board considers to be relevant to enable its shareholders to reach an informed decision on the offer. All documents must be written in Arabic and/or English, and include a translation as necessary. Further, all documents must state that the directors accept full responsibility for the accuracy of the information contained in the documents. In addition, shareholders should be advised to seek independent advice.[43]

The offeree must also provide information to the offeror to enable it to carry out

---

37 TMA-2.3.1 of the CBB regulations, Volume 6 – Capital Markets.
38 TMA-2.3.3 of the CBB regulations, Volume 6 – Capital Markets.
39 TMA-2.3.8 of the CBB regulations, Volume 6 – Capital Markets.
40 TMA-2.3.9 of the CBB regulations, Volume 6 – Capital Markets.
41 TMA-2.1.4 of the CBB regulations, Volume 6 – Capital Markets.
42 TMA-2.7.6 of the CBB regulations, Volume 6 – Capital Markets.
43 TMA-2.7.7 of the CBB regulations, Volume 6 – Capital Markets.

due diligence, including particulars of shareholders and any information that is material in the context of making the offer. In addition, the offeree is required to make available for inspection:

- its memorandum and articles of association;
- its audited consolidated accounts;
- the service contracts of its directors;
- written consents of professional advisers on material contracts in relation to the offer;
- reports of auditors or accountants in respect of profit forecasts; and
- any asset valuation certificates pertaining to the offer.[44]

Documents in relation to the financing arrangements of the offer or profit forecasts by the offeree should also be made available. The directors of the offeree are responsible for ensuring that all such information in relation to profit forecasts is compiled to the highest standards and there is an obligation to update this information as appropriate during the offer period. All documents must be filed with the CBB for comment before they are released. Thus, the CBB is involved throughout the entire offer process and will be able to influence the content of any announcements or documents.[45]

The CBB regulations set out restrictions on dealings before and during the offer. Limitations are put in place to prevent the disclosure of price-sensitive information either before, during or after offers dealing in shares in the offeree. Exceptions are set out, including where the proposed offer is not price sensitive in relation to the securities being dealt with. There is also a requirement of public disclosure of any dealings in the relevant shares by the offeror or the offeree during an offer period.[46]

(h) Equal treatment of shareholders

During the course of an offer or when an offer is in contemplation, neither the offeror nor the offeree or their advisers may provide information to some (but not all) shareholders. The relevant persons in relation to an offer must act with due skill, care and diligence in relation to all matters. Any time before or during the offer, the management of overall persons must maintain secrecy and confidentiality of the offer. However, precaution must be taken against the creation or continuance of a false market or the disclosure of misleading information.[47]

The CBB regulations provide that no special deals or arrangements with selected shareholders are permitted. The offeror may not make any arrangements for selected shareholders if there are favourable conditions attached which are not being extended to all shareholders without the CBB's consent.

(i) Acceptance of an offer

An offeror is obliged to publish an announcement on the date on which the offer

---

44 TMA-2.6.1 of the CBB regulations, Volume 6 – Capital Markets.
45 TMA-2.7.14 of the CBB regulations, Volume 6 – Capital Markets.
46 TMA-2.20 of the CBB regulations, Volume 6 – Capital Markets.
47 TMA-1.2 of the CBB regulations, Volume 6 – Capital Markets.

expires, is declared unconditional or is revised or extended. The CBB regulations set out certain details which must be disclosed in such announcement.[48]

4. Competition laws

Bahrain has no laws dealing specifically with economic competition. The Constitution states that "Any monopoly shall only be awarded by law and for a limited time".[49] The Commercial Companies Law provides that no merger or acquisition shall result in the monopolisation of an economic activity, commodity or particular product. However, the current Bahraini economy means that certain sectors are largely monopolised by government entities.

5. Foreign investment and ownership

Bahrain offers foreign investors an attractive investment choice as an offshore jurisdiction with no corporate tax (except in the oil and gas industry), and no restrictions on the repatriation of capital and profit. The incorporation of companies in Bahrain is also relatively easy in comparison to some of the more stringent incorporation regimes in neighbouring GCC countries. The Bahrain Investors Centre was set up in 2004 in order to facilitate the incorporation of corporate entities for both local and foreign companies.

The commercial registration of a company must list the activities to be undertaken. Certain activities are restricted to Bahrainis – for example, fishing, press, publishing and distribution houses, car rental, the supply of foreign manpower, the supply of oil products, gas bottling and distribution, book-keeping and accounting services, the import, export or sale of racing car fuel and cargo clearing.

In trade and retail, a minimum of 51% Bahraini ownership is required, while in travel and tourism activities, a Bahraini partner is required. Medical clinics and centres are licensed only to Bahraini and GCC citizens with medical qualifications (although this does not apply to hospitals), and a minimum of 50% of the capital of a pharmacy must be owned by a Bahraini pharmacist.[50]

The foreign investment restrictions in respect of certain activities will clearly be a consideration when assessing and structuring a merger or acquisition to be undertaken by a foreign individual or entity.

6. Merger documentation

In general, as for all significant transactions, parties in Bahrain will prepare formal documentation in respect of an acquisition or merger in order to deal with representations, conditions, financial matters, covenants, confidentiality and termination rights.

In addition to the standard market practice, mergers and acquisitions that fall under the CBB regulations will be required to enter into prescribed documentation and to make certain binding statements in respect of such transaction. This includes the

48 TMA-2.18 of the CBB regulations, Volume 6 – Capital Markets.
49 Article 117 of the Constitution of Bahrain.
50 Ministry of Industry and Commerce.

provision of a formal offer document through which an offer is made, which may not be withdrawn or decreased without the CBB's consent.[51] Acceptance of the offer must also be in the form prescribed in the CBB regulations. The directors of and professional advisers to a transaction are responsible for ensuring its compatibility with the law, and therefore careful attention must be paid to these documentary requirements.

7. Regulatory approval

All corporate entities in Bahrain must be licensed to undertake the commercial activities which they intend to carry out. While the Ministry of Industry and Commerce has general responsibility for commercial activities, a company may require further approval from the regulatory authority dealing with the specific sector in which it will operate. Therefore, a company may also require approval from a regulatory authority for any proposed merger or acquisition.

An example of this would be companies undertaking telecommunications activities, which are regulated by the Telecommunications Regulatory Authority. The acquisition of 5% or more of the shares in a telecommunications company imposes an obligation on the offeror to notify the authority of the transaction within seven days of acquiring the shares.

8. Employment issues

Employment in Bahrain is regulated by the Labour Law for the Private Sector (36/2012, as amended). Written contracts of employment must be at least as favourable as the Labour Law.

A large proportion of the workforce are expatriates and the Bahraini government has sought to address this by introducing 'Bahrainisation' measures, which require companies to employ a certain percentage of Bahrainis.

All foreign and local staff must be registered with the General Organisation for Social Insurance, which is responsible for levying social security taxes. The current rate of contributions is 19% for local employees and 4% for expatriate employees. Of the payments made in respect of local national employees, employers pay 12% and employees pay 7%. The tax covers old age, disability, death and unemployment.

The termination of employment entitles an employee to compensation of half the monthly wage for each of the first three years of employment and one month's wage for each subsequent year of service.

All foreign workers must have a valid work permit issued by the Ministry of Labour – employers of expatriate labour must pay an annual fee for such permits.

These requirements must be considered where an acquisition or merger is expected to lead to the termination of employment contracts. In particular, in accordance with the Labour Law, a merger shall not result in the termination of employment contracts. Any restructuring of a company and its workforce must take into account the minimum requirements for Bahraini employees.

Thorough due diligence must ensure that a company has complied with the Labour Law, as the new owner will become liable for any ongoing breaches.

---

51 TMA-2.5.1 of the CBB regulations, Volume 6 – Capital Markets.

9. Taxation

Except for companies in the oil and gas industry, companies and individuals in Bahrain are not liable to pay income tax. However, a company must pay municipality tax in respect of its commercial address – currently 10% of the rent payable for leased premises. All corporate entities must have registered business premises.[52] The only corporate income tax in Bahrain is levied on oil, gas and petroleum companies at a rate of 46%. There are no restrictions on capital and profit repatriation.[53]

10. Case study

A recently proposed acquisition in Bahrain demonstrated some of the uncertainty surrounding the CBB regulations and their application. The client, a UK-based investment firm, sought to acquire a 78.8% stake in a Bahrain investment bank by purchasing shares from a shareholder of the target, pursuant to a side arrangement in relation to the payment of a loan taken out by the target and to be repaid by the shareholder. The target was a public company listed on the Bahrain Stock Exchange.

The CBB regulations applied to the transaction as the client was obtaining a controlling interest of more than 30% of the voting rights of the target. However, as noted above, the regulations are drafted in such a way as to contemplate only acquisitions of 100% of an offeree company. Therefore, some of the rules and guidelines set out by the CBB regulations were not applicable to the proposed acquisition of a majority stake in a company. The client undertook negotiations directly with the selling shareholder, but under the CBB regulations, the client was required to approach the board of the target to make an offer. The board of the offeree was obliged to obtain written independent advice as to whether the offer was in the interests of the shareholders, which was then circulated among the shareholders. The board then made a recommendation as to the commercial merits of the offer, even though the offer did not involve the whole offeree.

In addition, the CBB regulations require that an announcement be made in respect of the offer to the board. However, a potential vendor must also make an announcement where negotiations are taking place between an offeror and shareholders holding more than 20% of the shares in a company and the company is subject to rumour or speculation about a possible offer. In this case, it was unclear which party was responsible for making the announcement in the form prescribed by the regulations and which party had to obtain approval of the announcement from the CBB.

The CBB regulations set out various provisions in relation to the timing and content of the documents to be disclosed once an offer has been made. The regulations require that all shareholders be provided with sufficient information and advice to enable them to make a informed decision about the offer. However, in the transaction at hand, this disclosure was not appropriate, as the offer was being made only to the selling shareholder.

---

52 Article 75(B) of Legislative Decree 21/2001.

53 *Doing Business in Bahrain*, Ernst & Young, page 73, "Taxation".

When considering the structure of the transaction, it was necessary to consider the CBB's restrictions on special deals or arrangements with selected shareholders, according to which favourable conditions cannot be extended only to a proportion of shareholders of an offeree, without the CBB's consent. It was clear that the CBB had to be involved at an early stage and would require a significant amount of documentation in order to understand how the transaction was to move forward. The CBB had a tight turnaround time in respect of disclosing information, which was problematic for a company operating overseas.

In addition, the transaction appeared to be subject to the requirements surrounding mandatory offers under the CBB regulations as the client was offering to purchase more than 30% of the target's shares. It was not in the client's commercial interests to make an open offer to all shareholders in order to acquire the specific shares of the selling shareholder. Therefore, the CBB was asked for an exemption from this requirement. The CBB was open to granting such exemption once a significant amount of documentation had been provided and a detailed explanation of the reasons behind the transaction had been given. The process required a large amount of sensitive commercial information to be shared – something that not all companies can undertake. Uncertainty also remains as to whether other exemptions will be provided going forward or whether, in light of the increase in mergers and acquisitions, the CBB will be more stringent in applying the regulations.

As the transaction involved the acquisition of a controlling interest of a bank licensed by the CBB, the CBB also had significant involvement in its role as the financial sector regulatory authority.

Egypt

Mohamed A Ghannam
Khaled Moussa
Helmy, Hamza & Partners

1. Structuring

1.1 Due diligence

Legal due diligence is normally carried out by requesting relevant documents, data and information directly from the seller or through its legal and/or financial advisers. In some transactions, a physical data room is set up; in more sophisticated deals, a virtual data room is created to assist multiple bidders and to maintain confidentiality.

The following factors will influence the scale of the due diligence process:

- the sophistication and organisational skills of the seller;
- the number of bidders involved;
- any elements of confidentiality; and
- whether the target is in a regulated sector.

The lack of electronic or online databases and search capabilities in the Egyptian court system and in other governmental agencies slows down the due diligence process, and it is generally difficult to obtain information without the target's cooperation. For instance, it is not possible to run an independent court search to find out whether the target is involved in any legal proceedings. Also, in many cases certain important searches relating, for example, to bankruptcy and mortgage certificates must be applied for by the target itself or by the holder of a power of attorney. In addition, the data discovered may not itself be up to date.

Practice varies in terms of the due diligence process, but a number of drafts are usually submitted to the purchaser, and 'red flags' are raised if and when a major issue is identified. Ideally, efforts should be coordinated with financial, tax and technical consultants to ensure that relevant information is exchanged and carefully analysed from different angles. In Egypt, tax matters are usually handled by specialist tax accountants rather than lawyers.

It is also important to agree with the purchaser on the scope of the due diligence and an appropriate materiality threshold. This will vary depending on the transaction structure and size, the nature of the business, its complexity and so on.

However, generally speaking, the legal due diligence report will cover ownership/title, corporate structure, change of control/ownership, governmental permits and approvals, material agreements and employment issues.

Certain regulated sectors may trigger additional special issues. For instance, under the Banking Law, a client's accounts and information are confidential and may not be disclosed without the client's written approval. The approval of the Central Bank of Egypt is further required for due diligence to take place in the first place. Once obtained, proper arrangements must be made to safeguard the identity of clients. Due diligence on banks is always carried out in a controlled data room, where strict restrictions apply to photocopying and access, and with clients' names deleted and confidential information strictly protected.

Although it is most common for due diligence to be led by the acquirer's advisers, in certain transactions the target will instruct a due diligence report (prepared by a reputable law firm) and make it available to all bidders, in addition to the due diligence carried out by the purchasers' counsel.

1.2 Evaluation and pricing mechanism

Generally speaking, the parties are free to negotiate the purchase price. Tax implications are usually important factors in establishing the price and legal structure. In addition, the sale and purchase of listed shares are subject to even more rigorous rules. In this regard it will be important whether the shares in question are deemed 'heavily traded shares' as defined by the Egyptian Financial Supervisory Authority (EFSA) and the Egyptian Stock Exchange (ESE). For heavily traded shares, if the price varies upwards or downwards by more than 10% of the opening price in the trading session, then trading on such shares must be suspended for 30 minutes, and will be suspended until the end of the trading session if the variation exceeds 20%. As regards non-heavily traded shares, if the price proposed varies upwards or downwards by more than 5% of the opening price of the trading session, then an application must be made to the ESE Trading Committee to obtain its approval of that price. The ESE Trading Committee has broad discretion in this respect. However, if the acquisition triggers a tender offer, the price restrictions do not apply.

Tender offer rules apply to any person that acquired or intends to acquire, whether alone or together with related parties, at least one-third of the share capital, voting rights or bonds convertible into shares of companies listed on the ESE or unlisted companies that offered securities in a public offering at any given time, either for cash, securities or a combination of both. Any person intending to effect a transaction of that nature must notify the EFSA and submit an offer to purchase 100% of the securities of the relevant company.

Furthermore, if the price of the tender is less than the average trading price during the six months preceding the application for the tender offer, then:

- the EFSA will request the target to appoint an independent consultant approved by the EFSA to prepare an evaluation report on the tender offer; and
- the target will be bound to issue a statement describing the opinion of the board of directors on the offer of the acquirer and its implications for the target, its shareholders and employees.

The independent consultant's report must be disclosed and the board of directors' opinion issued within 15 days of publication by the ESE of the main terms and conditions of the tender offer on its screens. The above rules are also frequently changed and reinterpreted by the EFSA and ESE.

Various disclosure rules are also applicable.

For the period from incorporation of an Egyptian joint stock company until the issuance of its financial statements for one full fiscal year, the purchase price of shares in the company may not exceed the par value of such shares.

The parties can choose a suitable evaluation mechanism for the target, taking into consideration commercial issues such as its line of business. However, relatively popular valuation methods include earnings before interest, taxes, depreciation and amortisation, discounted cash flow and price-to-earnings ratio.

1.3 Available structures

A transaction can be structured as a share acquisition. Transfer of title to the target's shares must be executed by a brokerage company licensed by the EFSA, even for unlisted shares. The mechanics of processing the transaction vary, but in all cases the transaction is effected through the ESE. The time required for execution of such transactions is approximately one to three business days. However, deals above a threshold of E£20 million require the approval of the Trading Committee and hence usually take approximately five business days.

No capital gains tax or withholding tax is levied on dividends for non-Egyptian tax resident shareholders. However, for Egyptian and Egyptian tax residents, capital gains tax is levied if the shares sold are not listed on the ESE.

The transaction could also be structured as share swap, merger, consolidation under a holding company or asset purchase.

Asset purchases are advantageous from a liability point of view, since to a large extent they shield the purchaser from past liabilities. However, the acquired assets continue to serve as security against certain obligations such as taxes, wages and social insurance. Capital gains and sales tax implications must also often be considered in an asset deal. The exact time required for the transfer of the assets will depend on the type of asset involved. For instance, transfer of title to real estate through the real estate notary is time consuming and can take several months. Generally speaking, asset deals are harder to structure and implement, since each type of asset must be transferred by a transfer instrument appropriate to that asset.

Choosing between the various structures available will be influenced by various factors, discussed further below.

(a) Share purchase

Existing liabilities: Given that in a share purchase the acquirer will indirectly assume the rights and obligations of the target, one of the important factors in deciding whether to choose this structure is the nature and extent of the actual and contingent liabilities of the target. In this regard, the agreement may provide that the seller will continue to be responsible for all or part of the vast majority of the target's pre-closing liabilities.

Tax: The target, and consequently indirectly the acquirer, will continue to be liable for any unpaid taxes for any period prior to the closing date. However, that liability is usually mitigated by the representations and in certain instances by a retention of funds or an escrow arrangement.

Regulatory considerations: As a general rule, the acquirer will not be required to obtain new government permits, approvals or licences in order for the target to continue as a going concern or for the continued performance of its activities as conducted prior to the closing date.

Acquisition of 10% or more of an insurance company or a bank requires prior regulatory approval.

Also, transfer of title to the shares of a company with operations in the Sinai Peninsula must be approved by the competent governmental agency.

(b) *Asset sales*

Tax: The purchaser will not be liable for any previous unpaid taxes or tax evasion, but may be subject to the payment of sales tax. However, the acquired assets are deemed as security for any taxes, social insurance and wages due, even for periods prior to the closing date. If any tax issues arise post-closing, the new owner of the assets (ie, the acquirer) will have to deal with them and, if applicable, claim reimbursement from the seller. Accordingly, it is recommended that acquirers include clear indemnification language in the asset purchase agreement to impose explicitly on the target the burden of settling and paying any such tax liabilities.

Regulatory considerations: Since the target will continue to exist as a going concern, all applicable governmental permits, approvals and licences will not be transferred automatically to the acquirer. Therefore, the latter will have to obtain or seek the re-issue/assignment of all governmental permits, approvals and licences required for the performance of the activities relating to the acquired assets. This is one of the important factors that should be carefully considered to determine the viability of an asset transfer.

Other considerations: In addition to the asset purchase agreement, the parties will need to enter into a special agreement to transfer any real property that forms part of the acquired assets. It is also common in these structures to have irrevocable powers of attorney issued to the acquirer to enable it to transfer such assets with all governmental agencies and the notary.

In order for the sale agreement of real property to be enforceable against third parties, it must be registered with the competent notary public office. However, an unregistered sale agreement is binding and enforceable between the parties from the execution date. It is recommended that the acquirer obtain a power of attorney from the target to represent the latter in connection with all matters related to registration of the sale agreement with the notary public office and to represent the target in relation to third parties and governmental and non-governmental entities.

The acquirer must ensure that new public utilities agreements and insurance policies are in place by the closing date, or that the existing agreements and policies are assigned to it; otherwise it will risk being unable to operate (if there is no supply of public utilities) or of operating uninsured assets (if there is no insurance coverage).

The General Authority for Investment and Free Zones, which acts as the company registrar in Egypt, takes the view that selling all or substantially all assets of a company triggers the implementation of liquidation proceedings and, ultimately, the winding up of the company in question.

Foreign investment laws and foreign ownership restrictions: Generally, Egyptian companies can be owned up to 100% by foreigners.

By way of exception, companies engaged in imports for commercial resale purposes and commercial agencies must be wholly owned and managed by Egyptians. Aviation companies must also be at least 60% owned by Egyptian nationals.

Foreigners are also restricted from owning any real property in the Sinai Peninsula, but are entitled to enter into usufruct agreements for a period of up to 99 years.

2. Acquisition agreement

(a) *Pre-acquisition agreements*

Confidentiality agreement: The parties to a potential acquisition may wish to enter into a confidentiality/non-disclosure agreement to regulate the sharing of information between them.

The confidentiality agreement must define clearly the confidential information in question. In certain cases, the existence of the acquisition agreement itself may be subject to confidentiality restrictions, although this would not work for listed companies, as they are required to disclose to the ESE any negotiations of a potential acquisition agreement to which they might become a party.

Exclusivity agreement: Under an exclusivity agreement, the obligor (usually the acquirer) covenants that it will not directly or indirectly solicit or encourage proposals relating to the contemplated transaction. This is fairly common and is usually included in the letter of intent or memorandum of understanding.

The potential acquirer must ensure that both the shareholders of the target and the target itself are party to the exclusivity agreement, in order to ensure that the exclusivity restrictions cover all transfers of the business in question.

Memoranda of understanding: Documents such as memoranda of understanding, heads of terms, letters of intent, expressions of interest and term sheets aim to set out the commercial agreement in principle. Such documents are usually non-binding, with a few exceptions, such as those relating to exclusivity, confidentiality, governing law and dispute resolution. Egyptian law puts great emphasis on the intent of the parties; hence, any such documents must make clear that they are not intended to create binding obligations.

The memorandum of understanding must have a longstop date to enable the parties to pursue a different transaction after a certain period of time has elapsed.

(b) *Acquisition agreements*

Pursuant to a share purchase agreement, the holder(s) of the shares in the target undertake to sell those shares to the acquirer. Title to the shares can be transferred from the target to the acquirer immediately upon signature of the agreement or can be postponed until satisfaction of certain conditions precedent to closing. The agreement can range from simple to fairly complex. Usually, the representations, limitation of liability and disclosure, in addition to the price release mechanism and adjustment, if any, will be heavily negotiated.

An important preliminary matter is the language of the documentation. In many sophisticated deals, the documents will be prepared in English. However, if a government or public entity is involved, or if the agreement must be presented to or approved by a government agency, then the documentation will be in Arabic or in dual Arabic/English format.

Pursuant to an asset purchase agreement, the target undertakes to sell to the acquirer the target assets and the acquirer undertakes to purchase them. Title and possession of the assets can be transferred by the target to the acquirer immediately upon signature of the agreement, or can be postponed until satisfaction of certain conditions prior to closing.

The parties to an asset purchase agreement are the target and the acquirer.

In asset deals, shareholder approval through an extraordinary general meeting will likely be required.

The following clauses are commonly applied to both share and asset purchase agreements, unless otherwise indicated below.

Conditions precedent to closing: Such conditions may include required internal approvals and governmental approvals or other third-party approvals (eg, where the target is subject to change of control restrictions). In addition, where the parties decide to sign the acquisition agreement before the material findings of the due diligence on the target have been cured, they may wish to include such cures in the sale agreement as conditions precedent to closing.

Further important conditions precedent to closing arise where the purchaser intends to finance the transaction with bank loans

In all cases, the acquisition agreement must have a clearly defined longstop date for the satisfaction of all conditions precedent to closing, and must clearly set out the consequences of failure to meet that deadline, as well as any apportionment of liability between the parties.

Pre-closing covenants: The acquisition agreement will include various negative covenants on the part of the target in order to assure the acquirer that the status and affairs of the target will not materially change in the period between completion of the due diligence and closing.

Purchase price: The acquisition agreement will define the purchase price and the terms of payment. The purchase price can be paid in Egyptian pounds or another currency. There is generally no foreign currency control, and foreign currency can be obtained from banks and licensed currency dealers. Transfers may be effected only through banks.

The acquirer will also want to ensure the accuracy of the target evaluation by incorporating in the agreement a price adjustment clause to verify the results on which the evaluation was based. Usually, such verification exercises are performed by a third-party expert; the acquisition agreement must specify the name of the expert who will fulfil this role or the appointment mechanism where no expert is identified, together with a description of the required verification process.

Representations and warranties: The acquisition agreement commonly includes certain warranties covering (among other things):

- title to the assets or shares in question;
- confirmation that they are free from encumbrances;
- compliance with law;
- possession of all permits and licences;
- employment issues;
- payment of taxes and governmental fees; and
- insurance, financial and environmental issues.

The extent of such warranties will be subject to negotiation.

Limitation of liability: The agreement may limit the acquirer's ability to claim against the target under it. This can be achieved by several means, such as:

- setting a cap for any compensation payable under the agreement;
- defining the validity period of the warranties set out in the sale agreement; and/or
- releasing the target from its obligations if the damage is compensated by a third party such as an insurer.

In addition, the seller's liability may be limited by reference to matters set out in any disclosure letter.

Choice of law clause: As a matter of Egyptian law, the choice of non-Egyptian law as the governing law of an acquisition agreement is valid to the extent that the chosen law does not conflict with public order, morality or any other mandatory rules of Egyptian law. In the event that legal proceedings are brought in any Egyptian court, a party wishing to invoke a non-Egyptian law must establish that law as a matter of fact before the Egyptian court. In practice, it is more common for agreements to be governed by Egyptian law, to avoid inconsistency with Egyptian regulations and to ease the conditions for implementation of the deal.

Notwithstanding the above, an agreement to transfer title to real property in an asset deal must be documented in a separate document and governed by Egyptian law.

Dispute resolution clause: Submission by the parties to an acquisition agreement to the jurisdiction of non-Egyptian courts will be legal, valid and binding as a matter of Egyptian law, except in relation to matters in respect of which of the Egyptian courts have exclusive jurisdiction (although some commentators consider such submission revocable, based on public order considerations). An Egyptian court which is petitioned by a party to resolve any dispute arising under the acquisition agreement will apply Egyptian law to determine whether it has jurisdiction to hear and resolve the matter.

A final judgment (including for a definite amount of money) issued by a foreign court will generally be recognised and enforced by the Egyptian courts without re-examination or re-litigation of the merits of the case, provided that:

- the foreign court offers reciprocal treatment in relation to Egyptian court judgments. Otherwise, the Egyptian courts will re-examine the merits of the case in the same spirit as the foreign court (in practice, reciprocity is difficult to prove, so the enforceability of foreign judgments issued in jurisdictions that do not have treaties with Egypt is uncertain);
- the Egyptian courts are not exclusively competent to hear the dispute which was the object of the foreign judgment and the foreign court is shown to have been competent to hear the dispute in accordance with its own laws;
- the parties to the dispute were duly notified and properly represented in the proceedings;
- the foreign judgment is final and conclusive (*res judicata*), in accordance with the relevant law; and
- the foreign judgment does not conflict with a prior Egyptian judgment on the same subject, and is not contrary to public order or morality in Egypt.

The Egyptian courts retain concurrent non-exclusive jurisdiction in relation to assets or entities located in Egypt or obligations that arose or were performed or should have been performed in Egypt.

Egypt is a signatory to the 1958 New York Convention on the Recognition and Enforcement of Foreign Arbitral Awards. Moreover, pursuant to the Arbitration Law (27/1994), international arbitration awards are enforceable in Egypt; therefore, arbitral awards issued in respect of an acquisition agreement will be enforced in Egypt, subject to some conditions. The following documents must accompany the application for enforcement:

- the original award or a signed copy;
- a copy of the arbitral agreement;
- an Arabic translation of the award, authenticated by the competent authority if the award was not issued in Arabic;
- a copy of the minutes evidencing the deposit of the award with the competent court in Egypt (usually the Cairo High Court of Appeals); and
- a copy of the notification of the award to the party against which the award has been made.

Egyptian law provides for the annulment of arbitration awards in the following specific exceptional cases:

- An arbitration agreement was absent, or has been nullified or terminated.
- A party to the arbitration agreement was fully or partially incapacitated.
- Either party to the arbitration was unable to present its case as a result of not

being given proper notice of the appointment of an arbitrator or of the arbitral proceedings, or for any other reason beyond its control or due process was not observed.

- The tribunal did not apply the agreed applicable law to the dispute.
- The composition of the arbitral panel or the appointment of the arbitrators was in conflict with the applicable law or the parties' agreement.
- The arbitral award dealt with matters not falling within the scope of the arbitration agreement or exceeding the limits of the arbitration agreement. However, if matters falling within the scope of the arbitration can be separated from that part of the award which contains matters not included within the scope of the arbitration, the nullity affects the latter only.
- A nullity that affects the award has occurred in either the arbitral award or arbitral procedure.

Annulment procedures must be initiated within 90 days of notification of the award to the party against which the award has been made. Filing an action for annulment does not stay or prevent execution of the award, unless so requested by the party against which the award has been made based on serious grounds that justify a stay. In the case of a stay of execution, the competent court must issue a final judgment on the action for annulment of the arbitral award within six months of the date of the stay order.

3. Employment law and pension issues

In share transactions, the target's legal personality will remain intact and it will continue to perform its obligations as employer in relation to its employees. By contrast, in asset transactions, the acquirer will assume the statutory obligations of the target in relation to the employees. In addition, Egyptian law encompasses the doctrine of 'acquired rights', whereby if a right or benefit has been habitually enjoyed by employees over a number of years, those employees may acquire the right to treat that benefit as part of their employment package. Thus, if bonuses or other benefits are habitually paid, the employer runs the risk that those will be construed as part of the employees' remuneration. Employees will continue to benefit from acquired rights post-closing and the acquirer is not entitled to change, alter or terminate such rights.

4. Approval process

In asset sales where the target is a company, the shareholders must approve the sale of the relevant assets in an extraordinary general meeting.

With respect to the acquirer, a board resolution approving the acquisition is sufficient for the purposes of Egyptian law.

5. Antitrust laws

The Competition Law (3/2005) provides that: "Persons with an annual turnover according to their latest financial statements exceeding E£100 million shall notify the Egyptian Competition Authority upon their acquisition of assets, property rights, usufructs, stocks, or the setting up of unions, mergers or amalgamations, or the joint management of two persons or more. The notification shall be made in accordance with the rules and procedures set out by the Executive Regulations to the Competition Law."

The term 'persons' includes "related parties that are composed of two or more persons, each having an independent legal personality, where the majority of stocks or shares of one of said parties is owned, directly or indirectly, by the other party or where the majority of stocks or shares in both parties are owned by one party. Related parties are also those persons who are subject to the actual control of another person. Actual control means every arrangement, agreement or ownership of stocks or quotas, regardless of their percentage, in a manner that leads to the control of the management or of the decision taking process."

Therefore, if the above threshold is exceeded by the parties to a proposed acquisition, the notification requirements of the Competition Law will apply. However, the obligation is merely to notify the Egyptian Competition Authority of the acquisition and not to obtain the authority's approval.

Jordan

Alia Nimry
Khalifeh & Partners

Under Jordanian law, mergers are governed by Articles 222 to 239 of the Companies Law (22/1997). The law distinguishes between a merger (typically involving the acquisition of a company) and a 'pure share sale'. Companies can purchase 100% of the shares of another company as a pure share sale transaction without being subject to Articles 222 to 239.

1. Structuring

1.1 Due diligence

(a) *Methodology*

Public records: The due diligence undertaken in connection with mergers involves checking the public records of the participating companies.

Official records of companies registered in Jordan are available for inspection at the Controller of Companies Department of the Ministry of Industry and Trade. Typically, official records can be inspected by anyone who has been authorised to do so. Such authorisations may be issued by any shareholders of the merging companies, any member of the board of directors of the merging companies or any government entity.

Public records of companies registered in Jordan are also available for public inspection on the Controller of Companies Department website (www.ccd.gov.jo), which contains a comprehensive database of Jordanian companies. Searches may be conducted using a company's registration number or name, or the name of any of its shareholders. The website also includes a database of IP rights (trademarks and trade names) registered in Jordan. IP rights searches may be conducted using a trade name/trademark, trade name/trademark registration number or company name. However, as this database may not be up to date, the information found might be unreliable.

Searches may also be conducted on the Ministry of Justice website (www.services.moj.gov.jo) for any litigation claims instituted by or against any merging company or any of their shareholders. Searches may be conducted by claim number, the name of any involved party or the date of scheduled court hearings. Such checks are not conclusive, however, as the database covers only cases filed and heard at Qasr Al Adel, the main court of first instance in Jordan, and does not include details of arbitration proceedings.

Public records relating to any movable or immovable assets in Jordan which are subject to formal registration requirements (eg, real property and vehicles) must also be inspected to establish whether any liens or other encumbrances are attached thereto.

Requesting documents: Due diligence also involves requesting various documents to determine, among other things, a valuation of the target, as well as any risks and liabilities affecting it. The documents typically requested in the context of a merger are outlined further below.

The law specifies no procedure or mechanism for requesting documents. It is left to the parties and their technical, legal and financial teams to agree and pursue their own procedures.

(b) Relevant information

The above checks and searches should reveal, among other things:

- particulars about the assets and capital (authorised and issued share capital) of each participant;
- authorised signatories;
- names of the members of the board of directors;
- the objects of each participant; and
- whether any company is subject to liquidation procedures.

In parallel, each participant will usually be requested to disclose certain documents, including:

- minutes of board meetings and general meetings, which should reveal any material issues that may adversely affect the company and thus the merger (eg, whether any loans or sales of assets or a material part of the business have been approved);
- licences and approvals necessary for the operation of the business. These may vary from company to company and will depend on the nature of the business. Examples include planning and environmental licences, and import/export licences;
- audited financial statements;
- lists of employees, remuneration, positions, nature of employment contracts (temporary or permanent) and key personnel;
- details of the organisational structure;
- lists of IP rights;
- the original title deeds to any movable or immovable assets which require registration (eg, vehicles, lands, properties or ships), to ascertain whether any liens, mortgages or other encumbrances exist;
- material contracts (these will vary depending on the nature of the company's business);
- data and particulars of major clients, in addition to the nature of business conducted with each client;
- a letter evidencing that, as of the date of the letter, the company has paid all taxes due and payable;

- a letter evidencing that, as of the date of the letter, the company has paid all applicable social security payments on behalf of its employees (if applicable); and
- a letter from its legal counsel outlining any legal claims, procedures or actions in which the company is involved in and the value of each claim.

1.2 Valuation and pricing mechanism

The evaluation and pricing mechanism used to determine each participant's equity value, including shares and assets, will vary, depending on whether the company is in debt or has any outstanding loans. Any debts and/or outstanding loans will be factored into the evaluation and pricing mechanism used to calculate the company's net equity value.

The Companies Law does not provide for a specific evaluation mechanism. It rather provides for the formation of an evaluation committee – comprising the controller of companies, auditors, a representative from each participating company and a suitable number of merger specialists – in order to determine the net equity of the shareholders and the participating companies as of the proposed date of effecting the merger.

However, the participating companies typically agree on a certain evaluation mechanism or formula for determining the price per share and the value of the assets of each company both prior to and again on the date of effecting the merger. The parties may also agree on a mechanism or formula for adjusting the price per share and/or of assets in the event of any material change between the date of signing the merger agreement and the date of effecting the merger. Any such agreement will be contractually agreed and will therefore be enforced through an undertaking by each party. Agreement on the evaluation and pricing mechanism, as well as its method of implementation, is essential to the merger and is among the most heavily negotiated issues between the parties.

1.3 Available structures

(a) *Mergers*

Mergers in Jordan may be effected in accordance with any of the structures identified in Article 222 of the Companies Law and outlined below, provided that the objects of the merging companies are similar or complementary.[1]

Upon effecting the merger, the corporate personalities of the merging companies identified by law will cease and all rights, liabilities and obligations incurred prior to finalisation of the merger will be transferred in full to the successor company.[2] The successor company will thus assume all liabilities and obligations of the merging companies.[3]

The merger structures set out in Article 222 of the Companies Law are as follows:

---

1 Article 222(a) of the Companies Law.
2 Article 222(a) of the Companies Law.
3 Article 238 of the Companies Law.

Merger of one or more companies into existing company or companies: In order for one or more companies (Company A) to merge into an existing company or companies (Company B) in accordance with the above structure, the procedures listed in the Companies Law must be complied with. The shareholders' meeting of Company A must approve the merger, and the assets and liabilities of Company A must be evaluated pursuant to the evaluation process set forth in the Companies Law to establish the value of Company A. Once this has been determined, the shareholders' meeting of Company B must pass a resolution to increase its share capital in proportion to the value of Company A and must also approve the amendment of its articles and memorandum of association to reflect the capital increase and any other changes as a result of the merger. The increase in share capital of Company B must be distributed among the shareholders of Company B in proportion to their existing shareholdings.[4]

Once all of this happens, Company A will cease to exist and Company B will be the legal successor of Company A.

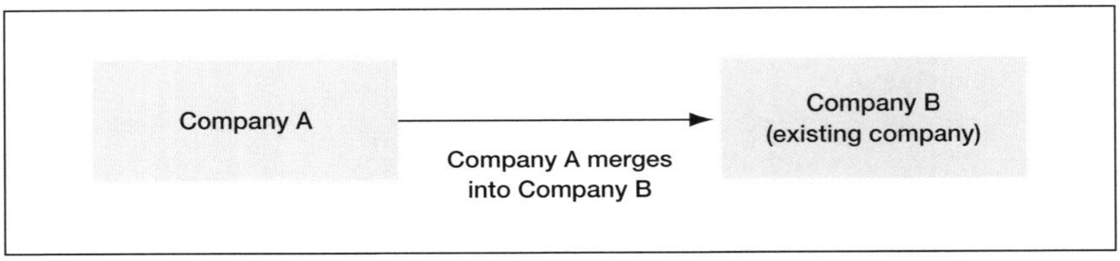

Merger of two or more companies to form a new company: In such a transaction Company A and Company C will cease to exist and the new company will be the legal successor of Company A and Company C.

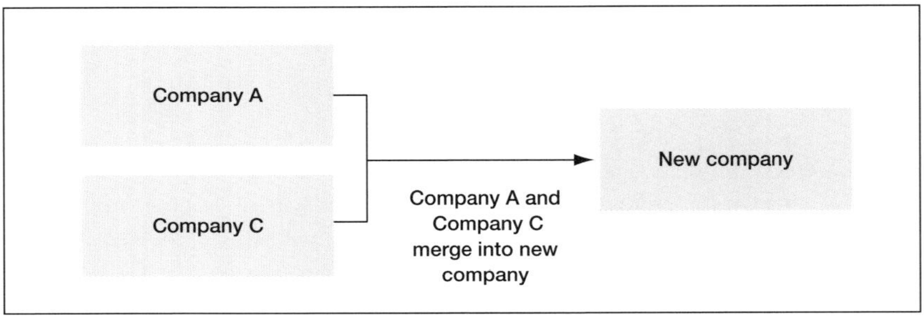

Merger of branch or agency of foreign company with existing Jordanian company to form new Jordanian company established solely for purposes of the merger: While this structure is provided for in Article 222 of the Companies Law, certain conceptual and legal obstacles hinder its application. In particular, a branch of a foreign company does not possess a separate legal personality; as such, it is conceptually difficult to understand how two branches would merge into a separate company.

4 Article 222(a) of the Companies Law.

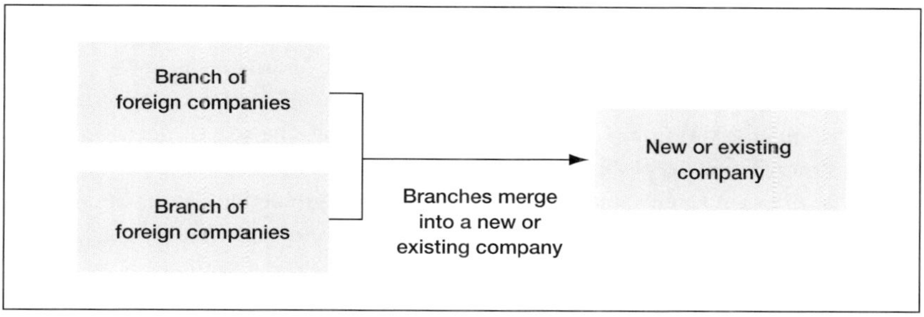

(b) ***Acquisitions***

The Companies Law provides for the acquisition of companies, in whole or in part, by other corporate entities.[5] However, in the context of mergers governed by Articles 222 to 239 of the Companies Law, acquisitions must relate to the entire share capital of a company. In order for such acquisitions to be valid, the following procedures must be undertaken:[6]

- The shareholders' meeting of the acquirer must approve a resolution on the proposed acquisition.
- The shareholders' meeting of the target must approve a resolution agreeing to the proposed acquisition.
- All approvals, announcements and procedures required under the Companies Law and the applicable Securities Law must be obtained or complied with, as the case may be, including the waiver of any pre-emption rights over shares of the target, execution of a share transfer deed in a form approved by the Ministry of Industry and Trade, and compliance with any share transfer lock-up period specified in the Securities Law, if applicable.
- The acquirer must deposit the purchase price for the acquired shares in a special account, to be distributed to the shareholders of the target in proportion to their shareholdings.
- The shareholders' meeting of the target must approve the amendment of the articles and memorandum of association and appoint a new board of directors.

(c) ***Alternative 'grouping' structures***

Alternative structures allow for companies to be 'grouped' under one umbrella. However, such groupings do not constitute a merger within the meaning of Articles 222 to 239 of the Companies Law, and as such do not attract the benefits which conventional mergers enjoy. For example, the companies and shareholders involved in a merger are exempt from all taxes which arise by reason of the merger or result therefrom. As alternative grouping structures do not enjoy those tax exemptions, stamp duties are levied on any transfer of shares in the amount of 0.03% (for private companies) or 0.05% (for public companies) of the value of the shares being transferred.

Several alternative grouping structures are available.

5 Article 222(b) of the Companies Law.
6 Article 222(b) of the Companies Law.

The first example is where Company X issues new shares, to which the shareholders of Company Y will subscribe (see graph below). Simultaneously with the issuance of new shares, the shareholders of Company Y will transfer their shareholdings in Company Y to Company X. Company X becomes the sole owner of Company Y. This structure may be problematic where Company Y's shares are transferred to Company X as an in-kind contribution (as opposed to a cash transaction), as the Ministry of Industry and Trade must form a committee[7] to ascertain the value of Company Y, which may be time consuming. Further, the committee's determination of the value of Company Y may differ from and/or contradict what has been agreed by the parties. If that happens, the parties will need to enter into side arrangements (which may not be legally enforceable) to document their understanding;

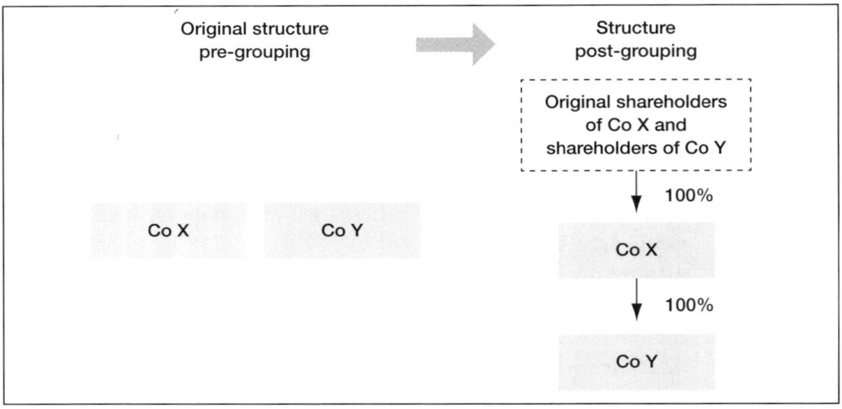

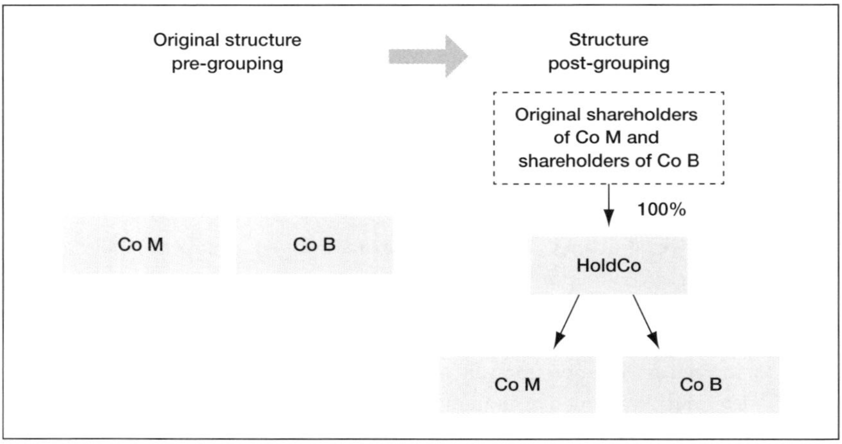

Alternatively, as shown in the second diagram, the entire share capital of the companies being grouped (Company M and Company B) may be sold by their

7 Articles 58 and 70*bis* of the Companies Law.

respective shareholders to another company established for the purposes of assuming ownership of those companies (HoldCo). Under this structure, the shareholders of Company M and Company B will incur registration fees for registration of HoldCo, as well as stamp duties in respect of the transfer of shares.

1.4 Structuring considerations

(a) *Merger versus grouping structure*

At the outset, companies must consider whether they wish to undertake a merger (within the meaning of Articles 222 to 239 of the Companies Law) or an alternative grouping structure. In this regard, the general consensus is that grouping may be a quicker process and require fewer governmental approvals and consents. Accordingly, alternative grouping structures may have a higher chance of success than a conventional merger.

In a conventional merger, the successor company (whether existing or new) assumes all obligations, liabilities and rights of the merging companies. By contrast, under a grouping structure, the obligations and liabilities of one company will transfer to another only through the execution of novation or assignment agreements. Novation is recognised and enforced by the Jordanian courts by virtue of Articles 993 to 1017 of the Civil Code (43/1976). In order for novation to be legally valid and enforceable, a number or requirements must be satisfied. One requirement which may be problematic in this context is that the novation instrument or agreement must be executed by all three parties – that is, the outgoing entity, the incoming entity and the surviving entity).[8] Further, the novation instrument or agreement must be notarised.[9] Notarisation costs are 0.0011% of the value of the novation instrument or agreement. As such, while novation is recognised and enforced in Jordan, the associated procedural requirements and costs may make the proposed grouping non-viable.

Additionally, in a merger the corporate personalities of the merging companies cease to exist and their registrations at the Ministry of Industry and Trade are simply cancelled. By contrast, under a grouping structure, a company that will cease to exist must be liquidated pursuant to the liquidation procedures of the Companies Law, which may be time consuming and costly.

If a merger is to be effected, the choice of structure will depend on the nature of the transaction and issues such as the overall objectives of the participants, the timeframe and the associated costs.

2. Merger procedure

An application must be submitted to the controller of companies at the Ministry of Industry and Trade for review, together with the following documents:[10]

- the shareholders' resolutions of the merging companies approving the

---

8 Article 996(a) of the Civil Code.
9 Article 1002 of the Civil Code.
10 Article 225 of the Companies Law.

merger and specifying the date on which the actual merger shall occur;
- the merger agreement entered into between the merging companies, duly executed by the authorised signatories on behalf of each merging company;
- the balance sheets of the merging companies, certified by licensed auditors;
- the financial statements of the merging companies for the two years preceding the date of the proposed merger, certified by licensed auditors;
- a preliminary evaluation of the assets and liabilities of the merging companies (actual value or market value); and
- any other documents required by applicable laws or requested by the controller of companies.

If the minister of industry and trade approves the merger application, an evaluation committee will be formed.[11] The evaluation committee will evaluate the assets and liabilities of the merging companies in order to substantiate the net equity of each shareholder of the merging companies as at the specified date of the merger. The committee will submit its report, along with the opening balance sheet of the successor company, to the minister of industry and trade within 90 days of the date on which the matter is referred to it;[12] the minister may extend this period by a further 90 days if necessary.[13]

2.2 Executive committee

The minister will form an executive committee comprising the chairmen and members of the boards of directors of the merging companies, and the companies' auditors. The committee's mandate mainly involves implementation of the merger, in particular by:[14]
- specifying the shareholding of each shareholder in the merging companies, applying the net equity evaluation made by the evaluation committee;
- amending the articles and memorandum of association of the successor company where this is an existing company, or preparing the memorandum and articles of association for a new successor company; and
- inviting the shareholders' meetings of the merging companies to approve the following (approval by a majority of 75% of the shares represented for each company separately is required):
  - the new or amended articles and memorandum of association of the successor company (as the case may be);
  - the results of the re-evaluation of the companies' assets and liabilities, and the opening balance sheet of the successor company; and
  - the final approval of the merger.

The executive committee shall furnish the controller of companies with the minutes from each shareholders' meeting within seven days of the meeting.[15]

---

11 Article 228 of the Companies Law.
12 Article 228 of the Companies Law.
13 Article 228 of the Companies Law.
14 Article 230 of the Companies Law.

2.3 Publication

On completion of the above procedures, the controller of companies will register the successor company and cancel any registrations of the merging companies.[16] The controller of companies will then publish notification of the merger in the *Official Gazette* and in two local daily newspapers. Details of the merger will be published for two consecutive days, along with a summary of the merger agreement, the results of the net equity evaluation as determined by the evaluation committee and the opening balance sheet of the successor company.[17]

2.4 New board of directors

The boards of directors of the merging companies will continue to function until the successor company has been officially registered and its accounts approved by the controller of companies. Once the successor company's independent accounts have been approved, the executive committee will manage the company for a period of up to 30 days, during which it will invite the shareholders' meeting to elect a new board of directors and auditors.[18] The management of the successor company will then be assumed by the new board and its operations conducted in accordance with its management structure.

2.5 Objections and annulment

Bond holders and creditors of the merging companies, and any shareholders that oppose the merger or have any outstanding shareholder loans or interests, may object to the transaction within 30 days of the date of publication, as described above.[19] Upon receipt of an objection, the minister of industry and trade will refer it to the controller of companies.[20] If the controller of companies fails to settle the objection within 30 days of the date of referral, the objecting party can contest the merger before the court. Any such objections or court proceedings will not affect or suspend the merger procedures.[21]

If a merger violates or fails to comply with the Companies Law, or if it contravenes public order, any interested party may instigate legal proceedings before the courts to contest the merger and request its annulment. Such claims must be instigated within 60 days of publication of the merger, as described above.[22] Any claim made must include a description of the grounds on which the objection is based and specify, in particular:[23]

- the grounds on which the merger agreement is claimed to be invalid or any material error in the evaluation of the net equity of the merging companies' shareholders;

---

15 Article 230 of the Companies Law.
16 Article 231 of the Companies Law.
17 Article 231 of the Companies Law.
18 Article 232 of the Companies Law.
19 Article 234 of the Companies Law.
20 Article 234 of the Companies Law.
21 Article 234 of the Companies Law.
22 Article 235 of the Companies Law.
23 Article 235 of the Companies Law.

- whether the merger involved an arbitrary use of rights, or would grant a direct personal interest to any member of the merging companies' boards of directors or to the majority shareholders of any merging company, at the expense of the minority shareholders;
- any grounds which led the objector to believe that the merger was based on deceit or fraud, or caused damage to the creditors; or
- whether the merger created a monopoly in a specific market, resulting in damage to the public economic interest.

Any such claims or legal proceedings will not affect or suspend the merger procedures, unless and until a final court decision is issued rendering the merger null and void. The court has discretion to grant the parties involved in the merger (mainly the merging companies) a grace period in which to resolve the issues. The court may subsequently dismiss the claim if the alleged violations/grounds are resolved prior to the issuance of the final court decision.[24]

With the exception of mergers that do not comply with the Companies Law or that contravene public order, the Companies Law does not address the consequences of objections to a merger. There appear to be no reported cases on the question of objections.

2.6 Personal liability

In order to prevent mergers on vexatious grounds, including fraud, the Companies Law recognises the personal liability of the directors and management of merging companies. The chairman, members of the board of directors and auditors of each of merging company are personally liable towards third parties for any claims against any such company for any liabilities or obligations which were not recorded or announced prior to the date of the merger.[25] Parties may be exempted from liability if they can prove to the court that they had no prior knowledge of, or are not responsible for, such liabilities or obligations.[26]

2.7 Tax

The successor company and the shareholders of the merging companies are exempt from all taxes and fees (including any share transfer fees imposed on the merger) which apply to or result from the merger.[27]

3. Regulatory considerations

Generally, applicable regulatory considerations depend on the sector in which the merging companies operate. There is no law or entity with exclusive responsibility for the regulation of mergers in Jordan. Some sector-specific regulatory issues/procedures are outlined below.

---

24 Article 236 of the Companies Law.
25 Article 237 of the Companies Law.
26 Article 237 of the Companies Law.
27 Article 224 of the Companies Law.

3.1 Insurance

If one of the participants to the merger is an insurer, it must also comply with the Regulation of Insurance Works Law (33/1999).[28] Where the terms of the Companies Law conflict with those of the Insurance Law, the latter will prevail.

Insurers can merge only with companies that are engaged in the provision of the same type of insurance services.[29] Further, no procedures relating to the merger can commence until an application has been submitted to the director of the Jordanian Insurance Commission, together with any required reports and information, and prior written approval of the commission's board of has been obtained.[30]

If the board of directors of the Jordanian Insurance Commission approves the merger in principle it will form a committee to evaluate the assets and liabilities and ascertain the net equity of the merging companies. The evaluation committee will report to the director of the commission no later than 90 days from the date on which the matter was referred to it.[31] The 90-day period may be extended following a decision of the board of directors of the commission.[32] If, following the review of the reports of the evaluation committee, the board of directors of the commission approves the merger, it will form an executive committee comprised of the members of the boards of directors of the merging companies and their respective auditors to commence the merger procedures.[33] The duties of the executive committee are the same as those set out in the Companies Law.

All insured persons (whether natural or legal) are entitled to inspect the merger agreement, which must be made available at the insurer's headquarters for 15 days after the merger has been announced in a local newspaper.[34]

Tax exemptions and incentives may be made available to the merging companies by decision of the Council of Ministers, following a recommendation of the board of directors of the Jordanian Insurance Commission and the Minister of Finance.[35]

3.2 Banks

Under Jordanian law, banks may be operated by public companies only. As such, and in addition to the requirements and restrictions set out in the Companies Law, banks must comply with the requirements set out in the Banks Law (28/2000, as amended).[36] Where the terms of the Companies Law conflict with those of the Banks Law, the latter will prevail.

A bank cannot commence any procedures relating to a proposed merger without the prior written approval of the Central Bank of Jordan.[37] No timeframe is specified within which the Central Bank must issue such approval.

---

28 Article 56(a) of the Regulation of Insurance Works Law.
29 Article 56(b) of the Regulation of Insurance Works Law.
30 Article 56(b) of the Regulation of Insurance Works Law.
31 Articles 57(b) and (c) of the Regulation of Insurance Works Law.
32 Article 57(c) of the Regulation of Insurance Works Law.
33 Article 57(d) of the Regulation of Insurance Works Law.
34 Article 58(a) of the Regulation of Insurance Works Law.
35 Article 58(d) of the Regulation of Insurance Works Law.
36 Article 76(a) of the Banks Law.
37 Article 76(b) of the Banks Law.

Once the bank's shareholders' meeting has approved the merger, this decision will be binding on all shareholders and any claims by minority shareholders will be limited to financial compensation.[38]

In the case of a merger between banks, the Central Bank of Jordan is responsible for appointing the members of the evaluation committee.[39] All other procedures and provisions stipulated in the Companies Law are applicable and must be complied with.

Subject to the provisions of the Companies Law, the following will be transferred by law to the successor bank:[40]

- all accounts, deposits, facilities tangible or intangible securities (without the approval of any person, beneficiary, account holder, mortgagor or mortagee); and
- all rights and obligations of the merging bank(s).

The successor bank will assume all rights and liabilities, and will be subject to all proceedings brought against or by any of the merging banks.[41]

4. Antitrust laws

The Competition Law (33/2004) applies to all production activities, trade activities and services in Jordan. It also applies to commercial activities conducted outside Jordan which result in commercial activities within Jordan.[42] Any practices, alliances or agreements, whether express or implied, which violate or eliminate fair competition are prohibited.[43]

4.1 Market concentration

For the purposes of the Competition Law, 'market concentration' means an activity which results in partial or full transfer of ownership or transfer of rights to use properties, rights or shares in a manner which would enable an entity or a group of entities to control (whether directly or indirectly) other entities or groups of entities.[44] Where an entity in Jordan wishes to undertake any activity that would affect competition in the market or strengthen the entity's dominant position in the market, it must obtain the written approval of the minister of industry and Trade where market concentration exceeds 40%.[45]

The entities responsible for approving such transactions must obtain the opinion of the minister of industry and trade as to the effect of such transactions on competition in the relevant sector.[46]

---

38 Article 77 of the Banks Law.
39 Article 78 of the Banks Law.
40 Article 79(a) of the Banks Law.
41 Article 79(b) of the Banks Law.
42 Article 3 of the Competition Law.
43 Article 5 of the Competition Law.
44 Article 9(a) of the Competition Law.
45 Article 9(b) of the Competition Law.
46 Article 9(c) the Competition Law.

4.2 Approval procedure

An entity that wishes to conclude a transaction that involves a market concentration must submit an application to the Competition Directorate at the Ministry of Industry and Trade within 30 days of executing the transaction agreement, together with the following documents:[47]

- the memoranda and articles of association of the parties to the agreement;
- the transaction agreement;
- a list of the products or services affected by the transaction;
- the financial statements of the parties for the preceding two years;
- a list of the board of directors of each party; and
- any other information or documents which the Competition Directorate may request.

The Competition Directorate will publicise the proposed market concentration transaction in two local newspapers, along with an invitation to any interested party to raise any concerns within 15 days of the date of the announcement.[48]

The minister of industry and trade, upon the recommendation of the director of the Competition Directorate, may:[49]

- approve the transaction, if it finds that the transaction would not adversely affect competition or the positive effects would outweigh the negative effects;[50]
- approve the transaction as long as the concerned parties undertake to perform and fulfil certain conditions specified by the minister of industry and trade; or
- reject the application and issue a decision to cancel/annul the transaction and restore the status quo prior to the transaction.

In all of the aforementioned cases, the minister of industry and trade must publish the decision in two local newspapers.[51]

The minister of industry and trade must issue a decision on the transaction within 100 days of submission of the application.[52] During this period, the parties to the transaction agreement must make no changes to the structure of the market or act in any manner which would endorse the transaction (any such actions may be deemed invalid or null by court order).[53]

The minister of industry and trade may cancel any approvals previously given for a market concentration transaction if:[54]

- the parties to the agreement violate any conditions under which the undertaking was approved; or
- the approved information or documentation is found to be misleading.

---

47 Articles 10(a) and (d) of the Competition Law.
48 Article 10(e) of the Competition Law.
49 Article 11(a) of the Competition Law.
50 This includes job creation, encouraging exports and attracting investment.
51 Article 10(d) of the Competition Law.
52 Article 11(c) of the Competition Law.
53 Article 11(c) of the Competition Law.
54 Article 11(d) of the Competition Law.

Decisions of the minister of industry and trade may be appealed to the High Court of Justice.[55]

5. Foreign investment laws and foreign ownership restrictions

51. Restrictions

The Regulation on Investments by Non-Jordanians (54/2000)[56] governs foreign investments in Jordan.

Pursuant to Article 3 of the regulation, a non-Jordanian investor may not own more than 50% of any Jordanian project or company which operates within certain sectors or activities. Such sectors and activities include the following:

- Trading activities:
  - purchasing goods and other movable assets with a view to leasing them, including machinery, equipment, transportation vehicles and equipment, rental cars, aircraft (without crew) and ships;
  - purchasing goods and other movable assets with a view to selling them at a profit;
  - offering trading services by bulk or unit;
  - importing and exporting goods (with the exception of imports to Jordanian borders);
  - distributing goods and services within Jordan; and
  - importing materials (with the exception of foods not made in Jordan).
- Services:
  - construction works (including associated engineering services);
  - agent and intermediary services;
  - currency exchange services (except services provided by banks);
  - travel agency services; and
  - restaurants.
- Transportation:
  - passenger and cargo transportation (with the exception of transportation on ships owned by non-Jordanians);
  - ship management services; and
  - storage services.

Article 4 of the Foreign Investment Regulation provides that a non-Jordanian investor may not own more than 49% of any project or company which operates within the following sectors or activities:

- scheduled or charter air transport services of passengers, cargo and mail; and
- aircraft leasing (with a crew).

---

55 Article 11(f) of the Competition Law.

56 Issued pursuant to Article 24 of the Investment Promotion Law and its Amendments (16/1995). Although the Investment Promotion Law and its Amendments (16/1995) has been replaced by the Provisional Investment Promotion Law and its Amendments (67/2003) and Provisional Investment Law 68/2002, its provisions will remain valid until they are replaced by others.

Article 6 of the Foreign Investment Regulation sets out sectors and activities which non-Jordanians are prohibited from participating in (whether partially or fully owned). These include investigation and security services, and sports clubs.

Except as provided in Articles 3, 4 and 6 of the regulation, and subject to any other restrictions under Jordanian laws, the ownership of a non-Jordanian investor in any other sector or activity is unrestricted.

5.1 Capital requirements

Article 7 of the regulation provides that any foreign investment must be of a minimum value of Jd50,000 (except where it relates to investments in public companies).

5.2 Council of Ministers

Article 8 of the Foreign Investment Regulation provides that the Council of Ministers may, on a recommendation of the minister of industry and trade, permit a non-Jordanian investor to own a higher percentage than that stipulated by the regulation in major development projects.

6. Merger agreement

6.1 Pre-merger agreements

(a) Confidentiality and non-disclosure agreement

The parties to a merger agreement or arrangement, as illustrated on the following page, may enter into a confidentiality agreement or non-disclosure agreement to protect confidential information disclosed in the process of negotiation and due diligence from unauthorised further disclosure or use. Jordanian law does not recognise punitive damages or self-help remedies. As such, if a party breaches the confidentiality agreement or non-disclosure agreement, the other party may bring legal proceedings against it and any award of the court will be based on actual damages incurred as a result of the breach. It is recommended to include a provision in the confidentiality agreement or non-disclosure agreement whereby the parties acknowledge that a breach of the agreement, and in particular any unauthorised disclosure or use of confidential information, will cause irreparable harm to the non-defaulting party.

In some cases certain restrictions may apply to a company's ability to disclose its confidential information to third parties. For example, the chairman, the members of the board of directors, the general manager and any employees working at a public limited company are prohibited from disclosing to any shareholder or third party information or data pertaining to the company which is deemed confidential and which was obtained through their post at the company or through performing any work for or at the company.[57] This excludes information and data disclosed pursuant to applicable laws. Anyone who violates this shall be removed from his post and

---

57 Article 158 of the Companies Law.

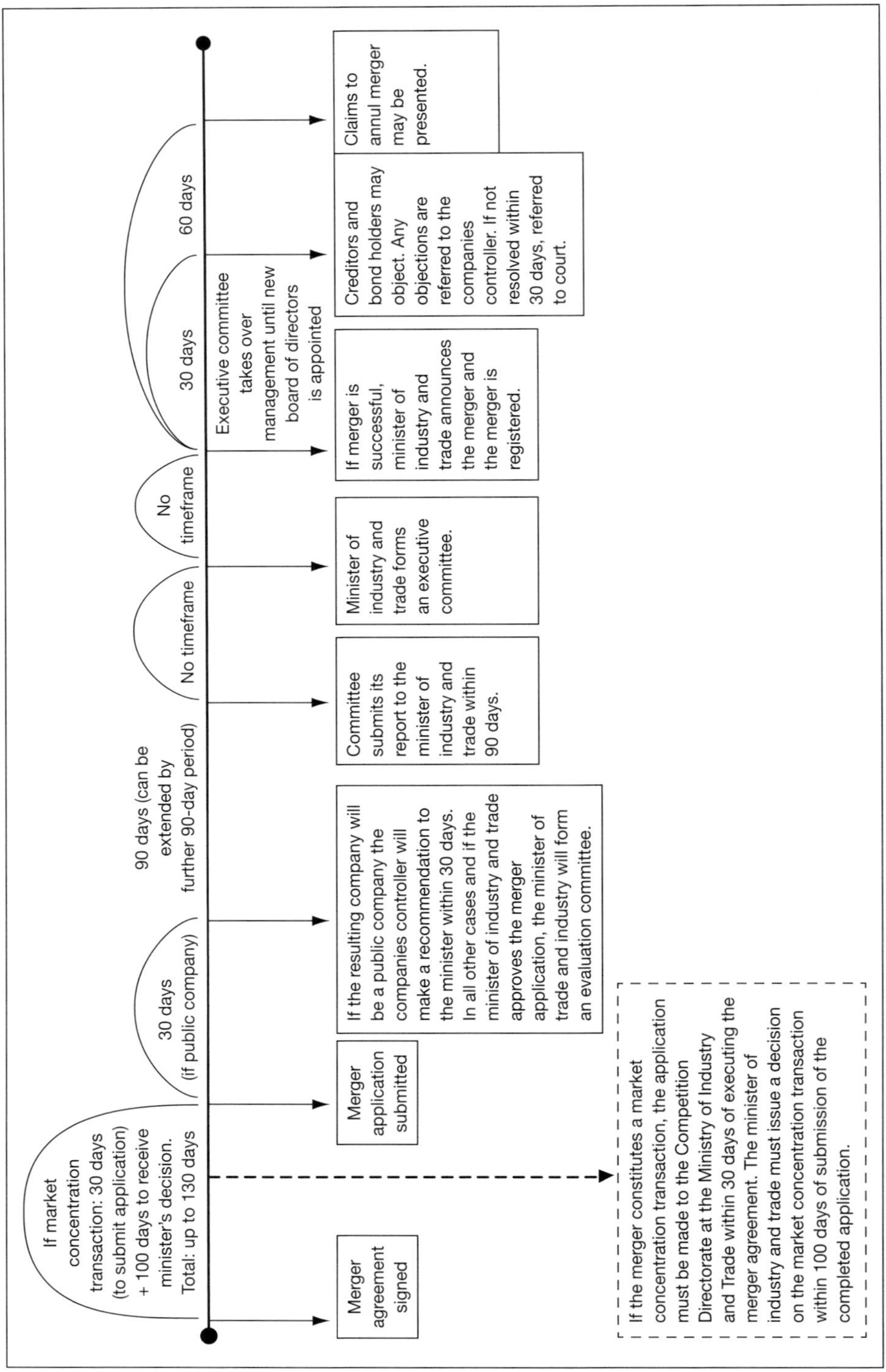
If market concentration transaction: 30 days (to submit application) + 100 days to receive minister's decision. Total: up to 130 days
30 days (if public company)
90 days (can be extended by further 90-day period)
No timeframe
No timeframe
30 days
60 days
Executive committee takes over management until new board of directors is appointed
Merger agreement signed
Merger application submitted
If the resulting company will be a public company the companies controller will make a recommendation to the minister within 30 days. In all other cases and if the minister of industry and trade approves the merger application, the minister of trade and industry will form an evaluation committee.
Committee submits its report to the minister of industry and trade within 90 days.
Minister of industry and trade forms an executive committee.
If merger is successful, minister of industry and trade announces the merger and the merger is registered.
Creditors and bond holders may object. Any objections are referred to the companies controller. If not resolved within 30 days, referred to court.
Claims to annul merger may be presented.
If the merger constitutes a market concentration transaction, the application must be made to the Competition Directorate at the Ministry of Industry and Trade within 30 days of executing the merger agreement. The minister of industry and trade must issue a decision on the market concentration transaction within 100 days of submission of the completed application.

required to compensate any damages suffered by the company. In such case the approval of the shareholders' meeting to release the chairman and the members of the board of directors from liability does not preclude legal liability.[58] The controller of companies, the company and/or any shareholder may bring legal proceedings for any disclosure of confidential information.[59]

It is not possible to determine conclusively whether certain documents or information constitute confidential information under the Companies Law, as the act does not provide a definition. However, a 'trade secret' within the meaning of the Illegal Competition and Trade Secrets Law of 2000 includes information:

- that is secret because it is not known in its final form or because of the accuracy of its contents, or because it is not 'easy' to obtain from persons dealing with such information;
- that has 'commercial' value (due to the fact that it is a secret); and
- whose holder/owner has taken reasonable measures to safeguard its secrecy and confidentiality.

Banks (which must be operated by public companies) provide another example of the application of restrictions on the disclosure of information. Article 72 of the Banks Law (28/2000, as amended) provides that a bank (within the meaning of the Banks Law) must maintain absolute secrecy in relation to client accounts, deposits, securities and deposit boxes, and is prohibited from disclosing such data (whether directly or indirectly) without the client's written consent. Existing and former administrative staff are prohibited from disclosing any information in relation to client accounts, deposits, securities and deposit boxes.[60] The prohibition expressly includes any person who by virtue or his profession, job, work or post (whether directly or indirectly) accessed such information, including bank employees and auditors. This provision also captures members of the board of directors.

Article 74 of the Banks Law provides certain exceptions to the prohibition on disclosure, under which it is permissible to disclose client information to third parties. The exceptions mostly relate to disclosure in relation to the Central Bank of Jordan or to auditors, or the sharing of client history information to ascertain the client's financial credibility. Article 75 of the Banks Law states that anyone contravening Article 73 will be imprisoned for a term of not less than six months, fined between Jd10,000 and Jd50,000 or both.

(b) Exclusivity agreement

As mentioned above, Jordanian law does not recognise punitive damages or self-help remedies. Thus, where a party breaches an exclusivity agreement, the other party may bring legal proceedings against it and any award will be based on actual damages incurred as a result of the breach.

58 Article 158 of the Companies Law.
59 Article 160 of the Companies Law.
60 Article 73 of the Banks Law.

(c) ***Memorandum of understanding***

A memorandum of understanding may be entered into between the parties to a merger to outline their intentions, and set out a road map and timeline to be followed. The memorandum may include confidentiality and exclusivity provisions, and those provisions as well as any applicable law provision will be binding on the parties; the remainder of the memorandum will generally be on a 'best endeavours' basis, although this may vary from case to case depending on the parties' specific intentions and arrangements.

The execution of a memorandum is not a legal requirement, but simply common practice (to set out initial commercial terms and understandings between the parties).

6.2 Merger agreement

(a) ***Scope of application***

In a merger involving a private shareholding company or limited liability company, the parties to the merger agreement are the merging companies (represented by their authorised signatories) and their respective shareholders.

Where the merger involves public shareholding companies, the parties to the merger agreement are the merging companies (represented by their authorised signatories), provided that the actual merger has been approved by the shareholders' meetings and the boards of directors of the participating companies.

(b) ***Important clauses***

The merger agreement will typically include an extensive list of conditions precedent, in particular due to the various governmental approvals required and the procedures relating to the evaluation committee and executive committee.

The agreement will also contain a detailed price adjustment mechanism to cater for:

- material changes which would affect the value of the companies involved in the merger between the date of signing of the merger agreement and the date on which the merger actually occurs; and
- the evaluations of the evaluation committee and verification of the executive committee, which could determine that the value of a company is higher or lower than the value agreed between the parties.

Typically, the agreement may also include (depending on the structure of the transaction):

- an agreement on a minimum percentage of shares to be allotted to a certain party as a condition precedent to implementing the merger;
- a mechanism or formula by which the parties agree to settle any differences arising pursuant to material changes or the evaluations of the evaluation committee and verification of the executive committee; and
- the execution of personal guarantees between the parties to transfer shares or settle any such differences, through the transfer of shares or through cash or in-kind payment.

Where a party fails to fulfil any of its obligations, the non-breaching party may bring legal proceedings for breach of contract only and cannot enforce the terms of such provisions.

(c) ***Representations and warranties***

A merger agreement typically includes all the 'standard' representations and warranties, such as the companies being duly incorporated and having all necessary permits and licences to conduct their business and operations.

Further, and depending on the nature of the particular transaction, representations and warranties given by a party may include items in relation to assets, employees, liabilities, debts, loans, arm's-length transactions, key customers, material contracts and so on.

(d) ***Liabilities and limitation of liability***

Limitations of liability in Jordan are not recognised. Any compensation ordered by the court would most likely be for actual damages sustained by the aggrieved party, as determined by a court-appointed expert. As such, any provision contained in a contract purporting to pre-determine liquidated damages, setting out an agreed amount of compensation or purporting to limit any party's liability may not be upheld by a court pursuant to Article 364 of the Civil Code. This article states that parties to a contract may contractually agree to estimated damages in case of contractual breach, but that "the court may in all cases and on the application of either party amend that agreement to render the estimation equal to the damage" suffered by a party. In other words, Article 364 reserves the right for the court to alter any predetermined figure for liquidated damages to reflect actual damage suffered.

(e) ***Choice of law clause and dispute resolution clause***

The laws of Jordan allow the parties to a contract to elect to apply the law of a foreign jurisdiction to their relationship, as long as the foreign law that is chosen does not contravene Jordanian public policy and morals. Any provisions under the foreign law that contravene Jordanian public policy or morals will be considered null and void, and as such will be unenforceable.

Article 28 of the Code of Civil Procedure further provides that the Jordanian courts may claim jurisdiction over a dispute instituted against a foreign party which has no domicile or residency in Jordan where, among other things:

- the subject matter of the action relates to property (movable or immovable) located in Jordan;
- the action arises from an obligation created in Jordan; or
- the action arises from an obligation performed or which should have been performed in Jordan.

A line of Court of Cassation cases has interpreted Article (28) broadly and held a waiver of jurisdiction provision invalid and unconstitutional in each case above. Such cases involved commercial agencies and situations where the Jordanian party was named as a defendant in legal proceedings filed by the foreign party in a

Jordanian court. In the latter cases, in dismissing the Jordanian party's lack of jurisdiction defence, the court reasoned that the submission to the foreign court's jurisdiction, as stipulated in the underlying agreement, was for the benefit of the foreign party, and as such, the foreign party could waive such right and pursue the defendant in its home country courts. In the former cases, the court used wide language that could be interpreted to mean that the court's interpretation of Article 28 will apply to all types of case. Accordingly, it may well be the case that if a contractual arrangement between a Jordanian party and a foreign party calls for the submission of the parties to the jurisdiction of non-Jordanian courts, and the Jordanian party institutes a legal action against the foreign party in the courts of Jordan notwithstanding, the foreign party's lack of jurisdiction defence might not be supported or upheld by the Jordanian court.

Where a party that obtained an arbitral award or a court decision seeks to enforce the decision in Jordan, it must file an enforcement request before the Jordanian court in accordance with the Enforcement of Foreign Judgments Law (8/1952) or the New York Convention on the Recognition and Enforcement of Foreign Arbitral Awards. Based on the Enforcement of Foreign Judgments Law, a Jordanian court may decline the request to enforce a court order in the following circumstances only:

- The court issuing the judgment is not competent.
- The party against which the judgment was made carried out no activities in the jurisdiction in which the court issuing the judgment has competence, did not reside in that jurisdiction or did not wilfully appear before the court and has not acknowledged its competence.
- The party against which the judgment was made was not notified of the summons to appear forwarded by the court issuing the judgment and did not appear before the court, despite the fact that it resided within the jurisdiction of the court or carried out its businesses there.
- The judgment was fraudulently procured.
- The party against which the judgment was made convinces the court that the judgment is not yet final.
- The judgment relates to a claim that will not be heard by the courts of Jordan due to conflict with public policy and public morals.
- The judgment was issued by any court of a country whose laws prohibit the enforcement of the judgment issued by the courts of Jordan.

This list reflects that of the Enforcement of Foreign Judgments Law. As Jordan is a signatory to the New York Convention, the terms of the convention have precedence over local laws when it comes to the enforcement of foreign arbitral awards covered by the New York Convention. Article 5 of the New York Convention provides a list of the events which might result in a refusal to enforce an arbitral award. As such, the application of the bullets above is limited to:

- foreign judgments issued by foreign courts; and
- foreign arbitral awards issued in countries that are not signatories to the New York Convention.

Jordanian courts, on enforcement of a foreign judgment or a foreign arbitral award, may not give effect to an indemnity for the costs of litigation, since Jordanian law imposes limits on compensation for costs of litigation awarded by the Jordanian courts.

7. Employment law and social security

For the purposes of the Labour Law (8/1996), an employee's employment (and employment contract) will remain valid and in force following a merger. In such event the original employer and the new employer shall be jointly liable, for a period of six months from the date on which the merger is effected, for the performance of obligations resulting from the employment contract that arose before the merger was effected. After six months, the new employer will be solely liable for the performance of obligations resulting from the employment contract.[61] This employer's liability relates to all of the employee's rights, not just pay.[62]

The Social Security Law (17/2010) makes mandatory the enrolment and registration of most categories of employee with the Social Security Corporation. This entails the payment of contributions by both the employee and the employer. Social security is deemed an entitlement for the purposes of the Labour Law and as such shall be treated in the same way as other labour-related rights.

It is unclear how the exact date on which a merger is effected is determined for employment purposes, particularly given the lengthy approval procedures involved.

In order to mitigate the risks for the original employer, the original employer may request that employees execute release agreements to waive their rights. For such document to be enforceable and valid, they must be executed by employees upon the cessation of their employment.

The parties to a merger agreement may agree among themselves how to allocate risks relating to employees. Such an agreement will not preclude liability, but it gives parties (depending on their agreement) the right to claim compensation from one another.

8. Approval process

8.1 Internal approvals

(a) Limited liability companies

The merger of a limited liability company must be approved by an extraordinary shareholders' meeting.[63] Unless the memorandum and articles of association stipulate otherwise, a quorum of shareholders holding at least 75% of the shares is required. It is permissible to increase the percentage required for the meeting to be quorate, but not to drop below 75%.[64]

The merger of a private shareholding company must be presented to the

61 Article 16 of the Labour Law.
62 The author wishes to thank Dr Sayid Mohmoud for his expert advice on the Labour Law.
63 Article 67 (a)(3) of the Companies Law.
64 Article 65(b) of the Companies Law.

extraordinary shareholders' meeting.[65] Unless the memorandum and articles of association stipulate a higher percentage, a quorum of shareholders holding at least 75% of the voting shares is required. In order to pass a resolution approving the merger, the approval of shareholders holding at least 75% of those voting shares represented at the extraordinary shareholders' meeting is required.[66]

(b) *Public companies*

The merger of a public company and/or the acquisition of the entire share capital of another company must be presented to the general assembly in an extraordinary meeting.[67] The presence of shareholders holding at least 50% of the listed shares is required for an extraordinary general assembly to be quorate. In order to pass a resolution approving the merger or the acquisition, the approval of shareholders holding at least 75% of those represented in the extraordinary general assembly meeting is required.[68]

8.2 Regulatory approvals

These are outlined in section 1.3 above.

(a) *Mergers involving public companies*

Where the merger involves a public company or will result in the establishment of one, the controller of companies will examine the merger application form, in addition to the supplementary documents, and submit recommendations regarding the proposed merger to the minister of industry and trade within 30 days of receipt of the application.[69]

(b) *Suspension of trading*

If the merging companies are public shareholding companies, the board of directors of each public merging company must notify the controller of companies, the Securities Commission, the Amman Stock Exchange Department and the Depository Centre within 10 days of the date on which the shareholders' meeting issues a resolution approving the proposed merger.[70] The trading of shares of the merging companies at the Amman Stock Exchange will be suspended as of the date of such notification and will be re-activated on the conclusion of the merger procedures and the registration of the resulting company.[71]

9. Post-merger issues

9.1 Employees – transfer, termination and end of service issues

The transfer of employees and the liabilities relating to such transfers are dealt with above.

---

65 Article 77(a)(3) of the Companies Law.
66 Article 67(d) of the Companies Law.
67 Articles 175(a)(2) and (5) of the Companies Law.
68 Article 175(b) of the Companies Law.
69 Article 227 of the Companies Law.
70 Article 226 of the Companies Law.
71 Article 226 of the Companies Law.

Where the resulting company wishes to terminate the employment of an employee, the amount of compensation payable to the employee will depend on whether the employee was employed under a permanent employment contract or a temporary employment contract.

The primary differences between the two are as follows:

- If the employer terminates the employment of an employee on a temporary employment contract, the employer must pay the employee an amount equal to the amount which would have been paid had the contract not been terminated (ie, the salary of that employee until the term of the contract expires).
- If the employer terminates the employment of an employee on a permanent employment contract, the employer will pay half a month's salary for every year of service which the employee has served or two months' salary, whichever is higher.

Additionally, where an employer fails to register an employee with the Social Security Corporation, the employer must pay the employee an 'end of service reward' in lieu of the social security corporation deductions. This applies to temporary and permanent employment contracts. The reward will equal one month's salary for every year of service.

9.2 Change of control provisions and third-party consents

The resulting company is the legal successor of the merging companies and as such, unless specifically agreed to contractually, it does not require third-party consents (except those governmental approvals noted in this chapter).

9.3 Assets

All assets of the merging company will be transferred to the resulting company by law. To this end, if the assets are registered in public records (eg, the Land Department), the name of the owner of the assets must be amended to reflect the name of the resulting company. This process may be time consuming.

9.4 Other post-merger issues

All official documents must be amended to reflect the name of the resulting company and all governmental entities must be informed of the change of name (eg, the Tax Department and the Social Security Corporation).

10. Case study

D Co specialises in the supply of energy in northern Jordan and A Co supplies energy in southern Jordan. Both companies felt confident that a merger would serve their commercial goals. As such, the companies decided to merge into a newly established company (X Co), comprising the shareholders of D and A. Both companies proceeded to the negotiation stages and a preliminary draft merger agreement was prepared, addressing issues of transferring the assets, customer data, know-how, IP rights and employees of D and A to X. In addition, financial advisers were appointed by D and A to substantiate the net equity value of each company, as well as to create a formula to be used to calculate the allotment of shares in X to the shareholders of D and A. The shareholders of D and A executed personal undertakings to abide by the allotment of shares as determined by the appointed financial advisers, regardless of the evaluation and allotment determined by the evaluation committee in accordance with the Companies Law. The negotiation procedures in relation to the actual mechanics of the merger – particularly the share allocation formula – extended for a period of seven months. Due to the lengthy approval procedures required by law to effect the merger and the difficulty in ascertaining the share allocation between the shareholders of D and A, the merger was not completed.

The author is grateful for the assistance of her colleague Duha Fayyad at Khalifeh & Partners in the preparation of this chapter.

Kuwait

Ramy El Demerdash
Philip H Kotsis
Sonia A Salah
Al Tamimi & Company

1. Introduction

In general, globalisation has positively affected business in Kuwait, although the Arabian Gulf region, including Kuwait, has not escaped the effects of the global economic crisis. In recent times, however, we have seen signs of the beginnings of resurgence in the Kuwaiti economy. Therefore, companies may soon consider the benefits of a merger or acquisition at both local and international levels.

Mergers and/or acquisitions can provide the opportunity for companies to build on strengths and limit or negate risks or weaknesses. Often large companies undergo restructuring with the objective of reducing market competition, and improving their financial position by increasing market share. Small or mid-size companies, by contrast, may consider mergers and acquisitions as a means of improving their market position and increasing profits.

1.1 Definitions

While the terms 'merger' and 'acquisition' are generally used interchangeably, in fact they represent two distinct business transactions, rather than a single corporate restructuring transaction, with differing features and consequences.

A merger occurs when two or more companies come together with the mutual purpose of forming a new separate entity. Accordingly, these individual companies will relinquish their respective corporate identities and combine their assets and operations to establish a new separate company. Neither company survives. Upon completion of the transaction the original individual companies will have consolidated to form a new separate entity. An alternative type of merger occurs when one or more companies is dissolved with all its liabilities subsequently transferred to an existing company.

Conversely, when one company purchases another company, and the purchased company is taken over by the purchasing company, this transaction is commonly referred to as an 'acquisition'. Therefore, in an acquisition the purchased company does not lose its legal identity as a company by merging into the purchasing company; rather, it ceases to exist as it is wholly taken over and subsists under the ownership and control of the purchasing company.

Often companies and individuals use the term 'mergers and acquisitions' when describing an acquisition to try to evade any negative connotations of a hostile takeover.

In summary, in a merger transaction, neither of the individual companies survives. Instead the companies are replaced by a newly-formed company. By contrast, in an acquisition transaction, one company ceases to exist when the other company takes control of it.

1.2 Regulatory framework

Various laws and governmental agencies are relevant to M&A transactions in Kuwait. No single, consolidated law regulates mergers and acquisitions; nor was there a specific regulator until the advent of the Capital Market Authority (CMA) in 2010.

The main laws that apply are as follows:

- the Commercial Companies Law (15/1960);
- the Commercial Law (68/1980);
- the Law concerning the Disposal of Shares of Joint Stock Companies and Securities (42/1984);
- the Law on Advertising Interests in Shares of Joint Stock Companies (2/1999);
- Ministerial Decree 60/1992 concerning Procedures and Conditions of Mergers and Evaluation of Company Assets;
- the Income Tax Decree (3/1955 – known as the Tax Law), as amended by Law 2/2008; and
- Executive Rules and Instructions of Kuwaiti Income Tax (Decree 3/1955), as amended by Law 2/1988.

In 2010 the Kuwaiti Parliament passed the Law concerning Establishment of the Capital Markets Authority and Organisation of Securities Activity (7/2010) (the Securities Law). This new law was brought into force to regulate and govern the organisation of securities activity, and applies to listed companies in Kuwait. It established the CMA as regulator under the supervision of the Ministry of Commerce and Industry (MOCI). The CMA's mandate includes the following:

- organising the activities of securities firms to ensure fairness, open competition and transparency;
- keeping the public informed about securities activities, publicising benefits and risks, to promote the development of securities activity;
- providing protection for those involved in the securities sector;
- reducing exposure to risks in the securities sector;
- applying a policy of total disclosure to promote fairness and transparency and to prevent conflicts of interest and the misuse of internal information; and
- enforcing compliance with relevant laws and regulations.[1]

Further, on March 13 2011 the Executive Bylaws of the CMA were published in the *Official Gazette* and subsequently amended on March 20 2011. The CMA Bylaws regulate and provide rules and guidelines governing securities activity, including the procedures for the acquisition of listed companies.

---

1 Article 3 of Law 7/2010 concerning the Establishment of the Capital Markets Authority and Organisation of Securities Activity.

The CMA Bylaws, however are silent on the subject of acquisitions of unlisted companies and mergers of listed and unlisted companies. The CMA recently issued guidance regulating mergers procedures (see below).

The Securities Law and the CMA Bylaws do not supersede the Commercial Companies Law, as the provisions in the Commercial Companies Law regulating mergers of companies in Kuwait are still in effect.

2. Foreign ownership restrictions and corporate forms

2.1 Foreign ownership restrictions

Under Article 23 of the Commercial Law, "no person other than a Kuwaiti may carry on business in Kuwait, unless he has one or more Kuwaiti partners, provided that the capital invested by the Kuwaitis in the joint trading firm is not less than 51% of the total capital of the trading firm". Therefore, a foreign entity wishing to participate in a Kuwaiti company would have to establish the company together with Kuwaiti partners, which must own at least 51% of the capital. Although this policy is protective in nature and designed to ensure Kuwaiti nationals have the opportunity to be involved in many activities conducted in Kuwait, foreign entities are not excluded from conducting profitable activities in Kuwait.

The foreign ownership restriction does not apply to citizens of, or entities established in, any of the members of the Cooperation Counsel for the Arab States of the Gulf (GCC). The GCC includes Bahrain, Saudi Arabia, the United Arab Emirates, Oman and Qatar. For purposes of the foreign ownership restriction rule in Kuwait, the law treats entities formed in and under the laws of a GCC member nation as Kuwaiti companies. Therefore, an entity based in a GCC jurisdiction is free to participate in Kuwaiti entities. The participation of such entity is treated the same way as participation by a Kuwaiti citizen or entity, and its participation is counted as part of the 51% minimum ownership rule.

Another exception to the restriction on foreign ownership was created by the Law Regulating Foreign Capital Direct Investment in Kuwait (8/2001 – the Foreign Investment Law). The Foreign Investment Law potentially allows foreign investors to own 100% of business entities in certain approved sectors and exempts the foreign investors from Kuwait income taxes for a limited term. The activities which can be conducted by foreign investors under this law are limited. Further, approval of such activities must be obtained from the Foreign Investment Bureau, which also monitors and assists in the administrative, legal and licensing process in conjunction with the relevant public authorities.

2.2 Available corporate structures

Various types of company can take part in mergers and acquisitions. Thus, the applicable procedures for each vary significantly.

Under the Commercial Law, foreign entities can establish a separate Kuwaiti legal entity either to conduct business in Kuwait, or to acquire an interest in the equity of an existing Kuwaiti company.

In the event that a Kuwaiti company is being established, the entity can take one of two forms under the Commercial Companies Law:

- a 'with limited liability' company (WLL); and
- a joint stock company (KSC).

2.3. With limited liability companies

Perhaps the most common corporate vehicle used by foreign companies setting up in Kuwait is the WLL company. The Commercial Companies Law defines a 'WLL' as a limited liability company consisting of a maximum of 30 people, each of whom is liable to third parties only up to the amount of their capital contribution. The Commercial Companies Law requires that a WLL have at least two, but no more than 30 partners.[2] A WLL may not be a public company, but may be converted to a joint stock company. The Commercial Companies Law requires the minimum capital of the WLL to be Kd7,500, but the MOCI may at its discretion raise that minimum sum depending on the objects of the company. The term of a WLL may be unlimited.

A Kuwaiti WLL requires 51% 'Kuwaiti' participation pursuant to Article 23 of the Commercial Law. This is most commonly achieved in practice via a Kuwaiti partner. This Kuwaiti partner will have to fulfil ongoing administrative functions at the MOCI and other governmental departments that deal only with Kuwaitis. Furthermore, the Kuwaiti partner will be the only party authorised to sign most documents on behalf of the company where governmental entities are involved.

Unlike other entities, share certificates are not issued for a WLL. Instead, the shares (or 'parts' as ownership interests in a WLL are sometimes referred to) held by partners in a WLL are recorded in the memorandum of association (the memorandum) of the WLL which is registered at the MOCI. Any transfer of those shares will not be effective until the memorandum of the WLL is amended by the signing of a deed of amendment before the Notary Public of the Ministry of Justice, which is then filed at the MOCI.[3]

One of the advantages of the WLL is that there is a degree of flexibility in designing its management structure, particularly in comparison with a joint stock company. A WLL can be managed by one or more managers, who need not be partners. They may act for a fee or gratuitously.[4] Under current MOCI practice, the managers may be foreign nationals, but only after an initial period as a start-up with the first manager being Kuwaiti.

Given that the memorandum of a WLL typically follows a standard form, most partners in a WLL enter into a form of partnership agreement to regulate the management and affairs of the company. Generally, partnership agreements are valid and enforceable as long as the provisions contained in the agreement are not contrary to public policy and law (eg, purporting to grant a foreign party more than a 49% beneficially interest in the company). The powers of the manager(s) are detailed in the memorandum, but in the absence of any provisions about powers, the managers will have full powers to act on the company's behalf.

---

2 Article 185 of Law 15/1960.
3 Article 197 of Law 15/1960.
4 Article 201 of Law 15/1960.

2.4 Kuwait joint stock companies

Another corporate vehicle used by foreign companies to set up an entity in Kuwait is a KSC. A KSC closely resembles shareholder companies as generally understood in the West. Any joint stock company incorporated in Kuwait is of Kuwaiti nationality if all of its shareholders are Kuwaiti and its registered office is in Kuwait.[5] There are exceptions to that general rule, however, which allow foreign entities to become shareholders of a KSC if necessary for the investment of foreign capital or to obtain foreign expertise. The Commercial Law specifies that some shareholders may be non-Kuwaiti where necessary to invest foreign capital or experience, provided that the proportion of capital of the Kuwaiti shareholders is not be less than 51% of the KSC's capital and as long as a licence is obtained from the relevant government authority.

Unlike a WLL, the number of shareholders in a KSC is not capped; the minimum is five.[6] Should there be fewer than five participants, nominee shareholders must be appointed and hold a small proportion of the shares of the KSC.

In a KSC, the liability of each shareholder is limited to the nominal value of its respective shares. All shares must be issued at its stated value, not at a value below par. Under the Commercial Companies Law, only one class of shares may be issued by a KSC. In addition, the rights attached to all shares in the KSC are equal in all respects, including rights in relation to the distribution of profits.[7]

The minimum capital of a KSC ranges from Kd250,000 to Kd2 million.[8] The amount of required stated capital will depend on the company's objectives. As with a WLL, the MOCI has the discretion, in practice, to increase the minimum capital required for the establishment of any KSC; it is not unusual for the MOCI to exercise that discretion.

3. Legal aspects of mergers and acquisitions

3.1. Acquisitions of a KSE listed company

In addition to regulations applicable to the organisation of securities' activity in Kuwait, the Securities Law and the CMA Bylaws also establish a supervisory framework for acquisition transactions, with specific provisions designed to protect minority shareholders during the acquisition process. Specifically, acquisitions of Kuwaiti joint stock companies that are listed on the KSE are governed by Chapter 7 of both the Securities Law and the CMA Bylaws. These new laws and regulations were implemented in 2010 to ensure that companies involved in M&A transactions act in the best interests of its shareholders, and the companies provide shareholders with sufficient information to make informed decisions. For example, the CMA Bylaws require that all shareholders of the target be treated equally by the acquiring company.

---

5 Article 68 of Law 15/1960.
6 Article 70 of Law 15/1960.
7 Article 63 of Law 15/1960.
8 Article 98 of Law 15/1960.

(a) ***Antitrust protection***

In the interest of fairness and competition, the CMA Bylaws require the acquirer to obtain the approval of the Competition Protection Agency in accordance with the Law concerning Competition Protection (10/2007) before proceeding with any acquisition procedures as set out in the CMA Bylaws. The Competition Protection Agency approval loop is intended to promote fair competition, and prevent anti-competitive behaviour such as price-fixing by ensuring that the acquisition will not prevent or harm competition in the Kuwait marketplace (eg, permitting a company to become so dominant that it creates barriers for new companies wishing to enter the same business or restrains the free flow of goods into the market).

(b) ***Protection of minority shareholders***

To protect the minority shareholders in an acquisition, the CMA Bylaws impose a ban on all parties (acquirer, target and any consultants) from furnishing information solely to some shareholders, but not to others during the period of acquisition offer or during the CMA approval process. This protection is to ensure that all shareholders, regardless of the size of their shareholding, are provided with the same information.[9]

Furthermore, the board of directors of the acquirer and of the target must supply their respective shareholders with sufficient information and relevant advice to enable them to reach an informed decision. Shareholders must be given at least 15 days to make an informed decision leading up to the date of the general assembly of shareholders called upon to resolve the acquisition transaction.[10]

(c) ***Acquisition offer of 51% to 100% of shares***

In order to make an acquisition offer for a Kuwaiti listed company, the acquirer must first receive approval from the CMA. An 'acquisition offer' is defined as an offer, attempt or request to obtain:

- all the shares of a listed company or all remaining shares within a listed company not already held by the acquirer, or its affiliated parties; and
- all remaining shares in the listed target held by other shareholders in the company (eg, where, the acquirer and its affiliated parties acquire a majority of the target's shares enabling it to control the board of directors).[11]

Within seven days of receiving the acquisition offer, the target company's board of directors must submit a letter to the CMA indicating its opinion and its recommendation to the shareholders. Upon receiving the CMA's approval of the acquisition offer, the target's board of directors must issue that opinion and recommendation letter to the target's shareholders.[12]

---

9 Article 251 of the CMA Bylaw.
10 Article 254 of the CMA Bylaw.
11 Article 247 of the CMA Bylaw.
12 Article 266 of the CMA Bylaw.

(d) *Information to be disclosed in acquisition offer*

With the need for transparency in mind, the CMA Bylaws require the acquirer and target to disclose an acquisition offer in any of the following situations:[13]

- if both the acquirer and target have reached an initial agreement to submit the acquisition offer;
- on the acquisition of shares of a listed company by a party – whether an individual or an entity – which results in an obligation to submit an acquisition offer under the provisions of the mandatory offer as set forth in the CMA Bylaws. This disclosure, however, may be delayed if all the relevant information is not readily available – it must, however, follow in a subsequent disclosure; or
- if the CMA finds that other events indicate that disclosure is necessary.

The CMA Bylaws also provide particular guidelines as to what type of information the acquisition offer documents must contain. At a minimum, they must include:[14]

- sufficient information about the acquirer and the target;
- details of the shares for which the offer is made, including any rights or restrictions attached to them;
- the total amount of shares being proffered;
- a complete description of how the offer will be financed, what the source of financing will be and who the main lender or the party arranging financing will be;
- details of all documents required and procedures to be followed in order for acceptance of the offer to be completed;
- a statement of any conditions or restrictions applicable to the offer and any relevant procedures;
- a schedule for the acquisition process;
- the number of equity shares and volume of any control shares of the acquirer in the target;
- the number of equity shares and volume of any control shares in the acquirer if it is an offer to barter with securities only;
- the number of equity shares and volume of any control shares in the target which is the subject of an offer in which the board of directors of the acquirer will have an interest, or which is owned or controlled by parties affiliated to the acquirer (including their names), or owned or controlled by persons that irrevocably accepted the acquisition offer before publishing the offer document (including their names); and
- any other information requested by the CMA.

The acquisition offer documents must also contain a statement indicating whether there are any agreements, arrangements or understandings between the

13 Article 257 of the CMA Bylaw.
14 Article 258 of the CMA Bylaw.

acquirer and any of its affiliated parties, any member of the board of directors of the target or any of its shareholders. This statement should also include complete details of any such agreement or arrangement. In addition, a statement must be issued indicating whether any shares to be acquired under the offer will be transferred to any other persons (stating the names of parties in any relevant agreement, arrangement or understanding, if any), and details of securities owned by such persons in the target, or a statement indicating that no securities are owned in this way.[15]

(e) Approval and publication of offer document

Once the acquisition offer documents have been prepared, they must be submitted to the CMA for approval before they can be published. The CMA will then issue its decision on whether to approve or withhold its approval within a maximum period of 10 days from the date of receiving the offer document and all the other documents, data and information requested by the CMA.

The CMA can withhold its approval if:

- the offer document does not comply with the provisions of the Securities Law or the CMA Bylaws;
- the offer is not accompanied by the required submission fees;
- the acquirer fails to submit the data required by the Securities Law or the CMA Bylaws; or
- the offer contains false information or has omitted data which might affect any shareholder's decision.[16]

Once the CMA does issue its approval of the acquisition offer documents, those documents will be published by the acquirer or on its behalf according to the time schedule established by the CMA.

Subsequent to publication of the offer documents, copies of the following documents must be made available until the end of the acquisition offer period:[17]

- the target's board of directors' recommendation regarding the acquisition offer;
- the memorandum and articles of association or any other similar corporate documents of the acquirer and target;
- audited financial statements of the acquirer and target for the preceding three fiscal years – if available;
- any valuation reports or letters;
- any document proving an irrevocable obligation to accept the acquisition offer;
- documents regarding financial arrangements related to financing the acquisition offer if such arrangements are revealed in the acquisition offer document; and
- any other documents requested by the CMA.

---

15 Article 259 of the CMA Bylaw.
16 Article 264 of the CMA Bylaw.
17 Article 267 of the CMA Bylaw.

The location of the documents (where they can be accessed and reviewed) must be indicated in the acquisition offer documents.[18]

In addition to the acquisition of more than 50% of the shares of a company, the CMA Bylaws also contemplate acquisitions of different amounts of shares, as discussed in the following sections.

(f) *Mandatory offer of an acquisition of more than 30% of shares*

A party, individually or jointly with its affiliated parties, must immediately submit a mandatory acquisition offer for all of the remaining shares from the same class, within 30 days of directly or indirectly obtaining equity ownership of more than 30% of the voting shares of a listed company. The CMA, however, can make an exemption from that rule if it appears to be in the best interests of the shareholders or on public policy grounds.[19]

Where an acquisition offer gives rise to a mandatory offer, the latter must be a cash offer amounting to at least the expected average daily price of a target share on the KSE target for the six years preceding the beginning of the offer period, as calculated by the KSE.[20]

For mandatory offers, the CMA Bylaws provide that the acquirer must submit its offer directly to the shareholders of the target (without having to hold a general assembly of shareholders of the target). Each shareholder will be permitted to sell its shares to the acquirer or keep them during the offer period decided by the CMA. If the mandatory offer requires a general assembly of shareholders to issue a resolution with regard to the acquirer or on any other such arrangement, then no shares relating to the mandatory offer may be acquired.[21]

(g) *Acquisition of between 5% and 30% of shares*

Another type of acquisition contemplated by the CMA Bylaws is that of at least 5%, but no more than 30%, of the shares of a listed company. When a shareholder holds approximately 5% or more of the shares of any company listed in the KSE, whether individually or jointly with its affiliated parties, and the shareholder intends to raise the percentage of its shareholding, then the shareholder must disclose its intention (under the disclosure of interests provisions of Chapter 10 of the Securities Law) and must submit relevant information to the CMA.[22]

A shareholder may increase its percentage of shareholding up to a maximum of 30% by the following methods:

- the purchase of shares directly through the KSE;
- the submission of an application to the KSE to hold an auction to purchase a specific number of such shares, but only after first receiving the agreement of a shareholder(s) who are willing to sell a specific number of their shares at a price agreed upon in advance, and following CMA and KSE conditions and

18 Article 267 of the CMA Bylaw.
19 Article 271 of the CMA Bylaw.
20 Article 274 of the CMA Bylaw.
21 Article 273 of the CMA Bylaw.
22 Article 269 of the CMA Bylaw.

requirements in holding the auction; and

- an announcement to the shareholders of the company of the submission of an offer to purchase a specific number of shares, at a specific price and within a specific period of time, provided that the CMA gives its prior written approval and the conditions and requirements laid down by the CMA are complied with.

(h) ***Reverse acquisition***

Another possible type of acquisition in Kuwait is a reverse acquisition. A 'reverse acquisition' is defined as any arrangement under which a listed company offers to its shareholders new shares in an unlisted company instead of shares in the same, and the new shares represent more than 50% of the voting shares in the listed company after acquisition. When a reverse acquisition is disclosed, the listing of the acquirer's shares will be suspended until the operation is complete. On completion of the reverse acquisition, the listing of the acquirer's shares will be cancelled, and the acquirer must submit an application for a new listing, as long as it meets the requirements for listing.[23]

(i) ***Acquisition where there are 'actual controlling parties'***

The CMA Bylaws also apply to the submission of an acquisition offer by one or more shareholders holding shares in both the acquirer and the target at whatever percentage would enable them to control the appointment of the majority of the board members, or to control resolutions passed by the board or by the general assemblies of the company in question. Such a shareholder is referred to as an 'actual controlling party'.[24] In these cases, the interests of the actual controlling parties must be disclosed to the shareholders in the acquisition offer before it is finalised, and that disclosure must be detailed (pursuant to the relevant provisions of CMA Bylaws). In addition to this disclosure, the board of directors for each company must confirm that the votes of the actual controlling party, and any affiliated party, will not be counted when passing a resolution regarding the acquisition offer in the general assembly of shareholders.

(j) ***New instructions regarding acquisitions***

In 2012 the CMA issued Instructions regulating New Restrictions and Procedures Concerning the Implementation of Acquisitions Procedures (the CMA Instructions). The CMA Instructions determine that Chapter 7 of the CMA Bylaws will apply if the target is listed on the KSE. The instructions apply where there is an acquisition of more than 30% of the capital of a listed company (for those exempted from making a mandatory offer).

Generally, the CMA Instructions require that in order for a company to implement an acquisition, it has to follow certain procedures in addition to those set out in Chapter 7 of the CMA Bylaws. These procedures include the following:

---

23 Article 289 of the CMA Bylaw.
24 Article 283 of the CMA Bylaw.

- disclosing the acquisition to the CMA and KSE when first agreed between the acquirer and the target;
- obtaining an approval from the Competition Protection Agency prior to proceeding with the acquisition;
- presenting an opinion from a neutral CMA-licensed investment consultant to the shareholders concerning the acquisition;
- providing the opinion and recommendations of the board of directors of the target with regard to the acquisition to the shareholders of the target and the CMA; and
- convening an extraordinary general assembly to pass a resolution regarding the acquisition offer by both the acquirer and the target. The resolutions by both companies should be forwarded to the CMA.

When the CMA has approved the acquisition offer, there are certain finalising procedures which must be completed by the acquirer at the KSE and the Kuwait Clearing Company. After concluding those matters, the implementation of the acquisition transaction will be published on the website of the KSE and in the *Official Gazette*.

3.2 Acquisitions of companies with limited liability

In Kuwait, an acquisition of a WLL can be a time-consuming transaction, since the MOCI is involved in all stages of the process (because changes to the memorandum of association of a company must be recorded in the MOCI registers).

In practice, the procedure for acquiring a WLL normally takes at least 60 days to be effected at the MOCI and in some cases, 90 days. The acquisition procedures include submitting an application on a form prepared by the MOCI, along with relevant documents including, but not limited to, the following:

- the memorandum and articles of association of the WLL and all amendments showing the capital structure of the WLL before and after the acquisition;
- a bank certificate showing that the share capital of the new partner has been deposited in an accredited bank in Kuwait;
- a financial statement for the last fiscal year; and
- minutes of the general meeting at which the acquisition was agreed.

After submitting those documents at the relevant department in the MOCI, the amendment of the memorandum and articles of associations will be publicised for the first time in the *Official Gazette*. The rationale is to provide any interested or potentially interested parties with notice of the proposed acquisition, and an opportunity to raise any (valid and reasonable) objections.

At the end of the objection period (normally two weeks), the amendment to the memorandum and articles of association is forwarded by the MOCI to the Ministry of Justice (the MOJ) for notarisation. Lastly, the MOJ sends back the notarised amendment to the MOCI to be recorded.

3.3 Acquisitions of unlisted joint stock companies

The acquisition of unlisted KSCs is regulated by Chapter 3 of the Commercial Companies Law. The Securities Law and CMA Bylaws do not apply to acquisitions of unlisted KSCs.

The Commercial Companies Law sets a few restrictions on acquiring shares in a KSC. For example, temporary shares may not be disposed of for at least 12 months and the company must have issued its first balance sheet covering a period of at least 12 months. Any disposal before that would be deemed invalid. In addition, founding shareholders of a KSC may not dispose of their shares until at least three years have elapsed from incorporation of the company (or else the disposal would be invalid).

All transfers of ownership in company shares must be officially and legally executed (as of the date of recording in the KSE registers) – otherwise, the transaction will be considered to have been implemented in violation of the provision of the Commercial Companies Law.

In sum, the ownership of shares may not be legally transferred to the acquirer or to third parties outside the KSE, and the transfer does not become legally valid until it has been registered in the shareholders' register.

3.14 Overview of mergers in Kuwait

Merger transactions are possible between WLL and KSC companies, either listed or unlisted (Commercial Companies Law). Mergers may also be implemented in relation to companies which are being liquidated.

There are two types of merger in Kuwait (Chapter 7 of the Commercial Companies Law):

- a merger conducted through the dissolution of one or more companies and the subsequent transfer of all its related liabilities to an existing company; and
- a merger where there is dissolution of two or more companies followed by the transfer of all their related liabilities to a newly-established company.

Prior approvals should be obtained from the appropriate authority in order to effectuate the merger (Commercial Companies Law). So, for example, in relation to banks, financial institutions and investment companies, prior approval should be sought from the Central Bank of Kuwait.

In addition to the above, advisers should consult the Ministerial Decree of 1992 (published by the MOCI), which sets out conditions and procedures for mergers between companies and rules about valuation of assets.

The Ministerial Decree provides that companies entering into a merger transaction should appoint neutral expert(s) to valuate the company's assets. That valuation must be notarised by a Kuwaiti court. It also requires that the merger agreement include certain information, such as:

- the objectives and purpose of the merger;
- the conditions of the merger;
- the initial valuation of the assets of the merger companies, including the date of the valuation, as well as relevant details about the person who conducted the valuation;

- the price which will be paid to the shareholders of the merging company and the basis of determining such price; and
- any other relevant information which might be deemed essential information by the regulatory authority.

When all necessary procedures have been finalised with the relevant authorities, the merger agreement should be registered in the commercial registry of the company and publicised in the *Official Gazette*. The merging company's creditors have the right to object to the merger agreement within a period of three months beginning with that date of registration.

4. Tax

According to Kuwaiti income tax law (Decree 3/1955), every corporate body (ie, a legal entity which is separate and distinct from its individual owners) carrying on business in Kuwait must pay tax on its Kuwait operations. A clear distinction is made between income earned by foreign entities from trading in Kuwait (which is taxable) and income earned from trading with Kuwait (which may not be taxable). Thus the supply of goods to Kuwait by a foreign entity which does not carry on any business in Kuwait will not typically create a tax obligation for the foreign entity.

In practice, however, tax is imposed on non-Kuwaiti corporate bodies only. Corporate bodies incorporated within the GCC and wholly owned by citizens of those countries are granted the same tax status as Kuwaiti citizens and are not required to pay income tax in Kuwait.

The Department of Income Tax (DIT) seeks to tax not only non-Kuwaiti corporate bodies, but Kuwait companies which have foreign corporate bodies as shareholders. So the DIT taxes the part of net profits of Kuwaiti companies that can be attributed to those foreign corporate shareholders. It is likely that the DIT would apply the same practice with respect to foreign corporate shareholders of GCC companies operating in Kuwait.

Kuwait shareholding companies must directly withhold 15% tax before distributing profits to shareholders in foreign and local companies.[25] However, Kuwaiti/GCC corporate shareholders can apply to waive such withholdings.

4.1 Phases prior to the M&A agreement

(a) Due diligence

A preliminary and vital stage of the merger or acquisition process is conducting a proper investigation and analysis of the target, commonly known as 'due diligence'. Due diligence is considered one of the most important exercises that potential partners/purchasers undertake as its goal is to reveal the financial status and legal liabilities of the target. In Kuwait, as in other jurisdictions, due diligence is divided into two parts: legal and financial.

---

25 Executive Rule 20 on Compliance of Fund Managers, Investment Custodians and Incorporated Bodies with Detaining and Paying Tax Due on the Distributions of Profits, part of the 2010 Executive Rules and Instructions of Kuwaiti Income Tax (Decree 3/1995, as amended by Law 2/1988.

Legal due diligence is normally conducted by an external legal counsel who reviews the legal documents relating to the target. Legal documentation may relate, but is not limited, to the following subjects:

- company constitution, such as the memorandum and articles of associations of the company and all amendments to them;
- agreements between the company and third parties;
- any current shareholder agreements;
- real estate, including title deeds of all the company's assets and lease agreements of the company's headquarter and related offices;
- insurance policies;
- antitrust compliance;
- intellectual property;
- labour, such as employment agreements and policies; and
- litigation and/or arbitration.

Having reviewed all of these documents, legal counsel will issue a report enabling the potential partner to assess the value of the company weighed against any risks.

(b) M&A agreement phase

When entering into a merger or acquisition, all potential partners usually have the same objective, which, for example, may be to make profits or expanding their business. So it is prudent to have a strategy in place to help avoid the risk of any dispute arising that could form an obstacle to the achievement of those targets. The M&A agreement gathers together all issues of potential conflict and provides a mechanism for the resolution of disputes.

Oral agreements can be valid for many types of transaction, if the conditions for such agreements are satisfied. Oral agreements, however, can heighten the chance of misunderstandings or even cheating or manipulation arising, so the disadvantages outweigh the advantages of oral agreements.

Written agreements provide more security to all parties and should reflect the agreement of all potential investors on issues relating to the management of the new company and other aspects, including rights and duties of the partners.

The main difference between an M&A agreement and the memorandum and articles of associations is that the latter is required by the regulating governmental authorities and can be disclosed to the public, whereas the M&A agreement is confidential and disclosed only to the partners. Another major distinction is that the terms of the memorandum and articles of associations tend to be more rigid, as they normally follow a standard template issued by the MOCI. In practice, the addition, removal or amendment of articles is rare.

By contrast, M&A agreements can include any terms negotiated by the potential partners. In practice, when the parties decide either to merge or to acquire another company, having agreed the commercial issues, they would normally seek the assistance of legal counsel to draft the agreement and to discuss issues which should be included in the agreement.

A priority issue should be the objective of the partners. The partners may well have different goals, especially when it comes to financials, capital contribution and the term of holding the business. For example, one partner might see a partnership as a short-term investment; another may have a longer-term arrangement in mind. It is therefore essential to include in the agreement, for example, a suitable exit scenario for both partners.

5. Conclusion

Advisers dealing with mergers and acquisitions in Kuwait must consult the body of rules and regulations affecting corporate restructuring transactions from the Commercial Companies Law to the Securities Law and the regulator's (CMA's) bylaws and instructions.

Lebanon

Nada Abdelsater-Abusamra
Abdelsater Abusamra & Associates (ASAS LAW)
Hala Raphael-Abillama
Raphael & Associes Law Firm

Business combinations can be a means to effect business expansion, access to capital, an increase in shareholder value or cash liquidity. There are two main types of business combination: business acquisition by equity transfer and business acquisition by asset purchase.

Mergers and acquisitions are the most common type of business acquisition by equity transfer transaction, but are not the only choice and not always the most advantageous option. Various considerations are to be addressed prior to entering into a business combination and deciding on the structure and potential implications of such a transaction.

1. Legal framework

In Lebanon, there is no law specific to mergers and acquisitions.[1] However, the Code of Commerce is relevant to joint stock companies (and probably to other corporate forms).

Companies in Lebanon may be constituted as general partnerships, limited partnerships, limited liability companies and joint stock companies, and may also be in the form of a holding or offshore company. In this chapter we use 'company' to refer to a joint stock company whose purpose is general commerce (and therefore excluding banks, insurance companies, telecommunications and media companies and other companies which may be subject to special regulations).

Business combinations can generally be divided into two main types: equity transactions and asset purchases. Equity transactions are sub-divided into mergers and acquisitions on the one hand and stock (asset) purchase transactions on the other. In all events, there is an acquirer and a target. The target is the company whose shares, assets or business are being transferred, or which is merged into another company resulting in a shift of the shareholders' equity interests. The acquirer is the company purchasing the assets or shares of the target, or the company that will absorb the target.

1.2 Acquisition by equity transfer

An equity transfer transaction may be structured as either a stock sale and purchase or an M&A transaction.

Stock sale transactions are straightforward share purchase transactions where the

1 The authors of this chapter have been entrusted with drafting a new M&A law as part of the team set up by the Presidency of the Council of Ministers.

acquirer enters into a share purchase agreement with the shareholders of the target. This transaction in theory involves one-on-one negotiations with each shareholder of the target, although it is not uncommon that various or all selling shareholders decide to negotiate with the seller through one representative appointed by them. As a result of the share purchase transaction, the acquirer may become the sole or controlling shareholder of the target. This chapter does not address stock sale transactions, instead focusing on mergers and acquisitions.

The words 'merger' and 'acquisition' are colloquially used interchangeably. However, in the technical sense of the term, 'acquisition' is a transaction whereby the acquirer (the 'absorbing company') acquires the other; as a result, the acquired company (the 'absorbed company') is dissolved and its shareholders hold equity in the absorbing company. The term 'merger' refers to the transaction whereby both companies combine to form one new company; both companies disappear and are merged into a new company (this transaction is also referred to as 'consolidation' in some legal systems).

1.2 Acquisition by asset purchase or purchase of a going concern

An asset purchase transaction is one where the acquirer purchases some or all of the target's assets and assumes some or all of the target's liabilities. Of particular importance in Lebanon is the transfer of a special type of asset owned by the target – namely, the 'going concern' also referred to as 'commercial establishment'.[2] Transfer of the going concern results in the acquisition of the target's business *per se,* but without acquiring the company itself or its shares. As a result of the asset purchase transaction, both the acquirer and the target may continue to exist.

2. Acquisition by equity transfer

The Code of Commerce does not specifically provide for mergers and acquisitions. M&A transactions are currently addressed by the Code of Commerce in relation to joint stock companies under Articles 210 to 213 of the Code of Commerce and Articles 15 to 18 of Decree Law 54/77 (on convertible bonds), as well as provisions governing increases of capital, dissolution and extraordinary general meetings.

In the absence of any statutory text governing M&A transactions for other types of company (eg, limited liability companies, general or limited partnerships), the view has been taken by experts and the case law that the provisions in the Code of Commerce applicable to joint stock companies can be extended to those other forms insofar as their nature itself does not preclude this, and as long as the statutory provisions governing the dissolution and increase of capital are complied with.

In this chapter we focus on joint stock companies.

2.1 Code of Commerce

(a) Merger

The term 'merger' is generally used in the Code of Commerce as referring to a

2 The Lebanese Code of Commerce was initially drafted in French.

transaction whereby a new company is created by the combination of two (or more) companies (Article 211 of the Code of Commerce) which will cease to exist individually (the 'absorbed companies' or 'dissolved companies'). Legal provisions governing the constitution of companies will apply to the creation of the new company (Article 211 of the Code of Commerce), and for the combined companies, the provisions on company dissolution apply.

(b) ***Acquisition***

The term 'absorption' is understood to refer to the process whereby a company (the 'absorbed' or 'dissolved company') is absorbed by another company (the 'acquiring' or 'absorbing company': Article 212 of the Code of Commerce). The absorbing company must comply with applicable formal and substantive requirements governing capital increase and the absorbed company must publicise[3] its anticipated dissolution.

2.2 M&A process and legal effects

(a) ***General concepts***

Simply speaking, M&A transactions start with a contractual agreement between the parties represented by their respective corporate bodies – the M&A agreement. Acquisitions are decided by resolution of the extraordinary general meeting of the acquirer and of the dissolved company separately. Mergers are resolved by an extraordinary general meeting of the dissolved companies and the constitutive assembly of the new company.

Both mergers and acquisitions necessarily involve the dissolution of at least one company (in a merger, two or more companies are dissolved). From the perspective of the dissolved companies, both transactions are significantly similar. When seen from the perspective of the acquiring/new company, mergers differ procedurally from acquisitions, in that the former involve the constitution of a new company whereas the latter involve an increase in capital. However, those differences are merely technical in reality, since the provisions for constitution and capital increase of joint stock companies are largely similar. We therefore consider the process for both mergers and acquisitions simultaneously, flagging any differences where relevant or significant.

Lebanese law does not require the constituent companies of a M&A transaction to have the same legal form; nor does it require them to have the same nationality.[4] In fact, there is no restriction on nationality. It is (technically at least) possible, therefore, to see a Lebanese company merge with or be acquired by a non-Lebanese company, subject to public policy considerations.

Nor does Lebanese law expressly address the issue of mergers and acquisitions of other types of company other than joint stock companies. At the same time, there is no requirement that all companies involved in the merger process be in the form of

---

3 The resolution of the extraordinary general meeting deciding the anticipated dissolution ought to be published at the commercial register in accordance with the provisions of the Code of Commerce, particularly Article 50.

4 Edouard Eid, *Commercial Companies*, El najwa, 1970, p 755, para 384.

joint stock companies. It is generally accepted that mergers and acquisitions can take place between companies of different legal forms[5] (eg, an M&A transaction between a joint stock company and limited liability company).

2.3 Stages of the M&A transaction

Although Lebanese law does not regulate the process of M&A transactions in any detail, based on legal and commercial practice[6] in Lebanon, the M&A transaction can be divided into two stages: preliminary and implementation.

(a) Preliminary stage

During the preliminary stage, the parties enter into negotiations on the general business aspects of the proposed transaction. At this stage only a very limited number of persons are involved and a confidentiality agreement is generally signed, often accompanied by an exclusivity agreement in which each signatory undertakes to abstain from entering into M&A discussions with any other parties. The preliminary stage itself may be divided into a very early stage, during which the M&A idea has not even been shared with all members of the board, and the stage where the transaction is still in its preliminary phase but the idea has been shared with the board of each of the companies so as to ensure that the negotiating persons have the necessary authority bestowed by their respective companies.[7]

Once the confidentiality agreement has been signed and the discussions advanced, a memorandum of understanding or 'M&A protocol' is signed setting out the general intent of the companies to explore the feasibility of the transaction subject to a due diligence review and to negotiations on the terms and conditions of the transaction.

The legal and financial advisers begin the due diligence review process. Usually, the absorbing company undertakes due diligence of the dissolved company; but it is not uncommon for the dissolved company also to undertake due diligence of the absorbing company. The due diligence process could be long or short, depending on the type of the company, its history and the nature of its business. Due diligence typically includes review of the following (as well as other) documents:

- basic corporate documents;
- other corporate documents for past years such as bylaws, minutes of extraordinary general meetings, board minutes;
- substantial contracts;
- employment agreements and employment-related information;
- any loans and other financial arrangements;
- past, pending or threatened litigation;
- deeds, titles and property rights;

---

5 *Ibid.*

6 The M&A process is mainly governed by the legal and statutory provisions. As detailed hereafter, this process is directed mainly by the board of directors as well as the financial and legal teams. The practice described in this chapter is not formally recorded in any official regulation; however, it is generally adopted by law firms specialised in M&A activity.

7 Edouard Eid, *Commercial Companies* (El najwa publisher, 1970), p 757.

- IP documents (for patents, copyright and trademarks);
- balance sheets for past years[8] and other financial documents; and
- tax liability analysis.

In parallel to the due diligence, the draft M&A agreement will be negotiated and drafted. The draft will be discussed at board level within each company.

(b) ***Implementation stage***

M&A agreement: Once approved by the board, the M&A agreement will be submitted to the extraordinary general meeting of each company for approval.

The M&A agreement must include at least the following:

- a description of the structure of the transaction;
- identification of the dissolved company(ies) and the new/acquiring companies
- the share exchange ratio;
- the extent of the dissolved company's liabilities and whether any debt guarantee is being provided;
- whether there are any existing convertible bonds;
- the bylaws of the acquirer as well as the proposed amendment to them either as part of or as an annex to the M&A agreement (recommended, but not mandatory); and
- draft bylaws of the new company as part of or as an annex to the agreement (recommended).

Share exchange ratio: The shareholders of the dissolved company become shareholders in the new/absorbing company. The merging company will increase its capital by issuing new shares in favour of the shareholders of the dissolved company in consideration for the assets of the dissolved company.

Several pricing structures and share exchange formulae are possible. The simplest and probably most common is a fixed exchange ratio. This refers to the number of shares that the new/absorbing company shall issue in exchange for each share of the dissolved company's capital.

Shareholder approval: Whether in mergers or acquisitions, one major milestone is the dissolution of one or more companies. Dissolution as a result of M&A transactions is a particular type of dissolution, different from ordinary dissolution – notably in that it does not result in liquidation and the distribution of assets.

Although Articles 211 and 212 of the Code of Commerce do not expressly stipulate that all provisions applicable to a proposed company dissolution shall apply to M&A transactions, it is generally admitted that legal provisions governing anticipated dissolution are applicable to the dissolving company.

---

8 The number of years is not specified, but will depend on the judgement of both the legal and financial teams. In general, legal counsel would want to analyse at least the past five years preceding the M&A transaction.

In this respect, and pursuant to Article 202 of the Code of Commerce on dissolution of joint stock companies, the approval of the M&A agreement by the dissolved company – and specifically, the decision to dissolve the company – requires a resolution of the extraordinary general meeting of the dissolved company with a minimum quorum of shareholders representing three-quarters of company capital present (attendance can be either personal or by proxy; the proxy conditions will vary from company to company, depending on any relevant bylaws). The decision must be resolved by a majority of shareholders representing not less than two-thirds of the shareholders attending the meeting. These quorum and majority requirements apply as a minimum, but the actual requirements could be higher if so stipulated in the bylaws.

Special attention should also be paid to other general due process requirements which must be strictly observed to avoid annulment of the resolution. For example, the shareholders must be properly convened and the correct notice period given, with the detailed agenda and all information necessary for shareholders to enable them to make an informed decision.

Publication of dissolution decision: Once the decision is duly resolved by the extraordinary general meeting in compliance with the applicable quorum, majority and other requirements, publicising procedures applicable to company dissolution must be complied with.

Creditors of dissolved company: Creditors of the dissolved company have the right to file an opposition to the proposed M&A transaction. Indeed, pursuant to Articles 213 and 208 of the Code of Commerce, the decision of the general assembly resolving the dissolution must comply with the same conditions applicable to decrease of capital with respect to preserving third-party rights. The resolution cannot be implemented unless it is published in the *Official Gazette* and as long as no creditor has filed an opposition to it within a three-month period. If any creditor does oppose the proposed transaction, implementation of the resolution will be suspended pending a court decision as to whether the proposal prejudices the rights of third parties. The court may declare that the transaction is not enforceable against the creditors if it appears that the assets of the new/absorbing company do not appropriately cover the new liabilities resulting from the transaction.

Any M&A deal will not be enforceable against the creditors of the dissolved company unless they have agreed to it (or unless they have not opposed it). In the event that the court decides that the transaction may prejudice the creditors' rights, the court may either require the target to settle its debts or grant the creditors guarantees under the M&A process.

In general, the assets and liabilities of the dissolved company(ies) will be transferred to the new/absorbing company. Some M&A transactions are structured in such a way as to exclude the transfer of liabilities of the dissolved company to the new/absorbing company. In such cases, the liabilities would, for example be assumed by the shareholders of the dissolved company. However, the validity of such a limitation of the liability of the new/absorbing company has been questioned.

Creditors of new/absorbing company: Lebanese law does not grant the creditors of the new/absorbing company any right to file an opposition with respect to the M&A deal, even though the latter may increase the liabilities and obligations of the merging/acquiring company.

Debtors of dissolved company: Nor does Lebanese law expressly regulate procedures for the transfer to the new/absorbing company of the dissolved company's receivables. It is generally understood, however, that all debtors of the dissolved company become debtors of the new/absorbing company upon completion of the M&A transaction.

However, some authors have argued that the M&A transaction should be notified to those debtors to be enforceable against them. In practice, this becomes relevant only where the contract between the dissolved company and the debtor has expressly prohibited the assignment of such debt. In any event, this is an issue that may be resolved by expressly incorporating the universal transfer principle into applicable M&A laws (as is proposed in the draft legislation currently before the Prime Minister's Office and the Lebanese Parliament).

Approval of bondholders: In the context of M&A transactions, the rights of holders of bonds that are convertible to shares in the dissolved company's capital must be taken into account (Decree-Law 54/77).

From the date of issuance of bonds convertible into shares, and during the period of existence of such bonds, the acquisition of the issuing company by another company, as well as the merger of the issuing company in one or several other companies within the framework of a new company, is subject to prior approval of the general meeting of the relevant bondholders (Article 15 of Decree-Law 54/77).

In the event that the meeting of bondholders does not approve the M&A transaction, or if the meeting fails to be held for lack of quorum, it is possible to dispense with the need for such approval.[9] However, such a decision of the board of directors to override the approval of the bondholders' meeting and dispense with it shall be immediately publicised in the *Official Gazette*, in a business newspaper and in a local daily newspaper.

The bondholders' meeting is entitled to take decisions based on a simple majority of those present – whatever their number – to authorise its representatives to file an injunction against the intended transaction with the competent commercial court within one month of the date of the last publication formality.

The court may dismiss the opposition, compel the issuing company to pay the value of the bonds or compel the absorbing company to provide guarantees to the bondholders.

In the event that the judicial decision is not enforced with respect to the payment of the bonds or provision of guarantees, the merger or acquisition remains unenforceable against an objecting bondholder.

9 Article 15 of Decree-Law 54/77.

Shareholder approval of acquiring/new company: In mergers, the rules of constitution must be complied with for the new company (Article 211 of the Code of Commerce). The shareholders of both dissolved companies together comprise the constitutive assembly of the new company.

The constitutive assembly will require a quorum of shareholders representing one-third of the share capital of the new company. Decisions must be resolved by a majority of shareholders representing at least two-thirds of the shares represented at the meeting. These quorum and majority requirements apply as *de minimis* levels; the actual requirements can be higher if so stipulated in the bylaws.

Usually, the merger transaction will be structured as a constitution and subscription by in-kind contribution, whereby the dissolved companies themselves constitute that in-kind contribution[10] to the capital of the new company. Alternatively, the transaction could be structured as a combination of cash and in-kind contributions. As such, merger transactions will be subject to evaluation by one or more court-appointed experts whose mission is to value the dissolving companies and determine the corresponding share exchange ratios (Articles 86 and 113 of the Code of Commerce). This court-appointed expert verification procedure could in some cases significantly hinder the merger process, especially in the event of dissenting shareholders and if the court-appointed valuation differs from the transaction valuation by more than 20%.

To the extent that the M&A transaction includes an invitation to public subscription, notice must be given in the *Official Gazette*, in a business newspaper and in a local daily newspaper containing, among other things, the company's name, address, capital, price of its shares, the value of in-kind contributions and other relevant information (Article 81 of the Code of Commerce).

In acquisitions, the absorbing company must comply with the applicable formal and substantial rules for capital increase (Article 212 of the Code of Commerce), which are substantially the same as for company constitution.

The extraordinary general assembly of the acquirer shall essentially resolve on the company's increase of capital, which shall be reserved to the shareholders of the dissolved company. Such a decision is resolved by the extraordinary general meeting with a minimum quorum of shareholders representing two-thirds of the company's capital present at the meeting (attendance can be either personal or by proxy, and the proxy conditions vary from one company to another depending on any relevant provisions of the company's bylaws). The decision must be resolved by a majority of shareholders representing not less than two-thirds of the shareholders attending the assembly. These quorum and majority requirements apply as a minimum; the actual requirements could be higher if so stipulated in the bylaws.

The acquisition will usually be structured as an increase of capital by in-kind contribution whereby the dissolved company itself constitutes the in-kind contribution.[11] Alternatively, the transaction could be structured as a combination of cash and in-kind contributions, in which case acquisition transactions will be subject

10 If the dissolved company holds cash equity, then the capital increase of the absorbing company will be a combination of in-kind contribution and cash contribution.

to evaluation by one or more court-appointed experts whose must value the dissolving company and determine the corresponding share exchange ratio (Articles 113 and 86 Code of Commerce). This court-appointed expert verification procedure could in some cases significantly hinder the acquisition process in the event of dissenting shareholders or when the court-appointed valuation differs from the transaction valuation by more than 20%.

To the extent that the M&A transaction includes an invitation to public subscription, publication must be made in the *Official Gazette*, in a business newspaper and in a local daily newspaper containing, among other things, the new/acquiring company's name, address, object, capital, price of its shares and value of in-kind contributions, and other relevant information (Article 81 of the Code of Commerce). The violation of the legal or statutory provisions concerning the increase of capital may result in the annulment of the operation, civil liability of board members, auditors, experts or breaching shareholders, potentially with criminal sanctions.[12]

3. Acquisition by asset purchase or purchase of going concern

Transfer of a going concern results in the acquisition of the target's business without acquiring the company itself or its shares. As a result of the asset purchase transaction, both the acquirer and target may continue to exist.

Indeed, a business in Lebanon may be operating as a going concern having no separate legal personality distinct from its owner (whether the owner is an individual or a company). The going concern is merely one of the owner's assets (usually the main asset), and the owner is fully liable for all of its business liabilities.

Depending on the circumstances of each deal, it may be more advantageous to structure the business acquisition as the transfer of the going concern itself. For the purpose of this chapter, we shall limit ourselves to the scenario where the target business is owned by a joint stock company (referred to as the 'target'), and start by describing the Lebanese legal concept of the going concern and what it includes.

3.1 Legal concept and components of going concern

Going concerns are governed by Legislative Decree 11 dated July 11 1967 (Decree Law 11/67). A 'going concern' is defined as the instrument of a commercial enterprise, comprised of tangible and intangible assets, whose organisation is directed towards the exercise of a commercial activity.

The Code of Commerce regulates various contracts that may be entered into in relation to the going concern, including in particular the business sale or transfer contract. Although apparently simple and straightforward, in practice the transfer of a going concern entails many technicalities and is governed notably by Articles 5 to

---

11 It would be rare to see an acquisition structured as a full cash contribution increase of capital of the absorbing company. But even in such a case, the transaction would still be subject to a court-appointed expert valuation where the shareholders of the absorbing company do not unanimously waive their priority rights to subscribe to the capital increase.

12 Fabia & Safa, *Code de Commerce Libanais Annoté*, vol II, 3rd edition, Articles 205 and 206, pp 41 and 42.

21 of Decree Law 11/67, as well as the general legal provisions governing sales and transfer contracts.

Acquiring companies may possibly prefer to acquire the business itself rather than the target, because that would allow for more flexibility in 'cherry picking' the assets to be transferred and reducing the risk of assuming unknown (or in some cases even known) liabilities. However, this risk can never be totally eliminated, and the acquirer will also need to consider any other potentially hurdles, such as any special legal procedural steps required in relation to third-party consents or pre-emption rights.

As under any agreement, the validity of the transfer of a going concern entails the valid free consent of the parties and the existence of an object and a cause.

(a) Target's consent

If the assets being transferred (the business components) constitute all or substantially all of the company's assets, the business sale or transfer contract will require the approval of the target's extraordinary general meeting, with a quorum equal to three-quarters of the capital.

(b) Assets being transferred

The subject matter of the business sale or transfer contract may, depending on the will of the parties, include the transfer of some or all elements of the business. In the absence of any express agreement between the parties with respect to the specific elements to be transferred, the transfer will capture only the company logo, business name, any leases and clients and customers. In any event, the transfer of a going concern will further entail the transfer of its customer base and its contacts list.[13]

On this point, commentators have made the point that if the client list has not been transferred at the effective date of the contract, the business sale or transfer contract could be null and void for lack of subject matter.[14] This legality may have several implications, including for anti-competition clauses, drafting of the business sale or transfer contract, and the definitions of assets, rights and liabilities included in the transaction.

In addition, there are legal conditions governing the publicising of the proposed transfer of a going concern, notably in order to be enforceable against third parties.

(c) Publicising the proposed transaction

In order to be enforceable against third parties, the transfer of a going concern must be:

- registered in the Commercial Register, including the names of the transferor and the transferee; and
- publicised in the *Official Gazette* and a local newspaper.[15]

---

13 Emile Tyan, *Droit Commercial*, vol 1, p 169– 184.
14 Mustafa Kamal Taha, *Fundamentals of Commercial Law*, Al-Halabi Publishers, 2006, p 216, para 229.
15 Article 12(1) of Decree Law 11/67.

Such notification is made at the expense of the transferee, and must be done within 15 days of signature of the business sale or transfer contract. A second re-publication is required within one week of the first notice.[16]

This publication procedure is of major importance, as it has significant implications for the legal status of the transfer. When the publication procedures have been properly completed, the transaction becomes irrevocable and so, for example, the target's creditors and landlord (where the transfer includes the lease of the business premises) have rights which they may exercise after publication (ie, after the theoretical completion of the transaction).

Any business sale or transfer contract should be structured so as to avoid or minimise these risks (ie, to exclude as many rights as possible – see further below). Factors to be taken into account include the price calculation, price payment method, liability guarantee and penalty clause where there are any undisclosed liabilities (or other similar issues).

(d) Rights of target's creditors

The creditors of the transferor have two rights:

- the right to stop payment of the business sale or transfer contract price; and
- the right to outbid the acquirer for an increment of at least one-sixth of the business sale or transfer contract price and subsequent equal increments.

Right to stop payment of business sale or transfer contract price: The target's creditors have the right to seek a court injunction requiring the acquirer to stop payment of the business sale or transfer contract price whether the creditors' debts have become due or not.

The creditor's right must be exercised within 10 days of the date on which the final publication formalities are completed.

The acquirer should refrain from paying the transfer price before the expiry of that 10-day period; otherwise, it may have to pay it again if the transferor's creditors so request. Moreover, if an injunction against payment of the price is requested within the 10-day period, the transferee should continue to abstain from paying the transfer price until a judicial decision in relation to the requested injunction is rendered.

Right to outbid transferee by an increment of at least one-sixth: Lebanese law[17] also grants the target's creditors the right to outbid the acquirer. Within 10 days of the date of completion of the publication formalities required by law, any creditor having sought such a 'stop-payment injunction' as well as any secured creditor having a pledge over the business, may request communication of the business sale or transfer contract and all relevant injunction applications.

The creditor may offer to acquire the business for itself or on behalf of a third party in consideration for a price that is higher than the business sale or transfer

16 Article 12(4).
17 Articles 18 and 19 of Decree-Law 11/67.

contract price by one-sixth. Such an offer can be made only if the price is insufficient to satisfy all creditors. In such an event, all interested parties may bid at a price that is one-sixth higher than the previous bid, and the business will be sold to the person that submits the highest bid within 20 days of the last publication formality. The acquirer may, in principle, participate in this auction.

Rights of landowner (where business sale or transfer contract includes transfers of leases): Under applicable law, whenever a business leasing premises is to be transferred, the landlord may either exercise its priority right to acquire the business or request revision of the lease under what is known as 'fair and just lease price'.

Landowner's priority right to acquire going concern: Despite any stipulation to the contrary in the lease agreement, transfer of the going concern entails *de jure* transfer of the lease, provided that the transferee complies with all obligations derived from the business sale or transfer contract and does not modify the nature of the business.[18]

Although the landlord's consent is not required for completion of the business transfer, the landlord can pre-empt a transfer after it is completed and published. This means that, except for transfers consequential to a public auction,[19] whenever the lease is part of the business sale or transfer contract, applicable law grants the landowner a priority right to acquire the transferred business for the same price agreed in the business sale or transfer contract on only one condition – that the landowner provide a bank guarantee to secure the deal.[20] However, this landlord priority right is limited in time and can be exercised only within 10 days of the landlord's official notification of the business transfer.[21]

It is therefore crucial that acquirers respect and very closely follow the official notification procedure, given that the 10-day limitation period will not start running *vis-à-vis* the landlord until the notification procedure is complete and the 10-day period has expired. As long as the procedure is incomplete, the transaction may be subject to annulment at the price stated in the business sale or transfer contract. There is legal precedent for these priority rights of a landlord: in one case where a landlord was not properly notified of the transfer (albeit that it was fully aware of the transfer), it was able to challenge the validity of the business sale or transfer contract and acquire the business several years after the contract had been entered into and at the same price as agreed in the original business sale or transfer contract, in spite of the fact that that price represented a gross undervalue at current market values.

Landowner's right to request just and fair lease price: Whenever a business is transferred, the landlord has the right to request the revision of the rental fee by judicial determination of a just and fair lease price (Article 9 of Decree Law 11/67). As under any contract, the transferor and the transferee have obligations towards one another upon conclusion of the business sale or transfer contract.

---

18 Article 9(1) of Decree Law 11/67.
19 Article 10(1) of Decree Law 11/67.
20 Article 10(2) of Decree Law 11/67.
21 Article 10(2) and Article 2 of Decree Law 11/67.

(e) ***Ownership transfer***

Transfer of business ownership is one of the most important obligations of the transferor in addition to its delivery and guarantee obligations. Transfer of ownership takes place between the parties upon signature of the business sale or transfer contract and, *vis-à-vis* third parties upon publication of the business sale or transfer contract in the Trade Register.

In the absence of any agreement between the parties with respect to the elements to be transferred, the transfer shall comprise only the company logo,[22] business name, lease and list of clients/customers.

It is possible, however, for the parties to agree on the transfer of other assets or liabilities of the business, such as trade books, debts, patents and trademarks. Those transfers will be subject to special formalities.

(f) ***Limitation of liability***

Rights and debts as well as books of trade can be transferred only if stipulated in the business sale or transfer contract.[23]

(g) ***Additional formalities***

As for the transfer of patents and trademarks, special formalities, in addition to those that generally relate to any transfer, must be observed.[24] Details of the transfer must be filed with the Ministry of Economy and Trade. The ministry will issue certification formalising the transfer of the IP right and the transfer will be publicised in the *Official Gazette.*

(h) ***Target's guarantee obligation***

The transferor, as seller, has the obligation to personally guarantee the business. For example, the business sale or transfer contract must mention the turnover and profit generated by the business in the past three years and the transferor must guarantee the accuracy of those figures subject to conclusion of the business sale or transfer contract, or else face payment of a penalty.

The transferor also has a legal obligation[25] not to start or be part of any competitor business which may obviously attract the clientele of the transferred business. In practice, the parties should include an express and valid non-compete clause, which must be limited in both geographical scope and duration in order to be valid and enforceable.

3.2 Taxation

A transfer of business may give rise to double taxation issues, for both the target and shareholders.

---

22 Article 5(2) of Decree Law 11/67.
23 Article 6 of Decree Law 11/67.
24 Article 7 of Decree Law 11/67.
25 Article 8 of Decree Law 11/67.

4. Conclusion

M&A transactions in Lebanon are not governed by any specific relevant legislation. While a general framework is enshrined in the Code of Commerce, no procedural details are to be found there or anywhere else. This leaves legal practitioners with only a scant and disparate legislative framework that fails to address issues of central importance to the M&A transaction itself and also to post-M&A issues, such as the protection of minority shareholders, dividend policies, exit procedures, corporate governance and investor matters, and other related issues. The success of any given venture will to a large extent depend on the specific contractual and legal procedures adopted by the parties, and on counsel's experience.

With those gaps and uncertainties in mind, and given the potential for mergers and acquisitions to enhance the business environment and help to attract foreign investment, the Lebanese Presidency of the Council of Ministers has set up a committee entrusted with amending the country's legal framework, inclusive of an overhaul of the Code of Commerce.

The authors would like to acknowledge the kind assistance of their colleague Serena Ghanimeh and their former colleague Joelle Abi-Haidar, who was recently admitted to become a judge.

Morocco

Mohieddine El Amari
El Amari & Associés
Sofia Layachi
Fonds Marocain de Développement Touristique (FMDT)

1. Deal structuring

1.1 Existing structures under the Moroccan legal system

Under Moroccan law, a transaction may be structured as a share purchase, an asset acquisition or a merger.

(a) *Share purchase*

Purchase of listed shares: Under Moroccan regulations, a 'takeover' is defined as a procedure by which a natural or a corporate body acquirer, either acting alone or in concert, publicly states that it intends to acquire, exchange or sell all or part of the securities that give access to the capital or voting rights (the 'stock') of a company, where that company's securities are listed on the Casablanca Stock Exchange (CSE).

Takeover bids are classified by Law 26-03 on Public Offerings on the Stock Exchange (the 'Law on Public Offerings'). Three types of transaction cover share purchases:

- tender offers – offers to buy in cash all or part of the stock of a target from its current shareholders at the price offered by the acquirer, which is normally higher than the listed price of the stock;
- public exchange offers – acquiring the stock of the target in exchange for other listed securities; and
- combined offers – a combination of a takeover bid and a public exchange offer where payment is made in cash and in listed securities. The local market supervisory authority, the *Conseil Déontologique des Valeurs Mobilières* (CDVM) will decide whether the offer is properly qualified as such by its acquirer; this in turn determining which set of rules will apply to the offer.

A draft takeover bid must be filed with the CDVM when the purchase of stock entails its holder then becoming the owner, directly or indirectly, of 40% of the voting rights of a listed company – except in cases where reaching such a threshold does not trigger a change in control of the company.[1]

The draft takeover bid must be granted preliminary clearance by the CDVM and

1 Article 18 of the Law on Public Offerings, combined with Article 1 of the Order of the Ministry of Finance and Privatisation 1874-04, setting out the percentage of voting rights that obliges the holder to conduct a tender offer (*BO* 5270 of December 2 2004).

by other relevant supervisory authority before a notice stating that a draft takeover bid has been filed can be publicised by the CDVM (Articles 24 and following of the Law on Public Offerings). The CDVM must issue final clearance within 25 days of the notice's publication date, but that time period can be extended by a further 10 days if the CDVM requires further information, documents or guarantees in relation to the payment of the stock from the bidder. During this period, trading in the target's stock will be suspended. At the end of its examination, the CDVM will pass on details of the draft takeover bid to the Ministry of Finance, which will then rule on its admissibility within two days.

The bid will be deemed admissible on final clearance by the CDVM and any other relevant supervisory authority. The decision is then notified to the acquirer, publicised and published in an official gazette within five days of the clearance, and trading in the target's stock is resumed.[2]

If during the takeover bid period the acquirer – acting alone or in concert – buys stock in the target on the open market at a price higher than the offer price, this will automatically result in an increase in the offer price to match the open market price. In the period following closure of the takeover bid, but prior to publicising the result, brokerage firms must ensure that buy orders relating to the target, submitted by the acquirer acting alone or in concert have been made at a price lower than or equal to the offer price.

Purchase of unlisted shares: The rules applicable to the purchase of unlisted shares varies depending on the legal form of the target. Several forms of companies are possible under Moroccan law. For example, Law 17-95 on joint stock companies and Law 5-96 on other legal forms of company[3] set out the applicable provisions to the purchase of unlisted shares.

Mostly, companies in Morocco take one of two legal forms: a *société à responsabilité limitée* (SARL) (limited liability partnership) or *société anonyme* (SA) (joint stock company). The SARL is the typical form for most medium or small-sized businesses. The SA is designed for larger, more formal enterprises and companies permitted to trade their shares on the CSE.

Shares in a SARL can be purchased by a third party only if the target agrees to it and admits the purchaser as a new shareholder in a shareholders' extraordinary meeting.[4] The shareholders may exercise their pre-emption right on the shares and prevent any third party from gaining access to the share capital and voting rights of the company. Such restrictions to the transfer of shares may be set out in the articles of association and in a shareholders' agreement in the context of a SA. If those restrictions were bypassed, the share transfer would be deemed void. Accordingly, buyers of shares in a SARL or SA where the company's articles of association restrict share transfers should, in order to avoid jeopardising completion of the deal:

2 Article 39 of the Law on Public Offerings.

3 Excluding civil law companies which are governed by the Obligations and Contracts Code (Dahir, September 12 1913).

4 Article 58 of Law 5-96 *sur la société en nom collectif, la société en commandite simple, la société en commandite par actions, la société à responsabilité limitée et la société en participation.*

- be aware of existing legal requirements that ensure the protection of the company's and shareholder's rights; and
- ensure that those requirements are fully complied with in a timely manner.

(b) Asset acquisition

In the context of an asset acquisition, the acquirer generally purchases all, or a substantial part of, the assets of the target. The transaction includes movable items, such as the machinery and equipment, and/or immovables, such as land and buildings.

An asset acquisition requires very specific due diligence processes, and specialised professional valuers to conduct the asset's valuation. An immovable asset acquisition requires:

- an extremely thorough and precise review of the registration of the asset with the Moroccan Land Registry and any other relevant authority;
- a search for the existence of any liens, pledges or mortgages; and
- a review of any permits authorising the operation of existing and contemplated activities.

Once the parties have agreed a purchase price, an agreement is entered into and should:

- define the scope of the transaction;
- provide for a comprehensive list of all purchased assets; and
- detail (perhaps in the schedules) amendments to any permits authorising the change in the ownership of the asset.

Sellers should note that they will be subject to heavy taxation on capital gains in asset acquisitions (ie, up to 20% for movable and immovable property).

(c) Merger

Under Moroccan law, a company can be absorbed by another company by means of a merger, or be part of a newly created company.[5] Either transaction can occur between companies with different legal forms, if it is authorised by the shareholders of both companies involved in the transaction.[6]

A merger triggers the dissolution without liquidation of the company which is absorbed, and its holdings, assets and liabilities are fully transferred to the absorbing company.[7]

On completion, the shareholders of the absorbed company become shareholders of the absorbing company, pursuant to the terms and conditions specified in the merger agreement.

The board of directors of companies under the SA legal form (*conseil d'administration*) drafts a report detailing reasons for the merger, from economic and legal perspectives. That report will also detail the share exchange ratio, valuation

---

5 Articles 222 and following of the Law on Joint Stock Companies.
6 Article 223 of the Law on Joint Stock Companies.
7 Article 224 of the Law on Joint Stock Companies.

methods used and any difficulties that need to be addressed. It should also disclose the existence of any relevant interest in the companies held by, or relationship between, the directors or members of the supervisory board if there is one.[8]

When at least one of the companies has its shares admitted to trading on the CSE, that report should be disclosed to the CDVM in accordance with the CDVM rules.

The draft merger agreement prepared by the general manager or board of directors should contain the following mandatory information:[9]

- legal form, corporate name and address of the head offices of all parties to the transaction;
- reasons, aims and objectives of the merger;
- designation and valuation of the assets and liabilities being transferred by the merger;
- terms and conditions of the transfer of shares;
- date from which the right to dividends will become effective, with any details about this right;
- date from which the operations are deemed to be executed by the absorbing or newly created company;
- date of the financial statements used as the basis for the terms and conditions of the merger;
- exchange ratio between the shares and compensation balance, if relevant;
- projected merger premium; and
- a description of any special rights being allocated to any group of stock holders.

When the merger is completed, all holdings, assets and liabilities of the absorbed or merging companies automatically become the property of the absorbing or new company. Unlike in asset transfers, there is no need to make a formal transfer of title in the context of a merger.[10]

However, some assets cannot be transferred automatically to the absorbing or new company. Leases and contracts containing change of control clauses must be carefully reviewed during the due diligence phase for this purpose. These clauses are often found in mortgages and other types of loan. The buyer will have to initiate talks through the target with the parties to material agreements entered into with the target to obtain a prior written agreement to the contemplated merger.

In the case of a merger by absorption between companies that are subject to corporate tax, only the merger premium deriving from the capital gain that results from investment in the absorbed company is included in taxable income. Accordingly, subject to certain filings and declarations, the merging companies are not taxed on the basis of capital gains resulting from the transfer of movable and immovable assets and equity from the absorbed company.

8 Article 232 of the Law on Joint Stock Companies.
9 Article 237 of the Law on Joint Stock Companies.
10 Article 224 of the Law on Joint Stock Companies.

Depending on variables such as timing, liabilities, tax issues or the nature of the assets involved, one of the three types of structure may be more attractive for the contemplated transaction.

1.2 Structuring options

Structuring considerations for companies in Morocco will be similar to those that apply in other jurisdictions. Share purchases trigger considerations relating to potential exposure to future risks (eg, could the target's liabilities result in claims?). For this reason, asset acquisitions can appear advantageous (as in other jurisdictions), since no seller's liability or debt is transferred to the buyer regardless of the size of the transfer. However, the opposite is true from the tax perspective: the fiscal cost of asset acquisitions in comparison with mergers by absorption make the latter much more attractive.

1.3 Due diligence

As in other jurisdictions, once the proposed transaction has been structured, its scope precisely defined and an initial share or asset valuation carried out, a legal due diligence process must be conducted by the buyer's side.

In Morocco, it is important to take into consideration the following facts when timing the different transaction phases and steps:

- Virtual data rooms are not very common, usually available only in the context of major, mostly cross-border, deals. Physical data rooms are more likely, but generally the buyer and its legal counsel will specifically request information from the target; and
- Legal and corporate information can generally be accessed only in person in the registries of the commercial courts (little information is available via computer databases or online).

Both considerations could have the effect of slowing down the due diligence or indeed, the transaction.

1.4 Language and execution of documentation

Article 5 of the 2011 Constitution establishes the Arabic language as the official language in Morocco.

While French has no official status, it has nevertheless acquired *de facto* status, due to its widespread use in education, the courts, politics, administration and across the media.

Accordingly, documentation is commonly drafted in either Arabic or French. If another language is used, the documentation should be translated and presented in a double column format.

Each page of all agreements, minutes and reports relating to the transaction should be initialled by the parties and every signature on all documents must be certified by local council services or, if the person who executed the document is abroad, by the local Moroccan consulate or a notary.

2. Merger control

The Moroccan merger control rules are set out in Law 06-99 on the Liberty of Prices and Competition of June 5 2000 (Law on Merger Control) and Decree 2-00-854 of September 17 2001. The regulators are the prime minister and the *Conseil de la Concurrence* (Competition Council).

All contemplated mergers fall within the 'scope of the control' and merger filings must be advised by the prime minister to the Competition Council, where:

- the transaction is likely to lessen competition, particularly by creating or strengthening a dominant position; and
- the parties to the transaction, or the target of the transaction, or companies which have economic connections with the parties or the target, have achieved together during the previous financial year over 40% of sales, purchases or other transactions on a national market of goods, products or services of a similar nature or substitute, or a substantial part of it.[11]

The concept of 'merger' is defined as any act, whatever its form:

- which involves a transfer of ownership or use of all or part of the assets, rights and liabilities of a company; and
- whose purpose or effect is to allow a company or group of companies to exercise, directly or indirectly, a decisive influence on one or more other companies.[12]

When a merger is deemed to fall within the scope of control of the Law on Merger Control, any of the parties to the transaction must notify the prime minister of the merger.[13] Depending on the likely impact of the merger on competition, the prime minister might decide to forward the case to the Competition Council.[14] The Law on Merger Control does not specify any particular timeframe for filing, so it appears that the parties to the transaction may notify the proposed merger at any time, as long as discussions among the parties have progressed sufficiently. No filing fees apply (to any of the parties).

The prime minister will review the proposed merger to determine whether it could significantly impair competition, in particular by creating or strengthening a dominant position, in which case the prime minister will refer the case to the Competition Council and notify the parties.[15]

The Competition Council will consider whether the proposed merger would make a contribution to economic progress such that a wider public policy benefit could offset the impact of the particular transaction on competition.

The 'competitiveness' of the parties or target will be judged in the context of international competition.[16]

---

11 Articles 6 and following of the Law on Merger Control.
12 Article 11 of the Law on Merger Control.
13 Article 10 of the Law on Merger Control.
14 Article 12 of the Law on Merger Control.
15 Article 10 of the Law on Merger Control.
16 Article 42 of the Law on Merger Control.

Notification suspends the merger, which cannot be completed without clearance from the prime minister.

Depending on the outcome of the Competition Council's assessment of the merger, the prime minister might go on to:[17]

- order the parties not to proceed with the transaction and remain in the status quo ante prior to the contemplated merger; or
- order remedies to be taken to resolve competition issues.

Where no notification is issued by the prime minister to the parties by the end of two months (or six months if the case has been referred to the Competition Council), the merger will be deemed to have been tacitly cleared.

Failing to file a merger triggers fines on the following scale:[18]

- corporate bodies – 2%–5% of pre-tax turnover achieved in Morocco during the previous financial year; and
- natural bodies – Dh200,000 to Dh2 million.

In addition, the prime minister can impose any necessary sanctions on parties to prevent the completion of an opposed merger and suppress all consequences of the transaction.

3. Foreign investment

Foreign investment is encouraged and promoted in Morocco – in particular since the promulgation of the Investment Charter in November 1995, which sets out measures to allow the free transfer of invested foreign capital and reduce the costs of investment.

No restrictions apply to foreign investments in most sectors and since March 31 2005 funds held by foreign non-resident individuals can be transferred without restriction.

In a few specific sectors, regulations apply to restrict foreign investment by non-residents. For instance:

- foreign investors may not acquire farmlands, although such land can be leased for periods of 99 years and special derogations can apply to foreigners who contemplate a farmland acquisition for tourism purposes;
- securities and bonds cannot be issued by non-residents on the stock exchange;
- there can be limits to the thresholds of shareholdings of non-residents in relation to the share capital of major banks where such holdings could trigger a change in control of the institution;
- regulations in specific areas of the service sector impose restrictions based on access conditions to a market (eg, in the maritime transport, telecommunications, entertainment or audiovisual sectors); this means, for instance, that the board of directors in the audio visual sector must include a minimum number of Moroccan nationals; and

17 Article 43 of the Law on Merger Control.
18 Chapter II of Title VIII of the Law on Merger Control.

- professional services provided by architects, doctors, engineers, lawyers, architects, etc are regulated, and access to these professions is subject to a number of criteria (eg, qualifications, residence, existence of a bilateral agreement between the country of nationality of the foreigner).

Morocco has been a party to the Declaration on International Investments and Enterprises of the Organisation for Economic Cooperation and Development since November 2009.

4. Case study

AA was a listed company that specialises in the production and supply of dairy products. It had a very significant share of the Moroccan market. BB was a major world player in the dairy business and an historic shareholder of AA (minority stake). AA's majority shareholder (CC) decided to sell its dairy activities. CC and BB negotiated for several months before entering into a memorandum of understanding which organised:

- the transfer of a large portion of CC's shares in the capital of AA to BB (granting it the majority of shares and voting rights) under some conditions precedent to be met within a certain timeframe; and
- the sale of the rest of CC's shares to the public on the stock exchange.

The listing of AA's shares was consequently suspended prior to the official announcement of the transaction (as mandated by market rules and regulations). Further to the announcement, the transaction was notified for prior approval to the office of the prime minister in compliance with competition regulations, such regulations allowing the prime minister to transfer the matter to the Competition Council. Having obtained competition clearance, BB and CC were able to sign the final share purchase agreement and close the deal. This was immediately followed by the filing by BB of a public tender offer on all listed shares of AA, an obligation imposed on BB by market regulations once it exceeded the 40% capital threshold. This was followed by the public offer initiated by CC to sell the rest of its shares on the market, primarily motivated by the need to maintain the liquidity of AA's shares on the stock exchange market. The whole transaction was a success, as the public offer was subscribed several times over the nominal amount.

Oman

Taimur Malik
Curtis, Mallet-Prevost, Colt & Mosle LLP
Alastair Neale
Jihad Al Taie Law Office

The financial challenges facing businesses all over the world have prompted many organisations to look towards consolidation as a means of survival. Meanwhile, others have embarked upon growth objectives to prepare for future opportunities.

Mergers and acquisitions in Oman have never been as common as in some other Gulf Cooperation Council (GCC) states and in Oman mostly relate to small and medium-sized businesses. Nevertheless, the fundamental principles to be followed in all such transactions are substantially the same.

This chapter examines mergers and acquisitions in the context of limited liability companies (LCCs) and joint stock companies. The most popular form of corporate vehicle in Oman is the LLC. An LLC requires at least two shareholders and there is no requirement in the laws of Oman for an LLC to have a board of directors. An LLC is easier to establish than a joint stock company and is subject to fewer regulatory rules under Omani law.

Many bigger companies take the form of joint stock companies which have higher minimum capital requirements and greater regulatory and compliance obligations. Publicly listed companies are commonly referred to as 'public joint stock companies'. The other form of joint stock company, essentially a private joint stock company, is known as the 'closed joint stock company'.

Closed joint stock companies are not listed on the Muscat Securities Market (MSM), although they are registered with it. The shareholders' register for joint stock companies is maintained at the Muscat Clearing and Depository Company (MCDC), whereas shareholders' information for LLCs is kept at the Ministry of Commerce and Industry (MOCI).

1. Structuring

The obvious initial decision in relation to an M&A deal is to decide upon the structure of the transaction. It is important to keep in mind that this choice will be affected by various factors including, among other things, any limitations in the laws and regulations in Oman and the outcome of the due diligence exercise.

1.1 Due diligence

A legal due diligence exercise in relation to the target will normally be carried out at the same time as the negotiations for the merger or acquisition of the business. Indeed, the acquiring party will rely on the results of the due diligence to decide the next steps.

(a) ***Methodology***

In most cases the due diligence report will take the form of a lengthy questionnaire covering different aspects of the operations of the target.

(b) ***Relevant information***

At the initial stage, one would expect to review the following general information/documents in relation to the due diligence of an Omani company:

- a copy of the constitutive contract;
- copies of any deeds of amendment of the constitutive contract since its incorporation;
- its Oman Chamber of Commerce and Industry membership certificate;
- an MOCI authorised signatories form;
- MOCI commercial registration information;
- the latest audited financial statements;
- the minutes of the last annual general meeting approving the accounts;
- evidence that all Omani taxes have been paid and are up to date, together with the company's tax file number and details of the tax manager;
- evidence that the company complies with applicable Omanisation targets;
- details of registration of all Omani employees with the Public Authority for Social Insurance (PASI);
- evidence that all social insurance contributions are up to date;
- the date of appointment of each authorised signatory and that person's signing powers (including bank mandates);
- copies of all leases of business premises and staff accommodation rented by the company;
- copies of all municipality licences for business premises and signboards;
- details of branches, if any; and
- details of any actual or pending litigation involving the company either as plaintiff or defendant.

In addition, the following information in relation to the company's board of directors may also be required for the purpose of preparing the due diligence report:

- the minutes of meetings of the board of directors of the company and any committee thereof;
- a list of directors identifying the chairman and managing director of the company, along with the following details:
  - the address and contact numbers of the directors;
  - the nationality of each director;
  - other directorships and business interests held by each director;
  - the percentage of shareholding in the company or any associated company for each director;
  - whether any of the directors are executive or non-executive; and
  - date of appointment and date of retirement if appropriate, of each director;
- details of annual remuneration, along with aggregate emoluments payable to the directors;

- a list of loans along with copies of loan agreements, if any, granted to the directors by the company;
- copies of service contracts/employment agreements, if any, between the company and any of its directors and its key executives;
- details of interest in shares, options, warrants, etc which each of the directors may have in the company;
- a copy of any power of attorney given by the company to its directors and/or officers;
- the appointment of nominee directors, including directors appointed at the instance of financial institutions or banks or by virtue of rights vested in such lenders or by debentures; and
- the names and addresses of persons, if any, who have been charged/designated by the board of directors with the responsibility for complying with the provisions of Omani laws and regulations.

As the due diligence progresses, the following additional information relating to the company's shareholding, financial commitments, contractual rights and obligations will also be required:

- a statement indicating the dates of any change in the authorised, issued, subscribed and paid up capital of the company along with copies of relevant resolutions;
- a list of the promoters (ie, the founder shareholders), along with their names, number of shares held, the list of companies in which they hold shares, along with the percentage shareholding held by them in such companies;
- any agreement or commitment to issue or transfer shares/conversion of loan into equity;
- any shareholders' agreement;
- any sanction letters (ie, letters or notices imposing penalties for breach of obligations or requiring the company to take specific steps) related to financing availed by the company;
- copies of any legal or commercial mortgages creating a charge on the company's property;
- particulars (together with copies) of all guarantees, performance bonds, letters of comfort or similar documents of assurance and any indemnities provided by the company or its directors for the benefit of the company;
- list of registered trademarks/copyrights;
- list of applications pending for registration of trademarks/copyrights;
- copies of all non-disclosure agreements and/or confidentiality agreements executed by the company;
- any other agreement entered into in respect of any IP rights and registrations;
- copies of all relevant industrial licences, environmental and health and safety permits and certificates; and
- a schedule (together with copies) of insurance policies showing types of risk covered, insurers, major exclusions and deductibles, and details of assets covered by the insurance.

(c) *Evaluation and pricing mechanism*

Royal Decree 4/1974 (Commercial Companies Law) provides that the net assets of the target shall be evaluated taking into account the latest audited balance sheet. It further provides that the procedures for evaluation of shares in kind provided in the Commercial Companies Law will apply in all other situations.

In the case of an LLC, with respect to contributions in kind, an auditor of a firm licensed to work in Oman must submit a report certifying the value of every member's contributions in kind to the capital of the company.

The value of the contribution in kind may also be determined by one or more experts to be appointed by MOCI, upon the application of the members and in accordance with the rules, regulations and policies decided by MOCI.

This will also apply in respect of mergers and acquisitions where the latest audit balance sheets of the merging companies or the target entity are not available.

Where the method for the acquisition of a listed company is by way of a private placement, the company needs to ensure that the issue price is not less than the average of the weekly high and low closing prices of the relevant shares quoted in the MSM in the previous 26 weeks or the average during four weeks before the date of official disclosure of the private placement agreement, whichever is higher.

1.2 Available structures under the legal system

The Commercial Companies Law provides for mergers to take place in two ways:

- by way of incorporation – that is, a dissolution of one or more companies and transfer of their liabilities/assets to an existing company; or
- by way of consolidation – that is, an establishment of a new company to which the liabilities/assets of all the companies to be amalgamated are transferred, and dissolution of such companies.

The legal steps required to be taken by the merging companies in order to approve the merger depend on the type of the companies involved in the transaction.

1.3 Structuring considerations

The most important decision in relation to an M&A transaction obviously relates to the structuring of the deal. In the case of mergers, the decision of whether to merge one company into the other company or to establish a new company depends to a large extent on the mutual agreement of the parties and their respective social and commercial considerations. Another important factor, in addition to issues relating to the assignment and assumption of all the rights and obligations of the merging company, is the transfer of employment visas of foreign employees of the merging company to the incorporating company or new company established by the merger.

In relation to acquisitions, the acquirer can decide whether it is more appropriate simply to go for acquisition of the assets of the target company or whether to acquire its shares.

(a) *Tax*

Under Royal Decree 28/2009 (Income Tax Law), the profits or gains made from the disposal of any asset, including disposal of the goodwill of the company or the trade name or trademark with respect to the activity or part thereof, will be considered as income for the purposes of taxation. However, profit on the sale of securities listed on the domestic capital market (MSM) is not subject to tax.

(b) ***Regulatory considerations***

In the case of certain companies such as those undertaking activities in the banking, insurance, electricity or water sectors, specific approvals must be obtained from the relevant regulatory bodies prior to any M&A activity.

If the target is a bank or an institution carrying out banking and financial activities, for example, the bidder must first obtain the approval of the Central Bank of Oman (CBO) and from the Capital Market Authority (CMA).

Similarly, in the case of companies in the electricity sector, approval for change of control must be secured from the Authority for Electricity Regulation Oman (AERO). Consideration will need to be given to the conditions of any AERO licence that the target company has, as well as the bidder's existing shareholding in companies operating in the electricity sector in Oman.

(c) ***Timeline***

In cases where regulatory approvals are required, in view of the information to be provided to the regulatory authorities and the fact that the parties have little control over the timing of the approval process, companies may find that they are in the hands of the regulatory authorities as to timetable.

In the case of mergers and acquisitions involving LLCs only, the timeline will depend on how efficiently the companies undertake the required procedural steps.

(d) ***Other considerations***

Oman has no foreign currency exchange controls. There are no restrictions on repatriation or remittance of funds abroad. The Omani rial is pegged to the US dollar at \$2.60/OR1. Both capital and profits are freely remittable.

1.4 Competition laws

There are no specific competition laws in Oman. There are industry-specific rules in relation to the maximum shareholding of a company (and its related parties/affiliates) in the companies undertaking activities in that industry. For example, companies with shareholdings in banking, finance and leasing companies need the approval of the CBO, which sets levels for maximum shareholdings in such companies. Similarly, companies with shareholdings in the power sector need approval from AERO.

The Capital Market Authority Law issued by Royal Decree 80/1998 (as amended) states that no single person or related persons up to second-of-kin may hold 25% or more of the shares of a public joint stock company without the prior approval of the executive president of the CMA. The Capital Market Authority Law also states that if the subject matter of such control or ownership is a bank or an establishment undertaking banking business, the approval of the Central Bank of Oman must be obtained beforehand in conformity with the Banking Law.

There are also certain restrictions on members of the board of directors of joint stock companies in relation to the number of board appointments that they can hold at a time.

In other words, in the absence of specific anti-competition rules, these sector-specific regulations and CMA approval requirements in respect of shareholdings of more than 25% in public joint stock companies serve as a control mechanism by which the CMA and the industry regulators such as CBO can check and prevent monopoly or anti-competitive trends in the market.

1.5 Foreign investment laws and foreign ownership restrictions

Those involved in mergers and acquisitions including foreign investment must also consider Royal Decree 102/1994 – the Foreign Capital Investment Law – which regulates foreign business presence. In general, non-Omani persons, whether natural or legal, are not allowed to conduct commercial, industrial or tourism business or to participate in an Omani company without an appropriate licence or clearance from the MOCI.

Under the Foreign Capital Investment Law, any foreign natural or corporate entity must obtain a foreign capital investment licence issued by the MOCI before commencing business in Oman (but in practice this is no longer required). The general rule is that a company with foreign participation must have a share capital of at least OR150,000 (with the exception, for instance, of engineering consultancy companies which must have a minimum share capital of OR200,000; and companies formed pursuant to the Oman-US Free Trade Agreement and companies established at the Knowledge Oasis Muscat, which can be 100% foreign owned with a minimum share capital of only OR20,000).

Foreign shareholdings in Omani companies can now be up to 70% without the need for any special permission (although the law provides for a lower percentage). (The 70% cap derives from Oman's accession to the World Trade Organisation in November 2000 and consequent liberalisation, with the secretariat of commerce at MOCI now permitting registration of companies with foreign shareholdings in LLCs up to 70% of the capital of the company). The articles of association of some companies (eg, banks) may require that such companies be owned at least 51% by Omanis.

In certain circumstances, foreign ownership can be increased beyond 70% with the approval of the Council of Ministers after a recommendation of MOCI. Such approval would be considered only for projects deemed critical to the development of the national economy. In such exceptional cases, the capital of the company must be not less than OR500,000.

If the merger involves the takeover of an Omani company (with some foreign shareholding) by another Omani company (also with some foreign shareholding), care must be taken to ensure that, in respect of the merged entity, the foreign investment limit of 70% is not exceeded.

Similarly, if a new company is to be established out of the merger of one or more companies, the provisions of the Foreign Capital Investment Law relating to share capital and foreign shareholding would need to be complied with.

2. Merger agreement

The merger agreement is the most significant document in relation to a merger transaction and it is important that all aspects of the transaction are adequately covered in this agreement. In any event, although there is no standard practice in Oman, it is likely that there will be a number of pre-merger agreements between the parties.

2.1 Pre-merger agreements

(a) *Confidentiality and non-disclosure agreement*

As a starting point, companies contemplating an M&A transaction will normally enter into confidentiality and non-disclosure agreements with the counterparties (and their representatives). The transaction advisers for a company will need access to a number of documents which are not in the public domain and the company providing this information will inevitably seek comfort in the form of confidentiality and non-disclosure agreements.

(b) *Exclusivity agreement*

In the event that the M&A transaction is consequential to an announcement by the target company to seek expressions of interest from other companies to purchase its assets or shares, it is likely that the target company will be approached by multiple interested parties. However, undertaking the financial, legal and technical due diligence of a business can be an expensive undertaking and most companies will prefer to enter into an exclusivity agreement with the target company. This agreement will be for a certain period and will normally give the bidding company the exclusive right to undertake all necessary steps to formulate its bid and negotiate with the target company during this period.

(c) *Memorandum of understanding*

A memorandum of understanding is usually the stepping stone to the main merger agreement. Depending on the stage at which a memorandum of understanding is entered into between the parties, the exclusivity clauses can be included in the memorandum instead of forming a separate agreement.

A memorandum of understanding is especially likely for an M&A transaction involving public joint stock companies and companies in sectors such as banking and electricity, which require additional regulatory approvals.

2.2 Scope

(a) *Parties*

The parties to the merger agreement will be the companies participating in the merger activity whether by way of incorporation or consolidation. Each party will need to undertake the required corporate action under its constitutive contract or articles of association to ensure that it has the necessary authority to enter into the merger agreement.

(b) ***Description***

The merger agreements can vary in length and scope depending on the type of merger and the size and nature of the merging entities.

2.3 Important clauses

The clauses discussed below will be included in almost all merger agreements.

(a) ***Merger, acquisition or purchase clause***

It should be set out at the beginning of the agreement whether the merger agreement relates to a merger by way of incorporation or consolidation. Another introductory clause should state whether the merger agreement is subject to any approvals, consents or other regulatory formalities.

(b) ***Representations and warranties***

The parties to the merger agreement will be required to provide certain representations and warranties. The scope of these representations and warranties to be given by one party will depend on the extent to which the other party is relying on information provided by the first party.

For example, the target company is likely to warrant that it is not party to any material litigation and that there has been no material depreciation or decrease in the net asset value of the company since the date of its last audited financial statements. This will normally be supported by confirmation from the auditors of the relevant company. Another representation may relate to the transfer of key employees of the target company to the other company.

(c) ***Liabilities and limitation of liability***

Depending on the structure of the transaction, the acquiring party will be interested in including a clause limiting its liability in relation to the target company. The Commercial Companies Law recognises the right of the parties to limit their liabilities in relation to each other in the merger agreement. There may also be a provision that part of the consideration will be payable only if the target meets certain financial targets.

(d) ***Choice of law clause***

The merger agreement and other related pre-merger agreements will normally be subject to the laws and regulations of Oman. The terms of the pre-merger and merger agreements need to be in line with the provisions of Article 13 of the Commercial Companies Law.

(e) ***Dispute resolution clause***

The dispute resolution mechanism will depend on the preference of the parties concerned. With respect to small and medium-sized M&A transactions, the parties are likely to agree to submit any disputes to the courts in Oman.

In relation to joint stock companies and especially companies with substantial foreign shareholding, the merger agreements are likely to include an arbitration clause (eg, under the Rules of Arbitration of the International Chamber of Commerce).

The courts will not usually interfere and freedom of contract between the parties will be respected by the courts, provided that there is no conflict with Omani public policy or laws of mandatory application. Oman has ratified the New York Convention on the Recognition and Enforcement of Foreign Arbitration Awards. In the event that arbitration is carried outside Oman, Royal Decree 36/1998 (Foreign Awards Law) is relevant and such awards would be enforceable through the Primary Court.

2.4 Employment law and pensions

Royal Decree 35/2003 as amended (the Labour Law) sets out the rights and obligations of employees and employers in great detail and companies contemplating M&A transactions in Oman will need to look at various issues in relation to employment matters.

For example, it is pertinent for such companies to evaluate in relation to the target company or the other merging companies[1] (normally as part of the due diligence and valuation process) the nature of any accumulated end-of-service gratuities with respect to the non-Omani employees and ensure that there are no arrears in relation to the PASI contributions and that the company complies with its Omanisation targets.

Companies also need to consider whether it will be necessary to terminate the services of any existing employees of the merging or target company. This is important because the Labour Law provides protection to employees against termination without cause and it is normal for courts to award compensation to employees in such cases. as the courts are not likely to accept a merger as a valid reason for dismissal.

In the event that a new company is to be established under the merger transaction, then the existing non-Omani employees will need to be transferred to the sponsorship/visa of the new company.

According to the terms of the Labour Law, the contracts of employment will continue to exist under a merger or acquisition transaction and the successors will be jointly responsible with the former employers for discharging all the obligations prescribed by the Labour Law.[2]

Particular attention also needs to be given to the Omanisation policy which has been implemented by the Ministry of Manpower (MoM) to promote the employment of Omani citizens. All companies must comply with its provisions. The Omanisation percentages for each sector are issued from time to time by the MoM

1 For example, the Labour Law states that "The dissolution, liquidation, closure or bankruptcy of the establishment or its merger with another establishment or transfer thereof by inheritance, sale, lease, assignment, legacy, gift or such other acts of disposal shall not preclude the discharging of all its obligations. Apart from the cases of liquidation, bankruptcy and the final authorized closure, the employment contract shall remain existent and the successor shall be jointly liable with the former employers for discharging all the obligations prescribed by the law subject to the established priority of the employees' rights."

2 Article 47 of the Labour Law.

and published on the MoM's website. New companies are expected to progressively achieve the Omanisation percentages applicable to their industries and agree on a development plan with the MoM in this respect; and they may be required to pay any applicable fines until they achieve the specified Omanisation percentage.

The submission of the Omanisation plan to the MoM is a condition of obtaining the labour clearance which is necessary to employ non-Omanis. The main aim of this policy is to encourage the employment and training of Omani citizens. The government in this regard has taken the following steps, which companies should be aware of:

- publishing and periodically amending a list of business activities restricted to Omanis only;
- specifying an 'Omanisation percentage' (ie, a percentage of Omani employees) for each sector and, within each sector, for the different job functions; and
- restricting some specific positions within all private companies (eg, receptionist, driver, human resources) to Omanis only.

The Omanisation percentages are declared by the MoM and apply for a period of four years or more.

2.5 Internal approvals

(a) LLCs

With LLCs, the merger will need to be unanimously approved by the shareholders of the company under the Commercial Companies Law and the constitutive contract of the company.

In the event of a merger by way of incorporation, among other things, the following steps need to be taken:

- The company intending to be merged must adopt a resolution to merge into the other company and to dissolve itself;
- The net assets of the company intending to be merged must be evaluated in accordance with the last audited balance sheet or under the procedure for evaluation of shares in kind provided in the Commercial Companies Law;
- The incorporating company must issue a resolution increasing its capital in accordance with the evaluation of the assets of the company to be merged; and
- The increase in capital must be divided between the members of the merged company in proportion to their shares.

The Commercial Companies Law requires that the merger announcement should be published in two consecutive issues of two daily newspapers and be registered in the Commercial Register.[3]

3 Article 13*bis* 8 of Royal Decree 4/1974, as amended.

The merger decision shall not be implemented until after the expiry of three months from the date of its registration in the Commercial Register.[4] If necessary, the minister of commerce and industry may reduce such period in a decision to be published in two consecutive issues of two daily newspapers.

The company's creditors shall, within the stated period, have the right to object to the merger by registered letter to the company, at which point the merger can be suspended unless:

- the creditors waive their objection;[5]
- the court passes a final decision rejecting the objection;
- the company satisfies that the debt is due; or
- the company provides sufficient security for its payment if it is a deferred debt.

If no objection is presented within the prescribed period, the merger will be considered final and the incorporating or new company assumes all rights and liabilities of the merging companies.

In relation to the rights and liabilities with respect to the merging companies, the Commercial Companies Law provides that once the merger is effective and registered in the Commercial Register, all rights and liabilities of the merged company shall, within the limits agreed in the merger agreement, be transferred to the incorporating or new company established under the merger without prejudice to the rights of the creditors.[6]

(b) *Public companies*

In the case of joint stock companies, the approval will require a resolution passed at the extraordinary general meeting of the company in accordance with the provisions of the Articles of Association of the company. The Commercial Companies Law requires that resolutions of the extraordinary general meeting be adopted by a majority of three-quarters of the votes cast in respect of a certain resolution, provided always that such resolution receives votes representing more than half of the company's share capital.

The Commercial Companies Law also states that, with respect to banks and investment companies, CBO approval is a pre-requisite for the implementation of any merger decision.[7]

2.6 Regulatory approvals

(a) *LLCs*

The merger decision cannot be implemented until the decision has been approved by MOCI.

---

4 *Ibid.*
5 *Ibid.*
6 Article 13*bis* 10 of Royal Decree 4/1974, as amended.
7 Article 13*bis* 4 of Royal Decree 4/1974, as amended.

(b) ***Public companies***

The merger decision cannot be implemented until the decision has been approved by the CMA.

2.7 Listed companies versus unlisted companies

Mergers and acquisitions involving listed companies take more time and are subject to greater regulatory and legal requirements and approvals compared with transactions involving only unlisted companies.

For example, there are disclosure requirements in relation to listed companies and any contemplated transactions, especially transactions that may result in a change of control, need to be disclosed through the electronic system of the MSM.[8]

Moreover, Royal Decree 80/98 (the Capital Market Law) provides that no single person or related persons up to second degree of kinship may hold more than 25% or more of the shares of a joint stock company whose shares are offered for public subscription, save by a prior approval of the executive president of the CMA (or his agent). Failure to comply with that rule will render the transaction null and void. The board of directors of the CMA has authority to specify the terms and conditions of that shareholding.

In the event that the acquisition of the controlling shares of a listed company is being conducted by way of private placement, then the private placement rules of the CMA will also need to be followed.

A public joint stock company interested in increasing its capital through private placement of shares to specific person(s) is required to convene an extraordinary general meeting to obtain the approval for such a proposal. The company is required to provide, along with an agenda, a summary of the proposal including pricing along with the rationale, identity and background of the proposed allottees, perceived value addition to the company and any other information the CMA deems necessary to be disclosed. Prior to the general meeting, the company is also required to obtain an undertaking from the persons to whom the private placement is addressed that they will pay the full value of shares on allotment.

Where persons to whom the shares are allotted are related parties, the company must disclose this fact to the shareholders in the notice of the general meeting showing the nature of interests related to the company. The resolution of the general meeting must include the names of the proposed allottees, the number of shares and the issue price.

On obtaining the approval of the general meeting, the company is required to submit to the CMA the initial draft of the prospectus containing the information and documents detailed in the CMA Executive Regulations. This will include an explanation of the advantages and benefits that will accrue to the company from the proposed subscription, and justification for selecting the method of private placement instead of a rights issue.

---

8 Article 20 (9) and Articles 291–9 of the Executive Regulations of the Capital Market Law (Decision No. 1 of 2009).

3. Post-merger issues

3.1 Employment issues

In order to employ a foreign worker in Oman, all requirements set out in the Labour Law must be satisfied. Under the Omani Labour Law, non-Omanis are prohibited from doing any work in Oman before obtaining a labour card, which will be granted only on satisfaction of certain conditions.

The labour card is granted at the employer's request, is valid for two years and is renewable. It can be granted only to foreigners whose age is not below 21 years and (with some exceptions) not above 60 years of age.

The Labour Law forbids foreign employees to work for an entity that is not their sponsor. Severe penalties have been established for all parties involved – that is, employee, sponsoring employer, employer who actually employs a foreigner without sponsoring him or her as an employee. Accordingly, it is very important to ensure in the post-merger scenario that all foreign employees are being sponsored.

3.2 Assets

During the M&A transaction, the assets of the merging companies will have to be assigned to the new company. Particular attention needs to be given to assets which require transfer procedures involving registrations, approvals etc.

The Land Law regime in Oman draws a clear distinction between the interests and entitlements available to Omanis and those available to non-Omanis. Only Omani nationals are entitled to the benefits of real estate on a freehold basis (except in integrated tourism developments such as The Wave Muscat). Companies which are wholly Omani owned and public joint stock companies which are 51% Omani owned may own real estate. The first element to be considered if one or more merging companies own real estate properties is whether the new company is allowed to acquire such properties.

The procedure for the transfer to be registered with the Ministry of Housing (MoH) involves the following steps:

- The buyer and the seller must appear at the relevant office at the MoH to sign the sale and purchase contract. If the buyer and/or the seller are companies, their authorised signatories must appear, provided that they have been authorised in writing by the board of directors or by the shareholders. The authorisation must be presented to MoH along with the authorised signatories form, the corporate documents of the company and the personal IDs of the individuals concerned;
- The seller has to submit the original title deed to MoH;
- The applicable fee (ie, 3% of the sale price) must be paid to MoH;
- MoH will then, upon verification of the title's authenticity and of the existence of encumbrances, and if no discrepancies appear between the information submitted and the information already registered, proceed with the filing of the transaction; and
- Once the transaction is registered, the new owner can obtain from MoH the title deed to the property.

This procedure is quite simple and straightforward. In normal circumstances, the total duration of the registration procedure is on average less than three weeks.

Moreover, any legal and commercial mortgages of the merging companies will have to be transferred to the new company in accordance with the procedures established by the relevant authorities.

In relation to commercial mortgages, notice should be given to MOCI, which may require formal consent from the mortgage holder for any change in the Commercial Register of the target. With respect to legal mortgages, notice should be given to MoH, which may require a deed of amendment or even a new legal mortgage. The government fee for registering any commercial mortgage (or change to a mortgage) is OR50 (US$130) and for registering any legal mortgage is 3% of the secured amount. There is no fixed fee in respect of the amendment of a legal mortgage.

A number of local legal, regulatory and procedural issues need to be considered by the parties before embarking upon an M&A transaction in Oman. Timely advice and assistance can improve the efficiency with which completion can be achieved.

Qatar

Grace Alam
Chadia El Meouchi
Marie-Anne Jabbour
Badri & Salim El Meouchi LLP

Qatar's booming economy, in parallel with general government policy, has driven several M&A transactions in recent years. The government has consequently amended the relevant laws and regulations. So, for example, a new chapter was inserted in the Commercial Companies Law (5/2002) by the Takeover Law (3/2010), which was promulgated on March 15 2010.

In addition, precedents have been established in recent years that assist parties and their advisers in completing M&A transactions efficiently.

1. Structuring

1.1 Due diligence

In the case of an acquisition, the acquirer will likely wish to carry out the due diligence, as it will wish to determine the true state of the company and any hidden liabilities or obligations that may attach to it.

In a merger, as the successor company will normally assume all rights and obligations of both parties to the merger, each will likely wish to carry out its own independent due diligence, to ensure that there will be no negative consequences from the merger.

(a) Methodology

Three key types of due diligence are usually undertaken:

- Legal – this generally focuses on the company bylaws, the terms on which it does business, ownership of the assets and any restrictions on the free use of such assets, and the extent of any potential liabilities. The process might identify legal issues that could affect the value or prospects of the company, as well as any preconditions or consents that must be satisfied to transfer ownership of the shares or assets of the company.
- Financial – this is usually undertaken by the company auditors, which will report on its commercial activities, management structure, employees, taxation, profitability, accounting systems/policies and premises. Often, information discovered by the auditors will then be passed to the lawyers to help with the legal due diligence.
- Technical – this will assess the actual business of the company.

In order to obtain the information necessary to produce the due diligence report, a questionnaire or due diligence list must be circulated to the relevant company. Once the necessary information has been collated, access to a data room should be provided in order to conduct the due diligence and produce the report.

(b) *Due diligence report*

Once the due diligence has been carried out, the due diligence report is produced. The purpose of the report is to introduce and highlight any particular issues that may affect the negotiations, especially with regard to price, warranties/covenants and liabilities.

This will involve highlighting any securities that exist over the company's property, including mortgages, pledges and guarantees granted over its assets, as well as loan amounts covered by such securities, any reimbursement plans in the event of default, and the company's ability to fulfil its obligations under such loans. The report will also specify any changes in the business that may result from the transaction (eg, change of control clauses), and any third-party consents or approvals which may be necessary in order to proceed with the transaction.

It will also reveal much more detailed information that was not previously in the public domain. This may help the acquirer to take a view on whether the target represents a viable investment. It may also flag up any problems which will need to be resolved before the transaction can proceed.

The due diligence report will mainly include the following information:

- an introduction summarising the proposed transaction;
- corporate due diligence – the basic corporate documents (ie, all incorporation and company documents, whether private or public, details of any subsidiaries; details of any increases/reductions in capital and of any listings on stock exchange, details of any ordinary or extraordinary general meetings) and all corporate finance documents (ie, credit agreements, lease financing agreements and all other agreements evidencing outstanding loans or guarantees undertaken);
- shareholder information – information on the number of shares held by each shareholder; the company books, including the members' register; shareholder communications and details of dividends paid in the last five years; any shareholder agreements or other documents relating to shareholders;
- securities issuance – samples of share certificates, details of any share option/purchase agreements and all other agreements relating to equity or debt securities;
- company dealings – agreements resulting from the day-to-day business of the company undertaken within its authorised scope of activities;
- financial information – information about bank accounts, changes in accounting methods, copies of any documents relating to charges, liens or mortgages or similar security documents;
- intellectual property – a list of all registered and unregistered IP rights, information about any IP licences and agreements, and information about any known infringements or challenges to IP rights;

- information technology – information about software licences, hardware and IT agreements;
- employment issues – copies of employment contracts governing the relationship between employer and employee, including information on each employee (eg, salary and benefits, details of any ongoing restrictive covenants);
- officers and directors – the identity of previous and current officers and directors, their duties, and the method, validity and term of their appointment. Information on any bonus agreements, severance plans, retirement agreements, details of any compensation paid to directors and officers since incorporation and any information about insider dealing must also be provided;
- insurance – a list of insurance policies, along with their term, warranty limits and any rights to assign or transfer such policies;
- litigation – all active litigation files submitted by and against the company and information about the parties, date of submission, relevant courts, facts, amounts claimed and latest proceedings, as well as all files relating to settled litigation and any issued judgments in favour of or against the company;
- properties and assets – all movable and immovable assets owned and leased by the company. For owned properties and assets, the due diligence report should identify the legal status of ownership and any securities over such assets and properties, taking into consideration foreign ownership restrictions and limitations. For leased properties and assets, the report should identify the parties to the lease agreements, the term of such agreements, the rent payable and the applicable conditions in case of transfer or assignment;
- related party transactions; and
- material agreements such as joint venture, partnership and management agreements, and any research and development agreements with third parties, highlighting the company's obligations and liabilities and the likely effect of the transaction on such agreements.

In addition to the related documents necessary to provide the above-mentioned information in the due diligence report, other information and documents that must be provided for due diligence purposes include the following:

- details of assets with a value of over $100,000, together with copies of all relevant insurance policies and details of the condition of those assets;
- copies of all permissions, licences, consents and regulatory authorisations, certificates of good standing and any other evidence of regulatory compliance;
- all tax returns or tax exemptions and related tax correspondence pertaining to the company since incorporation;
- matters relevant to the particular transaction- such as special environmental, maritime or other considerations; and
- any other material information that may not have been included specifically above.

1.2 Evaluation and pricing mechanism

In a merger by absorption, the target's assets should be valued by an expert appointed by the Qatari Civil Court according to Articles 158 and 274 of the Companies Law. That expert will be appointed following the submission of a request by the target to that court.

Article 274 of the Companies Law provides that a merger by absorption involves the following steps:

- The target decides on its dissolution.
- The target's assets are valued according to the provisions on the valuation of in-kind assets set out in the Companies Law.
- Based on the result of this valuation, the acquirer issues a decision to increase its share capital.
- The increased share capital is distributed to the shareholders in the merged company in proportion to their shareholdings.
- If the shares are equity instruments and two years have passed since the establishment of the acquirer, these shares may be traded as soon as they have been issued.

In-kind contributions are addressed in Article 158 of the Companies Law, which provides as follows:

> *It is possible for the company to have in-kind contributions, to be granted against participations which are not in cash or against evaluated rights. The founders of the company must request the Civil Court to appoint one expert or more to ensure that the in-kind assets were accurately evaluated. Such evaluation shall not be final unless approved by subscribers owning 2/3 of the cash contribution shares. The owners of the in-kind contributions shall not have the right to vote even if they are the owners of cash shares. The in-kind contribution shall only represent shares the value of which was already fully paid. The shares representing the in-kind assets shall not be delivered until the complete transfer of ownership of such assets to the company has been undertaken.*

The pricing mechanism is usually agreed between the parties. The law includes no requirements in this regard. Once the due diligence report has been issued, the parties, along with their auditors, will usually evaluate the price and the share value, and submit their offers.

1.3 Available structures

M&A structures in Qatar are governed by the Companies Law.

(a) Merger by consolidation

According to Article 275 of the Companies Law, a merger by consolidation takes place as follows:

- Both companies are dissolved.
- A new entity is established by the shareholders of the merging companies.
- The shareholders transfer the agreed assets of the dissolved companies into the newly incorporated entity.
- The parties run their combined business through that new entity.

(b) ***Merger by absorption***

According to Article 274 of the Companies Law, this structure takes place between two companies, Company A and Company B, as follows:

- Company A decides on its dissolution.
- Company A's assets are evaluated by an expert appointed by the Qatari Civil Court.
- Based on the above evaluation, Company B issues new shares by increasing its share capital.
- The newly issued shares are distributed to the shareholders in Company A in proportion to their shareholdings.

(c) ***Acquisition***

Acquisitions are governed by the Takeover Law. A 'takeover' is defined in Article 2 of the Takeover Law as a procedure through which one company directly or indirectly acquires part of another company's share capital, or obtains a majority of the voting rights in that company by acquiring all or part of its shares, by way of a general offer of exchange or by entering into a shareholders' agreement that does not contradict the interest and the objects of the target, or by any other legal means.

A takeover does not result in the elimination of the legal personality of the target; nor does it affect any of its rights and obligations towards third parties.

The procedure as set out in the Takeover Law is as follows:

- The shareholders' extraordinary general meeting of both the acquirer and the target must approve the takeover. Subsequently, these resolutions must be ratified by the Ministry of Business and Trade and published in two Arabic local and daily newspapers at the expense of the acquirer.
- The acquirer must increase its capital according to its articles of association and distribute the newly issued shares among the shareholders in proportion to their shareholdings.
- The transfer of ownership of shares from the target to the acquirer should be completed.
- If cash consideration is offered, the acquirer must pay the acquisition price, which will be held in a special account until it is distributed to the shareholders registered at the date on which the shareholders' extraordinary general meeting approves the takeover. If the consideration offered is in the form of shares, then those shares will be remitted to the target, which will distribute them to the shareholders registered at the time of the shareholders' extraordinary general meeting at which the takeover is approved.
- The target must undertake the necessary procedures to amend its articles of association and elect a new board of directors according to its articles of association.
- The acquirer must take all necessary measures to protect the minority rights of shareholders of the target, including offering to acquire their shares or voting rights in accordance with any decision in this respect of the Ministry of Business and Trade.

1.4 Structuring considerations

(a) Tax

Taxes in Qatar are governed by the Income Tax Law (21/ 2009) and its implementing regulations issued in 2011.

Article 2 of the Tax Law provides that an annual tax shall be levied on a taxpayer's total income that is subject to taxation and results from sources in Qatar.

Article 3 identifies what is regarded as Qatar-source income; this includes the sale of shares in joint stock companies or of quotas in partnership companies whose assets are mainly composed of real estate located in Qatar.

In addition, according to Article 12 of the Tax Law, every taxpayer undertaking an activity or generating income that is subject to tax must register for tax purposes with the tax authorities in accordance with specified timeframes and conditions.

According to Article 14(1) of the Tax Law, a taxpayer that commences an activity must submit a tax declaration stating its income subject to taxation and the amount of tax payable on such income.

All other taxpayers (those undertaking tax-exempt activities) must also submit a declaration.

Article 14(2) further provides that in the event of dissolution, the liquidator should submit the tax declaration within the period specified in the Tax Law.

With respect to a merger or acquisition, no tax will be due on the transfer of shares, quotas or assets, except as follows:

- The dissolved company in a merger should pay any due income tax in accordance with Article 14 of the Tax Law; and
- The total income from the sale of real estate by any company in Qatar, as well as the total income resulting from the sale of shares in joint stock companies or quotas of partnership companies whose assets which are mainly composed of real estate plots located in Qatar, is taxable.

The Tax Law applies a fixed rate of 10% of the income that is subject to taxation during a given fiscal year.

Pursuant to Article 4 of the Tax Law, the income of Qatari individuals who are resident in Qatar is exempt from income tax, including their share in profits earned from legal entities as partners or shareholders.

Qatari companies that are fully owned by Qataris are also exempt from such tax.

(b) Regulatory considerations

Regulatory considerations vary, depending on the adopted structure and the sector in which the companies operate. This section addresses only some of these regulatory considerations.

Merger by consolidation: The following approvals are required for a merger by consolidation:

- Ministry of Business and Trade approval of the shareholders' extraordinary general resolution issued by each company on their dissolution and liquidation; and

- Ministry of Business and Trade approval of the incorporation of the new entity.

If either of the participants is a joint stock company, the following additional requirements apply:

- The Ministry of Business and Trade must be notified of the time and place of the relevant shareholders' extraordinary general meetings, so that a representative can attend; and
- The new entity whose incorporation is approved by the minister of business and trade must take the form of a joint stock company.

If a participant in the merger is a bank or financial institution, as defined by the Qatar Central Bank, the prior approval of the Qatar Central Bank is required.

If a participant in the merger is listed on the Qatar Exchange, the prior approval of the Qatar Financial Markets Authority (QFMA) is required and the Qatar Exchange must be notified of the dissolution and merger decisions.

Merger by absorption: In the case of a merger by absorption, the Ministry of Business and Trade must approve the shareholders' extraordinary general resolution to increase the share capital and the value of the premium, if any.

If the company increasing its share capital is a joint stock company, the Ministry of Business and Trade must be notified of the date and place of the relevant shareholders' extraordinary general meeting, so that a representative can attend.

If a participant in the merger is a bank or financial institution, the prior approval of the Qatar Central Bank is required.

If a participant in the merger is listed on the Qatar Exchange, the prior approval of the QFMA is required both for the merger itself and for the capital increase. The Qatar Exchange must also be notified of the time and place of the relevant shareholders' extraordinary general meeting if the company increasing its share capital is listed on the exchange.

Acquisition: In the case of an acquisition, the Ministry of Business and Trade must approve the shareholders' extraordinary general resolution approving the capital increase and the value of the premium, if any. If the acquirer is a joint stock company, the Ministry of Business and Trade should be notified of the time and place of the relevant shareholders' extraordinary general meeting, so that a representative can attend.

If a participant in the acquisition is a bank or a financial institution, the prior approval of the Qatar Central Bank is required.

If a participant in the merger is listed on the Qatar Exchange:

- the QFMA's prior approval of the acquisition is required. The QFMA must also be notified of the time and place of the shareholders' extraordinary general meeting at which the capital increase will be approved, insofar as this involves the amendment of the articles of association. The capital increase further requires the QFMA's prior approval if the acquirer is licensed by the QFMA to undertake any of the financial activities listed in Article 4 of the QFMA Financial Services Regulations of 2009 (eg, custodial services, managing investments in securities, advising on securities); and

- the Qatar Exchange must be notified of the acquisition and, if the acquirer is listed, of the time and place of the shareholders' extraordinary general meeting at which the increase in share capital will be approved.

(c) ***Maximum ownership***

The approval of the Qatar Central Bank should be obtained where the acquirer is a bank and will own more than 20% of the capital in the target.

The approval of the QFMA should be obtained should one shareholder own more than 10% of the share capital of a listed company.

1.5 Duration of proceedings

A merger by consolidation involves the dissolution and liquidation of both companies and the incorporation of a new company, while a merger by absorption involves the dissolution and liquidation of one company only.

As the law is silent on the timeframe for completion of a merger or acquisition, it is not possible to determine a specific timeframe for closing. However, since mergers require the completion of more steps than acquisitions, the latter transactions are generally more efficient from a time perspective.

1.6 Antitrust laws

According to Article 10 of the Law on Protection of Competition and Prevention of Monopolistic Practices (19/2006), parties contemplating any transaction which will result in control or monopolisation of the market must notify the Committee for Protection of Competition and Prevention of Monopolistic Practices in advance. The committee will examine the notification and issue its decision on the transaction within 90 days of receipt.

However, Article 11 of the law provides that Article 10 does not apply to transactions which the committee considers would contribute positively to the development of the economy.

1.7 Foreign investment laws and foreign ownership restrictions

Pursuant to Article 2 of the Foreign Capital Investment Law (13/2000), foreigners may own up to 49% of the capital of a company incorporated in Qatar; the remaining 51% should be owned by Qataris.

Notwithstanding the above, Article 2 further allows a foreign investor – in specific situations – to obtain an exemption in order to incorporate a 100% foreign-owned subsidiary by submitting an application to the minister of business and trade, who will issue a decree providing for the exemption. Exemptions are available for foreign investors in the following sectors only: agriculture, industry, health, education, tourism, oil and gas, consultancy services, information technology, sports, culture and entertainment, and distribution.

The Council of Ministers has the authority to add any other economic activity to this list by official decision.

Foreign entities are prohibited altogether from investing in the fields of banking and insurance, except where permitted by decree of the Council of Ministers. Moreover, no exemptions are available where commercial agencies or the purchase of real estate is involved. However, Qatar recently lifted restrictions on real estate ownership by allowing foreign investors to own residential property in certain circumstances and in specific zones.

Article 2 of the Foreign Capital Investment Law provides that foreign investors may own up to 25% of the shares of Qatari companies listed on the Qatar Exchange, unless a higher percentage is provided in the company bylaws and the relevant percentage is approved by the Council of Ministers upon recommendation of the minister for business and trade.

2. Merger agreement

2.1 Pre-merger agreements

As Qatari law does not provide for pre-merger agreements, there are no provisions on the form or content of such agreements. In practice, however, the following provisions may be found in such agreements.

(a) Confidentiality and non-disclosure agreements

The purpose of such agreements is to restrict the use of information relating to the target and the transaction, and ensure that it remains confidential.

The agreement will likely specify the information which is classified as confidential – essentially, information of a sensitive nature. This will generally cover patents, know-how, trade secrets, client and employee data, and details of company structure, management and policies. The agreement will further specify any procedures that might be necessary in order to ensure confidentiality, such as the following:

- using reasonable endeavours to ensure that the relevant security measures and precautions are in place at all times;
- not copying or reproducing confidential information without ensuring that any such copies can be subsequently recovered and then returned or destroyed; and
- not making any public announcement concerning the potential transaction, potential partnering arrangements or any negotiations relating thereto, unless agreed by the parties in writing.

The agreement shall also provide for contractual remedies in the event of a breach of the agreement – usually an indemnity to be paid by the recipient. The amount of such indemnity will normally be determined in the agreement.

(b) Exclusivity agreement

As the acquirer will invest significant time and effort in the transaction, an exclusivity agreement is usually signed under which the target undertakes not to negotiate or enter into any other agreements regarding the company, whether directly or indirectly, for a specific period of time. The agreement will include contractual remedies in the event of breach by the target of the exclusivity obligation, which usually comprise an indemnity to be paid to the acquirer.

(c) *Memorandum of understanding*

The memorandum of understanding outlines the matters of agreement in the initial stages of a transaction and may also govern the relationship between the parties until they enter into a more formal agreement.

Often, the memorandum of understanding also marks the beginning of the due diligence process.

The memorandum can be binding or non-binding.

The issues which should be addressed in the memorandum include the following:

- Timeframe – the parties may agree to a projected timeframe within which the transaction should take place, in order to prevent either party from delaying negotiations.
- Confidentiality – the parties' confidentiality obligations will often be repeated in the memorandum, due to the importance of confidentiality and the desire of the parties to ensure that the confidentiality requirements are binding.
- Price – depending on the transaction, the issue of price may be considered. In many transactions this will depend on issues flagged during the due diligence process; however, in some cases price considerations may arise at this stage.
- Purpose – the parties will also agree to commence negotiations on a definitive purchase agreement.
- Termination – the parties will agree to terminate the memorandum either if they enter into a definitive purchase agreement or upon either party providing written notice.

A term sheet or a letter of intent may sometimes be concluded by the parties instead of a memorandum of understanding.

2.2 Parties and description

The parties involved in a merger or acquisition are as follows:

- the target, which may be a legal entity or an individual (a shareholder);
- the acquirer, which may be a legal entity or an individual (a shareholder);
- financial advisers, to handle the financial due diligence and evaluate the financial side of the transaction, on the basis of which it will be closed or cancelled; and
- legal advisers, to draft the relevant documents and contracts, advise on legal implications, conduct legal due diligence and develop/co-develop the deal structure, with a special focus on contingencies.

2.3 Important clauses

The merger agreement is the main binding document governing the transaction. The agreement will vary depending on the type of deal taking place.

The main provisions that must be included in the agreement in order to protect the parties are as follows:

- Price – this may have been agreed in the negotiations leading up to the merger agreement or, if previously agreed, may have been renegotiated as a result of the due diligence.
- Encumbrances – the shares/assets subject to the agreement should be transferred free from any encumbrances, except for those previously known and approved by the acquirer, which should be clearly detailed in the merger agreement.
- Rights – all rights attached to the shares will be transferred through the agreement, including rights to dividends, voting rights in the shareholders' meeting and any preference rights attached to such shares, such as matters reserved to the approval of the shareholder.
- Obligations – the target will want to ensure that all obligations attached to the shares/assets are transferred to the acquirer, in order to prevent it from incurring ongoing liability to any third party (eg, transfer to the acquirer of any pledge over the target's shares based on the acquirer's approval).
- Conditions precedent – these are requirements that must be fulfilled to ensure that the transfer of shares will be valid, such as obtaining all internal and regulatory approvals, depending on the activities conducted by the target and the acquirer. This list can also be useful in ensuring that all problems revealed in the due diligence are addressed before completion.
- Warranties – this is a list of statements made by the target regarding the state of the company at the time that it is transferred. Should it subsequently become clear that the company was not in the state that the target claimed, the acquirer may take legal action under the warranties in order to claim for any loss suffered.
- Covenants – these are promises made by the target about what it undertakes to do in the future. They may include management covenants detailing how the business will be run before the acquirer gains control, based on supporting documents such as management agreements, control at the level of the board of directors and business plans.
- Dividends – the acquirer will want to include a clause to ensure that it will receive all dividends declared by the company, regardless of when the accounting period ends.
- Entire agreement clause – this will state that the merger agreement and any other linked transaction documents mentioned within constitute the whole agreement. This ensures that anything said previously by the parties in any negotiation documents will not form part of the agreement.
- Miscellaneous provisions – these might include common provisions, such as:
  - a statement to the effect that the invalidity of a clause does not affect the remaining provisions of the agreement; and
  - provisions on *force majeure*, governing law (which is usually Qatari law) and dispute resolution (usually arbitration).

Representations and warranties: Common representations and warranties made by each company that is participating in the transaction include the following:

- It is a duly organised and validly registered company under the laws of its home jurisdiction.
- It has taken all necessary actions and has all requisite power and authority to enter into and perform the agreement, as well as the other documents referred to therein in accordance with their terms.
- Performance of the agreement does not violate or conflict with any law, decree, rule or regulation, or constitute a default under its bylaws.
- It shall, at its own expense, at all times from the date of the implementation agreement, perform or procure the performance of all things as may be required to give full effect to the agreement, including the execution and performance of all documents, acts and things, and the exercise of all powers available to it – including the convening of all meetings, the giving of all consents and the passing of all resolutions reasonably required.
- All executions and procedures required under the agreement shall be duly undertaken in compliance with any and all applicable Qatari laws, decrees, rules, regulations, orders, authorisations, circulars, direction and judgments, as well as the company bylaws.
- It will refrain from entering into any identical or similar agreement with another company.
- The facts contained in the due diligence prepared by it or on its behalf:
  - are true and accurate in all material respects; and
  - within the scope thereof, contained no material omissions.

With respect to the target's representations and covenants, the target acknowledges that:

- it is the sole legal and beneficial owner of the shares;
- the shares are free from all encumbrances; and
- the acquirer is entering into the agreement in express reliance on the warranties given by the target.

With respect to the acquirer's representations and covenants, the acquirer acknowledges that:

- it has the power to purchase the shares mentioned in the agreement and to execute any documentation relating thereto, and has taken all necessary actions to authorise such execution and performance; and
- the merger agreement, the shareholder agreement and the pledge agreement constitute the legal, valid and binding obligations of the acquirer enforceable against the target in accordance with their terms.

Choice of law clause: It is possible under Qatari law for the parties to choose a foreign law to govern their contractual relationship. Article 27 of the Civil Law (22/2004) provides that, with respect to the fundamental conditions of a contract and its implications, the contract shall be governed by the laws of the common nationality of the parties, and in case of different nationalities, the laws of the country where the contract was construed shall apply – unless the parties agree otherwise or it is understood from the circumstances that a different law shall apply.

However, Article 38 of the Civil Law states that the provisions of a foreign law governing a specific contract shall not apply to the extent that they are non-compliant with Qatari public policy and morality.

In addition, with respect to mergers and acquisitions involving companies registered in Qatar, Qatari law shall apply to such transactions and govern the possible structures and processes to be followed (eg, requisite internal and regulatory approvals). Such transactions should thus take place according to the structures, conditions and processes specified under Qatari law, in order to be accepted by the competent authorities.

Dispute resolution clause: The parties may decide that all disputes arising out between them shall be settled by the competent Qatari court, a competent foreign court or arbitration.

A foreign judgment or arbitral award shall be enforced in Qatar provided that certain conditions are met. These conditions, set out in Articles 379, 380 and 381 of the Civil and Commercial Procedure Law (13/1990), are as follows:

- Judgments and orders issued in a foreign country may be executed in Qatar upon the conditions determined in that country for the execution of Qatari judgments and orders.
- An order for execution of a foreign judgment or order will not be made unless it has been ascertained that:
  - the judgment or order was delivered by a competent court of the foreign jurisdiction;
  - the parties to the action were properly served with notice of proceedings and properly represented;
  - the judgment or order is capable of being executed by the successful party to the proceedings in conformity with the laws of the foreign jurisdiction; and
  - the foreign judgment or order does not conflict with a previous judgment or order of a competent Qatari court and is not contrary to public policy or morality in Qatar.

According to Article 381, Articles 379 and 380 shall also apply to arbitral awards issued in a foreign country.

3. Employment law and pension issues

Article 52 of the Labour Law (14/2004) provides, among other things, that an employment agreement does not terminate in the event of a merger, or where ownership or management of the employer is transferred to another party for any reason whatsoever. It further provides that the transferee will be jointly liable with the previous employer for the settlement of all rights of employees due by the latter.

In light of the above, employment agreements entered into with employees of the target will not terminate as a result of the transaction and their employment will be transferred to the acquirer.

Under Qatari law, these employment law considerations are covered only by the Labour Law, and by Article 52 specifically. Where either the employee or the acquirer wishes to terminate the employment agreement following the transaction, such termination should take place in accordance with the relevant provisions of the Labour Law and the provisions of the employment contract.

Pension plans are not required in Qatar, except for Qatari individuals employed by specific entities. These are governed by the Retirement and Pension Plans Law (24/2002), which contains no express provisions on mergers and acquisitions.

4. Approval process

4.1 Internal approvals

(a) Limited liability companies

Merger by consolidation: Each company participating in a merger by consolidation requires the following internal approvals:

- approval by the managers of each company of the decision to merge, to dissolve and to convene the shareholders' extraordinary general meeting for a resolution on the merger;
- approval of the merger by the shareholders' extraordinary general meetings of both companies, in each case by shareholders representing at least 75% of the capital (unless the bylaws also require approval by a specific number of shareholders present), according to Article 256 of the Companies Law. The shareholders' extraordinary general meeting will be quorate if shareholders representing at least 75% of the capital are present, unless a higher percentage is specified in the bylaws; and
- unanimous approval by the shareholders of both companies on the dissolution, unless the bylaws provide for a different majority.

Merger by absorption: In a merger by absorption, the target requires the following internal approvals:

- approval by the managers of the decision to merge and to convene the shareholders' extraordinary general meeting;
- approval of the merger by the shareholders' meeting, by shareholders representing at least 75% of the capital, as outlined above; and
- unanimous shareholder approval of dissolution, unless the bylaws provide for a different majority.

The acquirer requires the following internal approvals:

- approval by the managers of the decision to merge, to increase the share capital and to convene the shareholders' extraordinary general meeting; and
- approval of the merger and the share capital increase by the shareholders'

meeting, by shareholders representing at least 75% of the capital, as outlined above.

Acquisition: Each company participating in an acquisition requires the following internal approvals:

- approval by the managers of each company of the acquisition and to convene the shareholders' extraordinary general meeting for a resolution on the acquisition;
- approval of the acquisition by the shareholders' meetings of both companies, in each case by shareholders representing at least 75% of the capital, as outlined above; and
- approval of a share capital increase by issuing new shares by the shareholders' meeting of the acquirer, by shareholders representing at least 75% of the capital, as outlined above.

(b) Public companies

Public companies are incorporated in the form of a joint stock company and require the same internal approvals as those required by a limited liability company.

5. Post-merger issues

5.1 Employees

(a) Transfer

Every foreigner working in Qatar should be sponsored by an employer which is either a Qatari individual or legal entity.

Should the foreign national become an employee of another company, a transfer of sponsorship should take place.

According to Article 22 of the Immigration Law (4/2009), the Immigration Department at the Ministry of Interior may transfer the sponsorship of a foreigner to another sponsor by means of a written agreement (letter of non-objection) signed by the new sponsor and the previous sponsor, and with the approval of the Ministry of Labour (with respect to employees governed by the Labour Law). Following the transfer of sponsorship, the new sponsor shall replace the previous sponsor with respect to all of its obligations, and the old sponsorship shall be terminated and all related obligations shall be cleared.

Mergers and acquisitions can result in changes affecting employees' sponsors as follows:

- In a merger by consolidation, both companies will be dissolved and a new company created. The employees of both companies will become employees of the new company and their sponsorship should be transferred to the latter.
- In a merger by absorption, one of the companies will be dissolved and its assets will be transferred to the other company. Employees in the dissolved company will become employees of the acquirer and their sponsorship should be transferred to the acquirer.

- In an acquisition, both companies remain registered and there will be no change to the employer's identity. Therefore, no transfer of sponsorship of the employees will apply and employees remain under the sponsorship of the same company.

(b) *Termination*

The same termination issues as are outlined in section 3 above apply post-merger.

(c) *End of service*

End of service gratuities for transferring employees will be triggered by a merger or acquisition.

If the employment agreement is transferred according to Article 52 of the Labour Law (which provides, among other things, that the employment agreement does not terminate in case of merger with another company or the transfer of its ownership or its management to a party other than the employer for any reason whatsoever), the transferring employees will be deemed to have continuity of service.

However, where the employment agreement is terminated, Article 54 of the Labour Law applies. This provides that:

> *in addition to any sums to which the employee is entitled upon the end of his employment, the employer shall pay an end of service indemnity to the employee who has completed at least one year of service. This indemnity shall be agreed upon between the two parties, provided that it is not less than a three-week wage for every year of employment. The employee shall be entitled to the said indemnity for the fractions of the year in proportion to the duration of employment. The employment of an employee shall be considered continuous if it is terminated for reasons other than those stipulated in article 61 of this law (mainly ethical reasons) and he is returned to the service within two months of its termination. The last basic wage shall be the base for the calculation of the indemnity. The employer is entitled to deduct from this indemnity any amounts due to him by the employee.*

5.2 Change of control provisions and third-party consents

During the due diligence process, the report will highlight any change of control clauses and any third-party consents provided in the agreements concluded by the company that is subject to the due diligence.

Qatari law has no express provisions on change of control clauses; hence, those of the related agreements (if any) should apply.

In addition to any clauses in the relevant agreements requiring such consent, Qatari law requires third-party consents in the following cases.

(a) *Assignment of obligations*

In a merger or acquisition, the rights and obligations of one company are transferred, along with ownership, to another company.

An assignment of obligations requires creditor consent. Article 338 of the Civil Law relating to the assignment of debts provides that: "The assignment may not be effective towards the creditor unless it is approved by the latter. In the event where the debtor, or the assignee to whom the debt is being assigned, notifies the assignment to the creditor in order for the latter to grant its consent within a reasonable specific period, and [where] such period [has] passed without an answer from the latter, the silence of the creditor should be considered as a rejection of the assignment."

The provisions of the Civil Law governing the assignment of debts do not seem to exclude the possibility that creditors can waive consent by agreement with the debtor. This area of the law is open to argument (on a correct interpretation of Article 338). However, it is probably prudent to adopt a conservative approach and seek the consent of creditors prior to assignment.

(b) *Assignment of rights*

According to Article 324 of the Civil Law, a creditor may assign its right against a debtor without obtaining the latter's consent, except where such assignment is prohibited by law, by a contractual provision or by the nature of the obligation (eg, personal commitments).

Article 326 of the Civil Law provides that the assignment of rights may not be effective and opposable with regard to the debtor and third parties unless the debtor approves such assignment or is served with notice of the assignment.

Based on the above, the assignment of debts rights shall be effective:

- with regard to the assignee, by the act of assignment without the need for approval or notification of the debtor; and
- with regard to the debtor, pursuant to its approval or notification of the assignment.

Given that the Civil Law provides that the debtor must either approve the assignment or be notified of such assignment, a creditor may choose between either option, as long as nothing to the contrary is provided in the agreement executed between the creditor and the debtor in this respect.

(c) *Assignment of lease*

With respect to any lease that a company has over an asset that will subsequently be transferred to another company following the merger or acquisition transaction, Article 14 of the Lease Law (4/2008) will apply. This provides that "the lessee shall neither sublease nor assign the lease agreement, whether totally or partially, to third parties, unless the landlord grants his written authorization".

Article 14 may be interpreted in such a way that the landlord's approval of assignment of the lease or sub-lease is required, regardless of whether such approval was granted in the lease agreement (ie, before the tenant decides to assign or sub-lease) or at a later stage. This interpretation is supported by Article 26 of the Lease Law and Article 620 of the Civil Law.

5.3 Assets

Following a merger, the assets of one company will be transferred to another. An acquisition may also involve an asset transfer as a method of payment for the shares being acquired.

Article 277 of the Companies Law stipulates that all rights and liabilities of the target will be transferred to the acquirer or the successor company upon completion of the merger and registration of the company, as appropriate. The surviving or successor company will replace the merging companies in respect of all rights and liabilities.

Different transfer methods apply depending on the assets to be transferred, as outlined below.

(a) ***Transfer of real estate ownership***

According to Article 4 of the Real Estate Registry Law (14/1964), land in Qatar should be registered under the owner's name at the Real Estate Registry at the Department of Real Estate Registration and authenticated before the Ministry of Justice. Without registration, the ownership will be invalid.

(b) ***Transfer of vehicle ownership***

Article 26 of the Traffic Law (19/2007) provides that the seller and buyer of a vehicle should inform the Traffic Department at the Ministry of Interior of such sale within three days of the sale date. The initial owner will remain responsible for the vehicle until the vehicle has been registered under the name of the new owner.

(c) ***Transfer of IP rights***

Transfers of registered patents will not be effective with regard to third parties unless they are registered with the Patents Department at the Ministry of Business and Trade and advertised according to Article 13 of the Patents Law (30/2006).

Transfers of registered trademarks, trade names, geographical indications and industrial designs will not be effective with regard to third parties unless they are registered with the Protection of Industrial Ownership Bureau at the Ministry of Business and Trade, and advertised in national newspapers according to Articles 21, 37, 41 and 45 of the Law on Trademarks, Trade Names, Geographical Indications and Industrial Designs (9/2002).

(d) ***Transfer of lease rights***

According to Article 20 of the Lease Law, lease agreements should be registered with the Office of Registration of Real Estate Lease Agreements within 30 days of execution. The Lease Law does not expressly state whether the office should be notified in the event of assignment of a lease or sub-lease. It is the office's position that notification or registration of such assignments or sub-leases is not mandatory. However, it is recommended that assignments be notified and registered; otherwise, should a dispute arise between the parties to the assignment/sub-lease, they will not be permitted to submit any claim to the Leasing Dispute Settlement Committee, which is the competent authority to settle disputes concerning leases between the respective parties.

Saudi Arabia

Muhammad Arif Saeed
Dhabaan and Partners (in association with Eversheds)

1. Structuring

1.1 Due diligence

(a) *Methodology*

Legal due diligence is a crucial part of a potential acquirer's fact-finding exercise to analyse the financial health, value, operational weaknesses, and legal and regulatory compliance burdens relating to a target. It allows for the proper pricing of the underlying shares or assets to be acquired and prepares the acquirer to negotiate effectively.

Legal due diligence normally runs parallel to financial due diligence, with some crossover – for instance, in terms of asset ownership and potential liabilities under material contracts.

In a jurisdiction such as Saudi Arabia, legal due diligence can be a challenging exercise because public information on corporate entities (especially private businesses) is not readily available. An acquirer must depend largely on meaningful disclosure of material information and the production of corporate documents by the target. Awareness of cultural sensitivities which may discourage independent personal inquiries by an acquirer or its advisers can be helpful.

Availability of information and documentation for due diligence review could depend on a range of factors, including the target's standard of corporate governance, how professionally and effectively its business is managed, and its willingness to cooperate. An acquirer should be aware that information provided may not be complete or up to date; therefore, repeated requests and perseverance may be required to extract all useful information.

While sophisticated businesses understand the importance of due diligence and will normally be expected to cooperate in establishing a virtual data room to facilitate the process, in the case of less sophisticated businesses, advisers should expect to spend considerable time at physical data rooms to complete legal review of the information and documentation as it is made available.

Overall, acquirers should be extremely diligent in obtaining and vetting all available information to come to a reasonable understanding of the risks and liabilities involved in a given transaction.

(b) ***Relevant information***

Saudi Arabia is a regulated environment with prescriptive regulations in place governing various areas of business, in particular activities relating to foreign investment. As in other jurisdictions, it is not uncommon in Saudi Arabia to have a non-disclosure agreement signed in order to maintain confidentiality of any shared information. A due diligence request list should be prepared which comprehensively covers all aspects of the exercise and best suits the purpose (merger or acquisition of entities or business assets) and the target's line of business. The request list should adopt terminology that is generally understood in Saudi Arabia in relation to different types of corporate entity. For instance, a private company is normally known as a limited liability company.

Generally, any information that could materially affect the evaluation of a target, its business, assets, goodwill or the acquirer's decision will be relevant. Besides constitutional and regulatory matters, a legal due diligence request will seek information on the following aspects:

- licences and registrations;
- material contracts;
- long-term obligations;
- loans and financing obligations;
- assets and property ownership;
- mortgages or pledges over assets;
- insurance;
- employment and labour matters;
- sponsorship and visa issues;
- intellectual property;
- information technology;
- taxation and *Zakat* (a religious levy); and
- litigation (including threatened litigation or claims, if any).

A due diligence report will normally list the documents and information received from a target and set out the qualifications and assumptions as to the completeness or accuracy of the information received.

1.2 Available structures under the Saudi legal system

The typical forms of business merger experienced in Saudi Arabia are:

- private acquisition of shares in a target;
- private acquisition of a target's underlying assets and business; and
- acquisition of shares in a joint stock company (closed or listed).

A joint venture between two or more corporate entities through a contractual arrangement is the most common form of private acquisition transaction. A new special purpose vehicle may also be established to consolidate partners' resources in the joint venture.

In relation to a listed joint stock company (a public listed company), shares are generally acquired through either a restricted offer of shares or a takeover offer. These transactions are regulated by specific regulations issued by the Capital Markets Authority (CMA), and may be subject to foreign investment restrictions. Currently, foreign investment in Saudi listed shares is possible only through a swap arrangement pursuant to circulars issued by the CMA. However, a proposal for opening up foreign investment in Saudi listed shares is currently under consideration by the CMA.

For any of the above forms of transaction, consideration may be paid in cash, through the issue of securities or through a combination of the two.

The following legal corporate forms are available under Saudi law:

- companies with variable capital;
- cooperative companies;
- joint stock companies;
- general partnerships;
- joint ventures;
- limited liability companies;
- limited partnerships; and
- partnerships limited by shares.

2. Structuring considerations

2.1 Tax

In Saudi Arabia, tax primarily consists of corporate income tax, withholding tax and *Zakat*. For local companies, corporate income tax is assessed on the share of profit of the foreign partner in the local company. Generally, the maximum corporate income tax rate is 20%. Saudi and Gulf Cooperation Council (GCC) nationals and companies that are wholly owned by Saudi or GCC nationals are subject to *Zakat*. The *Zakat* rate is 2.5% of the higher of the Saudi/GCC share of the *Zakat* base, or the Saudi/GCC share of profit.

No specific rules in the income tax and *Zakat* regulations address mergers and acquisitions. A capital gain arising from the sale or transfer of assets is likely to be treated as normal business income and be taxed at the normal corporate income tax rate. No transfer fee, value-added tax, stamp duty or any other indirect tax is levied on the acquisition of shares or transfer of assets.

A target's tax position will have a significant bearing on any acquisition transaction. In certain circumstances, the target may prefer to realise part of the value of its investment as income by means of a pre-sale dividend so as to reduce exposure to a higher capital gains tax resulting from the sale of its shares.

In case of a foreign (non-GCC) acquirer, additional tax considerations may be involved and specialised tax advice should be obtained. For instance, there are withholding tax implications on payment of dividends to non-resident shareholders in a Saudi company. Interest expenses will also be subject to certain limitations under Saudi tax law.

Generally, chartered accountancy firms registered to practise in Saudi Arabia can advise on complex taxation matters. A foreign acquirer should seek advice with regard to the potential tax implications of a proposed transaction structure.

2.2 Regulatory considerations

The Companies Law (issued by Royal Decree M/6/1965) regulates mergers in Saudi Arabia and specifies the form that companies may take, the incorporation and corporate governance rules, and the applicable procedures in each case.

The articles of association or bylaws may prescribe the types of entity or the types of business activity with which a company can merge. This issue should be addressed at the outset to avoid any unnecessary complications in completing a transaction.

The Companies Law provides for mergers whereby:

- the participating companies merge to form a newly incorporated company, their assets and liabilities are transferred to the new entity and the merging companies are liquidated. The shareholders of the liquidated company receive shares in the new entity in exchange for their shares in the liquidated company; or
- one or more companies are absorbed by a surviving company. The shareholders of the absorbed company receive new shares in the surviving company.

A merger is valid if it is authorised by a properly publicised resolution adopted by each participating company in the manner prescribed for the alteration of its memorandum of association or bylaws. A merger resolution takes effect 90 days after the date of its publication. The creditors of merged companies may, during that period, object to the merger through registered letters addressed to the company. In such an eventuality, the merger will be suspended until:

- the creditors have waived their objection;
- the Board of Grievances has ruled, at the request of the company, that the objection is unfounded; or
- the company has offered sufficient security for satisfaction of the debt.

The Capital Markets Law (issued by Royal Decree M/30/2003) and its implementing regulations provide the legal framework for regulation of the capital market. The CMA, the stock exchange and the national securities depository centre are established pursuant to the Capital Markets Law.

The CMA is the apex regulator of listed securities, public joint stock companies, establishments involved in securities, asset management, investment banking and brokerage activities. It has the authority to issue regulations and guidelines for the implementation of the Capital Markets Law, covering, for example, licensing of financial intermediaries or authorised persons, initial public offerings, private placements of equity and investor protection relating to securities business in Saudi Arabia.

The Merger and Acquisition Regulations issued by the CMA in 2007 and the Listing Rules issued by the CMA in 2004 set out the basic regulatory framework for the regulation of:

- a restricted purchase of voting shares in a listed company which results in the acquirer owning or controlling 10% or more of such class of shares;
- a restricted offer of shares made by a public announcement in which the offer

is to purchase listed shares and such acquisition would increase the acquirer's ownership to 10% or more of the shares;
- a takeover offer whereby the acquirer acquires control of a listed company by acquiring more than 30% of the voting rights in such company or a right to appoint 30% of the directors; and
- a reverse takeover whereby a listed company offers the shareholders of a private company (limited liability company) its new shares in exchange for the shares of such shareholders, provided that the number of shares to be issued by the listed company under such arrangement results in the shareholders of the private company owning more than 50% of the shares in the listed company.

The general principles under this framework require the boards of directors of the acquirer and the target, as well as their respective advisers, to act fairly and in the best interests of their respective shareholders. A public announcement of the offer must be made under certain circumstances, and both the acquirer and the target must fulfil their responsibilities, including those relating to dealings in the target's securities or disclosure pertaining to the same under the regulatory framework. A firm intention to make an offer should be announced together with the terms of the offer, the identity of the acquirer, details of any existing holding in the target and any conditions to which the offer or publication of offer documents is subject. If appropriate, an offer must contain terms relating to compliance with the Competition Law as well. The offer period is determined by the CMA in accordance with the regulatory framework, and all conditions (including settlement of payment) must be fulfilled according to the timetable adopted for completion of the takeover.

2.3 Social considerations

Sharia is the fundamental law of Saudi Arabia, and primarily governs contractual arrangements and interaction between parties generally. *Sharia* is a collection of principles derived from different sources, but principally the Holy *Qur'an* and the *Sunnah* (the witnessed sayings and actions of the Prophet Muhammad). The broad and general nature of the *Sharia* means that Saudi courts can be expected to apply a combination of discretionary powers and established legal principles in the review and interpretation of business documents. This flexibility, combined with the absence of an established precedent system and the liberal exercise of discretionary powers by authorities during the regulatory process, can make it difficult to predict with certainty the correct interpretation and ultimate enforceability of transaction documents.

Matters relating to transfer of employees, liabilities relating to end-of-service benefits and general social security issues for employees and Saudisation policy should be carefully reviewed during a legal due diligence exercise and efficiently handled in the post-merger or post-acquisition scenario to avoid any regulatory implications.

2.4 Other considerations

The Saudi government authorities and agencies may exercise considerable discretion in regulatory matters. Because of a lack of transparency and existence of internal guidelines and circulars (that may not be shared with the public or be changed without prior notification), the parties should be aware of the latest practice and regulatory position that may affect certain elements of a transaction.

2.5 Antitrust laws

The Competition Law (issued by Royal Decree M/25/2004) aims to protect and encourage fair competition and provides a means to combat monopolistic practices affecting legitimate competition.

The Competition Law applies to all entities active in the Saudi market, except for public corporations and wholly owned state companies.

Specific provisions in the Competition Law deal with mergers and prohibit any merger or acquisition which creates a dominant market position or restricts market entry, and which may therefore result in anti-competitive behaviour such as price fixing and restrictions on the free flow of goods and services.

Under the Competition Law, an application for approval of the transaction should be filed with the Competition Protection Council by the parties at least 60 days prior to completion in respect of any merger or acquisition which may otherwise violate the Competition Law. The council is required to notify the entity of acceptance or rejection within 90 days.

2.6 Foreign investment laws and foreign ownership restrictions

The Foreign Investment Law (issued by Royal Decree M/1/2000) and its implementing regulations regulate foreign (non-GCC) direct investment in licensed activities in Saudi Arabia. Following Saudi Arabia's accession to the World Trade Organisation in November 2005, the foreign investment regime has been liberalised to some extent. Investments are allowed in every sector, except those contained in the Negative List issued by the Supreme Economic Council.

The business activities currently on the Negative List and prohibited for foreign investment include:

- exploration, drilling and production of oil and gas;
- manufacturing of military equipment;
- road transportation;
- real estate investment in Mecca and Medina;
- real estate brokerage;
- printing and publishing services (with a few exceptions);
- audiovisual and media services;
- recruitment services;
- commercial agencies and franchises; and
- fisheries.

Certain capital investment, market access and ownership thresholds apply to some activities that are open to foreign investment. For instance, foreign ownership of up to 75% in wholesale and retail businesses is permitted subject to foreign investment of a minimum Sr20 million.

The acquisition of a local business by a foreign investor requires a foreign investment licence from the Saudi Arabian General Investment Authority (SAGIA), in addition to any industry-specific licences, such as in the healthcare, pharmaceuticals, mining, telecommunications and banking sectors. Advice in relation to the structural options and legal requirements of the licensing process should be obtained in addition to advice on any tax implications.

3. Merger agreement

3.1 Pre-merger or pre-acquisition agreements

(a) ***Confidentiality and non-disclosure agreement***

Confidentiality and non-disclosure agreements are generally acceptable and enforceable under Saudi law. As a matter of practice, non-disclosure agreements are executed between the parties to a merger or acquisition of private businesses. However, in the event of a breach of such an agreement, the aggrieved party will be entitled to recover only any direct and actual loss arising from that breach.

(b) ***Exclusivity agreement***

An exclusivity agreement which seeks to prevent parties from negotiating with a third party pending conclusion of discussions between the parties in relation to a merger or an acquisition transaction will, subject to any restrictions under the *Sharia* principles, normally be enforceable under Saudi laws.

However, in the event of breach of such an agreement, the aggrieved party will be entitled to recover only any direct and actual losses arising from that breach.

3.2 Merger or acquisition agreement

Depending on the nature of the transaction, an acquisition of shares will mainly involve:

- a share sale and purchase agreement;
- a shareholders' agreement (where less than 100% of the shares are being acquired);
- an amendment to the articles of association;
- an escrow agreement (depending on the payment mechanism); and
- other necessary documents to complete the transaction.

An asset purchase agreement will be relevant where the subject of an acquisition is business assets instead of shares.

(a) ***Scope***

Parties: The parties to an agreement should be clearly identified and must possess legal capacity and authority to enter into the agreement. In the case of corporate entities, proper authorisation from the owners/shareholders is required. Where more than one selling shareholder is involved in a sale and purchase of shares, all such shareholders should be parties to an agreement, unless proper authorisation has been given to one such shareholder by way of a valid power of attorney to represent the others.

Description: The parties' intention and their understanding of the terms of a sale and purchase agreement should be clearly set out in an agreement. The agreement should be free from '*gharar*' (uncertainty). The Saudi courts may deny or modify the enforcement of contractual obligations in an agreement in strict accordance with its terms if, in their opinion, a strict enforcement would be inequitable under *Sharia* principles.

(b) ***Important clauses***

Merger, acquisition or purchase clause: An agreement for merger or acquisition should clearly set out the intention of the parties by recording the terms of the merger or acquisition and the payment method or share swap arrangement, as the case may be.

The consideration or purchase price should be set out in clear terms, and if there is a deferred payment component then this should preferably be definite and not contingent, although adjustments to any material adverse change or to offset any established liabilities or claims should be possible.

Payment can be made through an escrow arrangement if the parties agree.

Representations and warranties: Because of the risk of lack of complete and accurate information or transparency in disclosure of information by a target, and due to the need to rely on information provided by the target, it is important to cover any deficiencies through proper representations and warranties in transaction documents. The representations and warranties should be valid both at the time of the signing of the transaction documents and on completion.

A sale and purchase agreement may contain conditions precedent to cover any measures to be taken by the parties to regularise any matters before the transaction is completed.

Indemnities: Any representations and warranties given by the parties should be covered by appropriate indemnities against:

- any liabilities prior to completion;
- any representation or warranty that proves to be misleading or inaccurate; or
- any third-party claims.

However, the Saudi courts may enforce indemnities only to the extent of actual loss. Indemnity for legal costs is unlikely to be enforced and then only for reasonable legal cost.

Liabilities and limitation of liabilities: In case of breach of a duty or failure to perform an obligation, an aggrieved party will be entitled to seek compensation for direct and actual proven losses. Liability cannot be limited by agreement between the parties, because the principle of limitation of liability is not recognised under *Sharia*.

Where any provision of an agreement is construed as an undertaking by a party to pay a penalty, the Saudi courts are unlikely to enforce that provision, or will effectively amend it by allowing recovery only of the actual loss occurred.

Choice of law: Sale and purchase agreements are the most common method for the acquisition of private business or shares in a target. Typically, such agreements are governed by Saudi law, in particular where the parties involved are Saudi and no cross-border aspect is involved in the transaction.

Shares in a listed company are normally acquired through a formal takeover offer. Such transactions are governed by the CMA's Mergers and Acquisition Regulations and Listing Rules, as discussed above.

In a cross-border transaction (where a foreign party is involved), the parties may opt for a foreign law as the governing law of the sale and purchase agreement and other related transactional documents. There is no restriction under Saudi law in this respect and parties are free to elect a foreign law as the governing law. However, the doctrine of conflict of laws is not recognised in the Saudi legal system; therefore, a Saudi court will not be bound by a choice of foreign law and will invariably apply Saudi law to any matter before it.

The choice of law is largely dictated by dispute resolution and enforcement considerations. A foreign party can benefit from a choice of foreign law and forum if a dispute is to be brought and enforced outside of Saudi Arabia, but there will be a disadvantage if the dispute is to be brought before the Saudi courts or a foreign judgment is to be enforced in Saudi Arabia.

Dispute resolution: The choice of law and forum clauses are largely dictated by the presence of foreign elements (foreign parties, assets outside Saudi Arabia and convenience of obtaining evidence) in a transaction.

Where parties agree on Saudi law as the governing law of an agreement or resolve disputes in Saudi Arabia, dispute resolution through local arbitration offers an alternative to court proceedings. However, arbitration proceedings under the Arbitration Law are supervised by the Board of Grievances and an arbitral award is not final unless it has been validated by the Board of Grievances. This means that arbitration proceedings lack finality, as an award can be challenged before the Board of Grievances. Therefore, it may take a very long time to attain finality for enforcement. However, once validated, an award is as good as a court judgment and may be enforced in a similar manner.

For enforcement of a foreign judgment in Saudi Arabia, two conditions must be satisfied: reciprocity of enforcement and compliance with *Sharia* and public policy of Saudi Arabia. Currently, the Board of Grievances has the principal jurisdiction over all commercial disputes and is responsible for the enforcement of foreign judgments in commercial matters.

Saudi Arabia has acceded to the New York Convention on the Recognition and Enforcement of Foreign Arbitral Awards, so theoretically enforcement of foreign arbitration awards in respect of all member states to that convention is possible in Saudi Arabia.

However, as a matter of policy, in relation to convention member states, the Board of Grievances will enforce only such provisions of a foreign arbitration award that, in its sole discretion, do not conflict with *Sharia* principles or public policy of Saudi Arabia.

Generally, the enforcement of foreign judgments or foreign arbitration awards in Saudi Arabia is unpredictable and there are few precedents of successful enforcement. To overcome these hurdles, a foreign party may consider electing Saudi law as the governing law of an agreement, with arbitration in one of the GCC member states (eg, Dubai or Bahrain). This approach would have the benefit of a *Sharia*-compliant award and ease of enforcement because of the GCC's resolution on reciprocal enforcement of judgments and arbitration awards among the GCC member states.

4. Employment law issues

Article 18 of the Labour Law (issued by Royal Decree M/51/2005) regulates the treatment of employment contracts in case of a merger or acquisition.

It provides that if the ownership of an entity is transferred to a new owner, or if there is a change in the structure of an entity as a result of a merger, restructuring or otherwise, the terms of employment contracts shall continue to remain in force and the original employer and the new employer shall be jointly liable for salary accrued prior to the change in control or transfer of ownership and for any other amounts due to an employee.

The original employer and the new employer can agree to transfer all payment obligations due to employees to the new employer. An acquirer may therefore be obliged to accept all employees employed by the target, and both the acquirer and the target will continue to be jointly liable for the cost and obligations of maintaining the existing terms and conditions of the employment contracts. It is advisable for an acquirer to procure indemnification from the target (and, where the target is being liquidated, from the shareholders of the target) for any and all losses and liabilities incurred with respect to employees prior to the change of control.

An acquirer must assess whether the target meets the requirements of Saudi nationals for employment in terms of the Saudisation policy, which requires that at least 30% of employees be Saudi nationals for a business with 20 or more employees. A business that does not achieve the requisite levels of Saudisation may not be allowed:

- to sponsor new expatriate employees;
- to renew the residency visas of existing employees;
- to renew commercial registration of the business itself; or
- to amend its memorandum of association or bylaws to change its shareholding.

Moreover, businesses that fail to meet the Saudisation levels may not qualify to receive benefits from government-affiliated funding programmes or to bid on government procurement contracts.

5. Approval process

5.1 Internal approvals

(a) *Limited liability companies*

In a private acquisition of shares or underlying assets of a target, the shareholders must pass a resolution at a duly convened meeting approving the sale and stating that they waive their statutory pre-emptive rights under the Companies Regulations. Such a resolution must be passed in the manner prescribed in the memorandum of association. The resolution must be publicised in the manner prescribed for the publication of alterations to the memorandum of association of the merging entity.

(b) ***Public companies***

In relation to the acquisition of a joint stock company, a shareholders' resolution of the acquirer authorising a takeover offer should be passed. The responsibilities of the acquirer and the target in relation to public announcements through the stock exchange as set out in the CMA's Market Conduct Regulations (issued in 2004) should be satisfied.

Under the CMA's Mergers and Acquisition Regulations, a public announcement of an intention to make an offer is required when the offer is notified to the board of directors of the target. The announcement must contain:

- the terms of the offer;
- the identity of the acquirer and details of its existing holding in the target;
- all terms and conditions and consents required by law to which the offer may be subject; and
- details of any indemnities involving the acquirer, the target or any person acting with them in relation to the subject securities.

Before notification of a firm intention of offer is made, the target must make a brief announcement, on a no-names basis, that a potential acquirer is considering making an offer. Given the impact that such announcement may have on the share price of the target – in the sense that it may become the subject of rumour and speculation – the CMA may, at the target's request, set a time limit for the potential acquirer to clarify its intention in respect of the target.

5.2 Approval by regulators

(a) ***Limited liability companies***

A duly notarised sale of shares or asset transfer agreement between the shareholders of the acquirer and the target must be filed with the Ministry of Commerce and Industry for approval. In the case of a sale of shares, a shareholders' resolution amending the articles of association should be signed before the relevant notary public by the parties or their duly authorised representatives.

The relevant constituent document (eg, the articles of association and commercial registration certificates) should be amended accordingly to reflect the post-merger or acquisition position.

Where a foreign acquirer is involved, a foreign investment licence from SAGIA is required. If the target is already established pursuant to a foreign investment licence, then an amendment to that licence is required to reflect the change in ownership structure.

Subject to approval from the Ministry of Commerce and Industry, a transfer of shares takes place before a notary public by execution of amendments to the articles of association to reflect the change in shareholding. The amendments are then published in the *Official Gazette* and the commercial registration certificate of the target is amended in accordance with the change in ownership.

A merger resolution passed by the shareholders of the merging entity takes effect 90 days after the date of publication. Where a creditor objects to the merger within that period, the merger is suspended until:

- the creditor has waived its objection;
- the Board of Grievances has ruled that the objection is unfounded; or
- the company has offered sufficient security to the satisfaction of the debt.

If no objection is made within that period, the merger is considered valid.

(b) *Public companies*

In an acquisition of a joint stock company, the takeover offer is made by an offer circular, which must be approved by the CMA and presented to the target. The board of directors of the target should circulate the offer circular to the shareholders of the target, setting out a recommendation as to whether the shareholders should accept the offer.

In accordance with the takeover timetable, the offer circular and the circular of the board of directors must be publicised, and presented to and approved by the CMA. The same offer must be made to all shareholders of the same class of shares in the target.

Compliance is essential with the notification and announcement requirements and their timings as prescribed by the CMA's Merger and Acquisition Regulations and Listing Rules.

6. Post-merger issues

6.1 Employees

In relation to employees, a change of employer triggers the need for employees' consent. In case of expatriate employees, transfer of sponsorship (which requires the original employer to issue a no-objection letter to the transfer) is required. Specialised advice on visa and residency aspects is generally necessary.

The original employer and the new employer can agree to transfer all payment obligations in favour of the employees to the new employer. The acquirer is therefore obliged to accept all employees employed by the target, and both the acquirer and the target will continue to be jointly liable for the cost and obligations of maintaining the existing terms and conditions of the employment contracts.

6.2 Change of control provisions and third-party consents

Generally, an agreement for sale of shares or underlying assets in an acquisition contains representations as to the non-existence of any change of control provision in relation to third-party agreements, and requisite third-party consents are included as conditions precedent.

A legal due diligence of material third-party contracts (eg, with suppliers) should reveal any change of control provisions. However, to secure an acquirer's interest, it is important to back the seller's representations with appropriate warranties and indemnities.

6.3 Assets

In general, there is very little regulatory control over the transfer of assets in Saudi Arabia. However, any items such as property and cars will require change of registered ownership.

Any leased assets may require change in the lessee's details or other terms and conditions, depending on the nature and terms of the relevant lease agreement. Similarly, any insurance policies in place may require changes in the beneficiaries' details.

Tunisia

Mohamed Zaanouni
Zaanouni Law Firm

1. Structuring

In recent years in Tunisia we have seen mergers and acquisitions to be the preferred mode of growth for large companies both from the perspective of expansion and diversification, since they allow businesses both to accelerate growth and reduce costs and risk. The integration of firms through a merger naturally involves joining different corporate cultures, management and communication styles, corporate histories, rules and procedures and the Tunisian legislature has been incrementally building up statutory provisions on the subject.[1]

Fusion acquisitions arise in all sectors of economic activity in Tunisia, but are most frequent in the industrial sector, followed by the service sector.

In practice, M&A activity in Tunisia in general tends to involve the joining of companies operating in the same sector of activity and in the same markets.

Within the industrial sector, M&A activity is most common in the textile sector (29%), the mechanical engineering industry, and the electric (14%) and chemical industries (14%).

Mergers can involve the acquisition of either shares or assets.

Cross-border mergers are not the same as domestic mergers. There are fundamental differences in the transaction process itself and advisers must also take into account the diversity of the rules in the different jurisdictions. A first step is obviously to identify which country's law applies to the transaction.

1.1 Due diligence

In any acquisition, due diligence essentially entails trying fully to establish the current state of the target, especially all obligations, including debts, pending and potential lawsuits, leases, warranties, long-term customer agreements, employment contracts, distribution agreements, compensation arrangements and so on.

(a) *Methodology*

To ensure the success of a transaction, it is advisable to take the following actions:

- understand the objectives of the transaction;
- develop mutually agreed procedures;
- provide professional strategic, commercial and financial due diligence

1 Law 91-64/1991 (as amended and enhanced), completed by Law 93-83/1993, Law 95-42/1995, Law 99-41/1999, Law 2003-74/2003 and Law 2005-60/2005.

informed by regional intelligence;
- provide regular reports linking commercial and financial issues to the strategic objectives of the corporation;
- facilitate decision making and transaction negotiations; and
- assist with post-transaction implementation procedures.

(b) ***Relevant information***

All relevant information must be gathered and shared. This should include:
- legal and organisational structure, including board of directors, bylaws and composition, as well as information about any subsidiaries;
- financial data (eg, assets, liabilities, audits, revenue history, current financials, reserves and real estate holdings);
- current budget information detailing revenue, revenue sources and expenses;
- service data showing volumes, capacity and utilisation;
- contracts and agreements including any pertaining to revenues and expenditures, contracted personnel, service delivery agreements and lease agreements;
- human resources data, such as organisational charts, salary and benefits data, policies regarding leave, and information about staff turnover and length of service;
- retiree benefits and obligations; and
- any active or pending lawsuits.

Due diligence assists companies in understanding and implementing effective risk management control mechanisms and processes.

(c) ***Evaluation and pricing mechanism***

The target obviously needs to be valued: assigned a value or range of values, to assist the transfer process. But it should be noted that the valuation process is not intended to establish a selling price for the target: at the end of the day the price will be whatever the buyer and seller agree.

1.2 Structuring considerations

(a) ***Tax***

Tax due diligence review plays a critical role in any transaction. It is not just about uncovering and quantifying contingent liabilities, although this is obviously important. Taxes can represent a large cost burden, but also a rich source of cashflow savings if properly managed.

The vast majority of deals fail to achieve targeted returns by not capturing or maximising upside benefits or by not identifying hidden liabilities and downside risks. A well-conducted tax due diligence, in conjunction with legal and financial reviews, should expose these issues and opportunities and help achieve a successful investment.

(b) ***Regulatory***

There is growing demand for expertise in helping businesses to cope with the challenges associated with new regulatory frameworks in Tunisia. With new corporate sanctions programmes now emanating from financial institutions such as the World Bank and regional development banks, the need for businesses and investors to control regulatory risk has never been more pressing.

(c) ***Timeline***

Notification of any transfer agreement must be made to the minister of trade:

- at any time if the agreement is still in draft form; or
- within 15 days of the date of signing the agreement, of publication of the purchase/exchange of rights or obligations or of the acquisition of a controlling participation.[2]

Therefore, the parties can sign the transfer agreement before filing it with the minister of trade or before clearance is obtained, provided that they comply with the legal obligation of notification within 15 days of signing the agreement, and that they refrain from taking any irreversible measures.

The minister of trade's decision will be announced within a maximum of six months of the date on which complete notification is received. Within this six-month period, the minister of trade can refer any apparent market concentrations to the Competition Council, which in turn must give its opinion within a timeframe not exceeding three months.

The Competition Council will weigh up whether the agreement or draft agreement contributes to any broader economical and social issues in Tunisia which it might consider compensates on policy grounds for any apparent interference with competition.

Where it finds abuse of a dominant position resulting from a concentration, the Competition Council may suggest to the Ministry of Trade[3] that the related company or group of companies must amend, add to or terminate all agreements through which the concentration was implemented (or proposed to be implemented), even where there has been compliance with procedures in the merger control law.

(d) ***Geographical considerations***

The risks associated with financing projects can vary significantly according to the geographical location of the project. While many projects that banks are asked to consider financing are in compliance with national legislation and permit requirements, they may fall short of international standards and best practice. A detailed understanding of the project's political and legal framework is required in order to judge the extent to which national requirements meet the risk management needs of international financial organisations.

---

2 According to Law 91-64/1991, as amended and completed by Law 93-83/1993, Law 95-42/1995, Law 99-41/1999, and Law 2003-74/2003, Law 2005-60/2005, and Decree 1215/1995.

3 Or it might take a decision jointly with the Minister of the relevant sector.

(e) Other considerations

Retain local legal counsel: A key starting point is to understand the legal and regulatory environment of the country/(ies) in which a target is located or does business. It is also critical that the attorney selected has significant experience working with multinational corporations, and 'speaks the same language' from a risk management and compliance perspective.

Determine formation and ownership: At times, the identity of owners, the existence of voting blocs or shareholder agreements or the powers of an individual to speak on behalf of the entity or owners is not clear and cannot be determined solely by a review of public records.

Understand reputation and risk: Another key area for diligence is reputation, not only of the target entity, but also of its key officers, directors and owners.

Know the political risks: Recent political events in the country highlight the political risk of doing business. The goal in conducting political risk due diligence is to help determine the non-commercial risks that may arise in conducting business.

1.3 Antitrust laws

The legislation controlling merger activities in Tunisia is Law 91-64/1991 (as amended). The aim of this legislation is to ensure that the merger process does not raise competition issues by altering the structure of the relevant market.

Law 91-64/994 applies to any merger likely to create a dominant position in the local market, or a substantial portion of it. It defines a 'merger' as any transfer of property, or of the use of all or part of the property, or of rights or liabilities of a company, such that this enables a company or group of companies to exert a decisive influence directly or indirectly on one or more companies.

According to Article 7 of the law, the companies involved in the merger – whether they are parties to the agreement or target companies – must between them meet two criteria to satisfy competition requirements:

- The combined market share of the previous business year must not exceed 30% of the sales, purchases or all other transactions in the local market for goods, products or substituted services; and
- The combined turnover in the local market must not exceed Td3 million ($2.4 million).

If the companies, when combined, would meet the above criteria, they must notify the minister of trade of the proposed merger.

Tunisian merger law does not provide different thresholds for financial institutions.

1.4 Foreign investment laws and foreign ownership restrictions

Under the rules of the Investment Incentives Code (Law 93-120/1993), foreign investments in Tunisian industries and services are unrestricted. The investment must, however, be declared to the Agency for the Promotion of Industry.

Services not wholly engaged in export will be subject to other authorisations.

Tunisia is a signatory to the Euro-Med Association Agreement, along with the member states of the European Union. The agreement came into force on March 1 1998, with the parties committing to creating a free trade area between themselves by the year 2010.

On mergers and acquisitions, the Euro-Med Association Agreement provides in Article 36(1) that:

> *All agreements between undertakings, decisions by associations of undertakings and concerted practices between undertakings which have as their object or effect the prevention, restriction or distortion of competition;*
>
> *– abuse by one or more undertakings of a dominant position in the territories of the Community or of Tunisia as a whole or in a substantial part thereof; (...) is incompatible with the proper functioning of the Agreement, as it may affect trade between the Community and Tunisia. (Article 36(1)).*

According to Article 36(2): any practices contrary to this Article shall be assessed on the basis of criteria arising from the application of the rules of Articles 85, 86 and 92 of the Treaty establishing the European Community.

Due diligence tends to seek to evaluate whether:

- the project is feasible as conceived;
- the project is financially viable;
- the capital, operating and maintenance costs are reasonable;
- jurisdictional, market and environmental issues have been adequately addressed; and
- the project has the potential for a positive net present value.

2. Merger agreement

Relevant legislation controlling the merger process in Tunisia jurisdiction spans the years 1991 to 2005.[4]

2.1 Pre-merger agreements

(a) Confidentiality and non-disclosure agreement

A non-disclosure agreement is more than a commitment to keep information secret. It also seeks to prevent the other party from using your confidential information for their own benefit. As the old saying goes, 'ideas are as free as the wind'. Copyrights can protect your 'expressions' of an idea (eg, a novel, software code, photograph or painting); and a patent can protect an idea used to create a non-obvious and useful invention. But ideas are free to copy – so they need to be protected as 'secret' by non-

---

4 Law 91-64/1991, as amended and completed by Law 93-83/1993; Law 95-42/1995; Decree 1215/1995; Law 99-41/1999; Law No. 2003-74/2003; and Law 2005-60/2005.

disclosure agreements, preventing other parties from using such ideas freely (a well-drafted non-disclosure agreement should limit the purposes for which the confidential information may be used).

(b) ***Exclusivity agreement***

In any negotiated corporate acquisition, there is a substantial risk that the deal will not be consummated. Another party may approach the target with an alternative, presumably higher-priced, acquisition proposal.

Unless there is an exclusivity agreement, a board of directors has broad discretionary authority to decide whether to proceed with another merger.

(c) ***Memorandum of understanding***

A memorandum of understanding is a document used in mergers to express a convergence of wills between the parties. It is often used in cases where parties either do not intend a legal commitment or cannot yet enter into a legally enforceable agreement.

2.2 Scope

(a) ***Parties***

Each party to a merger agreement must provide details of its name, position and address and, where a contracting party is a corporation, its legal form, registered office and company registration number. The contract must be signed by its legal representative or failing that by a person specially authorised to bind the company under the contract in question.

(b) ***Description***

The merger contract will be generally based on the language of the memorandum of understanding and the intent of the parties.

The merger agreement governs the conditions and terms of an acquisition. This contract is a legal document and is prepared before the acquisition.

This agreement contains all pertinent information relating to the merger and begins with an opening paragraph that lists the price of the business deal and details of what the purchase includes. Other items included in the agreement will be representations and warranties, covenants, conditions, indemnification, and termination procedures and remedies.

2.3 Important clauses

(a) ***Merger, acquisition or purchase clause***

The parties agree that, in the event of any dissent to the merger agreement or any relevant merger matter raised by their respective shareholders in accordance with the law, they must proceed with the purchase of the shares owned by the dissenting shareholders in accordance with the Corporate Merger and Acquisition Act and Commercial Company Law respectively. The shares so purchased by the parties shall, to the extent permitted by laws and regulations and with the permission of the competent authority, be cancelled on the record date. The registration of this share cancellation should be carried out together with registration of the cancellation of outstanding shares of parties upon dissolution of the latter.[5]

(b) Representations and warranties

Regardless of the structure of the transaction, merger and acquisition agreements will involve representations and warranties.

The seller and buyer will make representations and warranties to each other in the acquisition agreement. The seller's representations and warranties typically make up the largest part of the acquisition agreement. Representations and warranties serve three important purposes:

- informational – the seller's representations and warranties, coupled with the buyer's due diligence, enable the buyer to learn as much as possible about the seller's business prior to signing the definitive acquisition agreement;
- protective – if the seller's representations and warranties prove to be untrue in the period between signing and the closing, this will provide a reason for the buyer to walk away from, or possibly to renegotiate the terms of, the acquisition.
- supportive – the seller's representations and warranties provide the framework for the seller's indemnification obligations to the buyer after the closing.

(c) Choice of law clause

Choice of law and forum clause in contracts will often state that the contract clauses are to be interpreted under the laws of a particular state or jurisdiction.

In general, when the parties are nationals, Tunisian law will apply.

(d) Dispute resolution clause

The parties should attempt to resolve any dispute arising out of or relating to the contract by negotiation, but where this is not possible, the parties may resort to the Tunisian judicial system.

2.4 Employment law and pensions

The Tunisian employment code (Law 27/1966) and Decree 1974-0499/1974 apply to employment and pension issues. Pension issues are usually not the first concern of the parties involved in a purchase and sale transaction, but pension liabilities could be significant so should feature when considering any corporate transaction. Pension issues can affect the amount of due diligence required, the purchase price, representations and warranties, and obligations of the buyer to transferred employees. The key is to obtain as much information as possible about all pension plans involved and seek expert pension advice as early as possible in the process.

---

5 See Article 319 (Chapter Four), *Des Sociétés par Actions* in *Code de droits des Sociétés.*

2.5 Internal approvals

(a) *Limited liability companies*

Article 412 of the Commercial Companies Code provides that:

> *the merger may bring companies of the same shape or companies of different forms. However, it must in any case lead to the formation of a limited company, a limited liability company or company limited by shares. The merger of one or several foreign companies with one or more companies should lead to the Tunisian Incorporation of a company whose majority stake is to be held by Tunisian persons or entities.*

(b) *Public companies*

In terms of acquisitions, no Tunisian regulation obliges companies to inform the public of such transfers or proposed transfers, but law firms and business may be allowed to request certain information.

2.6 Cultural issues

As most M&A activities in Tunisia involve family businesses, there are fewer problems concerning integration, corporate culture and organisation than are experienced elsewhere. Merger and acquisition may constitute a preferred mode of growth for large companies, in terms of both expansion and diversification, since they allow entrepreneurs both to accelerate growth and reduce costs and risk.

3. Post-merger issues

3.1 Employment issues

Contracts of employment for employees and executives of each company involved in a merger are automatically sent to the newly created company. These employment contracts legally remain effective.

3.2 Change of control provisions and third-party consents

Tunisian merger control regulation applies only where one of the following thresholds exists:

- The participants' combined market share in the previous business year exceeded 30% of all sales, purchases or other transactions in the local market for goods, products or services; or
- The participants' combined turnover in the local market exceeds an amount fixed by decree (ie, Td20 million pursuant to Decree 2005-2038/2005).

3.3 Assets

The aim of the Tunisian merger control regulation is to ensure that the merger will not hinder effective competition on the market and will not alter the market structure. The Tunisian merger control regulation applies to any merger that is likely to create a dominant position in the local market or a substantial part of it. The Competition Council will consider public policy issues (ie, the interests of economic and social progress, such as whether local companies' competitiveness on the international market may be enhanced) in deciding whether wider benefits may outweigh competition issues.

3.4 Other post-merger issues

The post-merger integration phase covers the operational part of the merger. It is often in this phase that the success or failure of a merger begins to become apparent.

Issues demanding attention at this stage include:

- communicating the new strategic objectives and the new vision of the merged organisation;
- implementing a new shared corporate and management culture;
- developing a new management structure for the new organisation – in particular, overcoming any leadership problems;
- uniting formerly separate divisions from both former organisations;
- harmonising management compensation and management incentive systems;
- overcoming language barriers and country-specific cultural differences;
- overcoming staff suspicions of the other organisation ('us versus them' syndrome);
- filling management positions;
- allocating responsibilities;
- integrating knowledge transfer between units; and
- maintaining customer relationships during the integration phase.

Many mergers break down because of failures in one or more of these areas.

4. Case study

The Société Tunisienne de Banque (STB) was established in 1957. It was the first national bank to be established following Tunisian independence. Initially operating primarily as a development bank, it has now fully become a commercial bank. In 2000 it merged with two development banks – the Bank for Economic Development of Tunisia (BDET) and the National Bank of Tourist Development (NTDB) – creating the first banking group in the country. The main owners of the STB are currently the state directly, and public enterprises. The merger was the largest ever in Tunisia, and took over three years to bed down.

STB now plans to merge with Banque de l'Habitat in the largest ever bank merger in Tunisia. It will create a giant with a market capitalisation of around Td1.1 billion. The new entity will be the country's largest local bank, with total assets in excess of Td11 billion – nearly double the total assets of BIAT, which is currently the largest local bank with total assets of Td6.1 billion.

The net banking income of the new bank will stand at Td431 million and net income at around Td93 million. In addition, the new bank will have 207 branches, employing over 4,200 people.

In terms of banking intermediation, credit to customers will be in the order of Td8.4 billion and deposits around Td7.5 billion.

United Arab Emirates

Steven Bainbridge
Al Tamimi & Company

1. Introduction

The United Arab Emirates comprises seven individual emirates: Abu Dhabi, Dubai, Sharjah, Ajman, Umm Al Quwain, Ras Al Kamiah and Fujairah. Each of the seven emirates is subject to UAE federal law.

In several of the emirates, and in particular Abu Dhabi and Dubai, there are a number of free trade zones. Each has its own distinct set of corporate laws and regulations. Enterprises established within such free zones are considered 'offshore' – that is, beyond the borders of the United Arab Emirates from a legal perspective. The Dubai free zones incorporated under the Dubai Technology and Media Free Zone Authority umbrella are a prime example of specialist trade zones – or 'business parks', as they are labelled – set up to promote and support particular economic activities with pertinent infrastructure and business tools. For example, Media City is the business park for media-related ventures; Internet City is dedicated to technology companies such as IBM and Microsoft; and Knowledge Village is the business park for education and research.

Typically, free zones have two general classes for licensing business activities situated within their legal boundaries. So, for example, a licence issued by Internet City to IBM will not be the same as the licence issued to a sandwich kiosk operating in Internet City providing services to patrons working in the same free zone.

The corporate laws of the individual free zones are in many cases similar, but there are important differences between them. Besides the particular laws and regulations designed specifically to create economic spaces to promote and facilitate one or more of the particular business activities that a free zone may have been designed to foster, most UAE federal laws and regulations are also applicable throughout the territory of each free zone. Most UAE companies are governed by the federal Commercial Companies Law (8/1984).

One exception to this general statement is the Dubai International Financial Centre (DIFC). Due to the particular nature of its business sector specialisation (ie, banking and financial services), which were previously subject only to federal control and regulation, the DIFC has effectively been granted the status of a 'super' free zone. Accordingly, many federal and local Dubai laws have been made inapplicable within the territory of the DIFC. The DIFC has therefore been obliged to draft and implement virtually all of its laws and regulations from scratch, and has taken the opportunity to devise and construct a relatively comprehensive and sophisticated corporate and regulatory regime.

The DIFC also offers something very different from all other free zones in the United Arab Emirates: a common law framework with which many international investors and industry global players are very familiar. As part of this common law framework, the DIFC has its own common law judiciary and court system that operate separately from the onshore UAE civil law judicial system. In keeping with the self-sustained financial centre structure, the DIFC also has a specialised independent regulator in the Dubai Financial Services Authority, modelled on the UK Financial Services Authority.

For the purposes of this chapter, we focus on the laws of the United Arab Emirates as applicable to M&A activity within the United Arab Emirates only (ie, outside the free trade zones, unless expressly stated otherwise).

2. Structuring

2.1 Valuation

At the outset of any acquisition transaction, cost will be one of the principal driving factors. It will be rare for parties not to have aired strong views on valuation at an early stage. Indeed, cost considerations often go to the heart of the deal and will generally be a significant driver for the parties contemplating the transaction in the first place. There are various methodologies for determining an initial share valuation and this exercise will usually be completed by the target in conjunction with its financial advisers.

In respect of a listed entity, objective market factors make this process more straightforward. In the case of an asset purchase, there are also objective markets and, to the extent that the assets are not unique, it is largely only the assignment of a value to goodwill that can be vexing. This can be considerably different in terms of share acquisitions for a private entity.

Where there is no objective market for shares in a limited liability company or a private joint stock company (Article 215 of the Commercial Companies Law defines a 'private joint stock company' as a company founded by at least three people and whose shares may not be floated to public subscription), the parties may face a greater challenge in arriving at a fair valuation of shares and may have more work to do to reach accord on what constitutes a mutually agreeable consideration. Independent valuators can be chosen and the parties can agree in advance to accept resulting valuations. However, in a perfect world, the valuation process should remain open at least until after the due diligence (legal and financial) has been completed, as the results will inform valuation.

2.2 Due diligence

(a) Methodology

With few exceptions, an acquirer cannot know what it is purchasing or how to assign a meaningful value to the target without first conducting thorough legal due diligence. This core fact-finding exercise cannot be supplanted as the most meaningful indicator of the constitutional, financial, regulatory and operational wellbeing of a corporate entity. Legal due diligence, often conducted concurrently with financial due diligence, provides the substance for negotiations and key provisions in the documentation of the M&A process.

Legal due diligence is a challenging task in a jurisdiction such as the United Arab Emirates, where the preferred structure of a corporate entity – even for enterprises with considerable operations and resources – is the limited liability company, which can often be a vehicle for family interests managed by only a few key individuals. While there is no inherent legal concern with this corporate structure (in fact, such companies are often characterised by their highly motivated core management team), experience suggests that record keeping can tend to be less than optimal. This has direct implications for the potential purchaser in understanding exactly what is being purchased.

Public information on corporate entities is limited in the United Arab Emirates. For example, where corporate and litigation searches may yield considerable information in more established jurisdictions, this will not be the case in the United Arab Emirates (informal searches with the help of local counsel are possible, but should be relied on solely for comparisons against disclosures by the vendor). Primarily, an acquirer must depend on disclosure of material information concerning the target by the vendor.

The availability and quality of corporate documentation and information for review cannot be taken for granted. In practical terms, this means that an acquirer should brief its legal due diligence team to be persistent and repetitive in its demands for information where it suspects there may be more information than is provided in response to initial queries. Experience suggests that due diligence personnel need to establish reliable and direct lines of communication to stimulate timely and accurate production of information from the target.

On the other hand, there are examples of corporate entities that are well organised in terms of corporate governance, record keeping and organisational set-up (particularly in the case of limited liability companies which have governmental stakeholders). But without a significant body of independent information against which to check disclosed information, buyers need to be aware of the risk that information provided may be incomplete. Management interviews and cross-checking for inconsistencies towards the end of the due diligence process can provide significant assurances where third-party sources are unavailable.

Issues to stay on top of at an early stage in the process, upon identifying a potential target, include:

- the engagement of financial advisers with regional experience;
- the presence of in-house legal personnel and sound corporate practices; and
- the target's readiness for participation in a due diligence review.

These factors will affect timelines and budgets for proceeding with a meaningful due diligence review and indeed the broader transaction.

(b) Relevant information

Any due diligence request list should be tailored to reflect the relevant UAE corporate structure of the target and account for its operational circumstances. Failure to tailor the initial request with knowledge of UAE law and practice can start the crucial due diligence process off on the wrong foot. Particularly in respect of foreign investment in the United Arab Emirates, there has been an unfortunate tendency to rely on replicated request forms used in the United Kingdom or in one or more US jurisdictions. While these forms may provide a reasonable starting point, counsel and management for a UAE-based target will be quick to recognise that many items on such a request list will result in 'not-applicable' responses and a number of key issues such as local operating licences and land ownership may not be given due coverage and attention.

An acquirer should seek all information that could materially affect its reasonable understanding of a target entity, its business, assets, goodwill and so on. It is standard practice for an initial legal due diligence request to seek information in each of the following categories (subject to tailoring for sector or other factors):

- corporate history;
- affiliates and/or group structure;
- constitutional documentation;
- list of directors and shareholders (eg, internal registers, minutes);
- capitalisation table;
- operating licences;
- Chamber of Commerce membership;
- recent financial statements;
- details of loans, financing and charges;
- material contracts;
- change of control triggers;
- assets and real property ownership;
- intellectual property;
- mortgages, liens or pledges over assets;
- insurance;
- employment details;
- information technology;
- environmental matters; and
- litigation issues (contingent or otherwise).

A due diligence report would typically be requested in the form of either:

- an exceptions-based report which covers only 'show stoppers' or key findings on issues such as contingent liabilities or regulatory hurdles that would likely impede the transaction at hand; or
- a comprehensive report that examines the full spectrum of possible details relating to broader picture of the target's operations, assets and liabilities.

In either case, an interim 'red-flag' report is usually prepared in brief to inform negotiations and raise any deal breakers or significant valuation issues. This interim report can re-focus the direction of due diligence and illuminate any restructuring or organisational issues that should be dealt with by the vendor in advance of closing.

Whether the due diligence report is exceptions based or comprehensive, if one or more parties is unfamiliar with UAE law, the executive summary section should be crafted with substantial focus on issues that may be jurisdiction specific.

2.3 Available structures under the legal system

In the United Arab Emirates, businesses may combine in a number of ways. Most commonly, a business may be acquired by a purchaser buying either the shares of a company carrying on a particular business or the business and assets of the commercial concern itself.

Business fusions in the United Arab Emirates also include classic partnerships and joint ventures, which take effect when two or more business entities come together either pursuant to a straightforward contractual arrangement or by contributing resources to a new joint venture special purpose vehicle owned jointly by the joint venturers. In addition, under UAE law two or more distinct commercial entities can merge such that one or more will effectively be dissolved while transferring all of their business, assets and liabilities to another by means of a formal merger arrangement.

While there are various potential methods of merger and acquisition in the United Arab Emirates, the difference between them lies in the position of the shareholder. Shareholders of merged companies typically exchange shares for shares in the new entity; whereas in an acquisition, the target is usually acquired as a going concern and its shares are transferred to the shareholders of the acquirer for cash or debt, giving the acquirer effective control over the assets and liabilities of the acquired target. The terminology, in practice, is often blurred and recent trends show that M&A activity is largely weighted towards acquisitions.

The typical forms of business merger in the United Arab Emirates are the acquisition of shares in a target or the acquisition of a target's underlying assets and business. Although a number of different corporate formations are recognised, the following legal corporate forms are the primary entities most commonly encountered in M&A practice:

- private joint stock companies;
- limited liability companies; and
- public joint stock companies.

2.4 Structuring considerations

(a) Tax

The laws relating to taxation in the United Arab Emirates are relatively scant. There is no universally applicable system in operation relating to the levy of personal or corporate revenue, capital, withholding or sales tax. Excise duty applies to the import of products into the United Arab Emirates at a standard rate of 5% in common with the other members of the Gulf Cooperation Council (GCC) customs union. It is not expected that direct taxation will be implemented in the near future and indeed most of the free zones have guaranteed that no tax will be payable by corporations or individuals active or working there for a particular period – usually 50 years. Some industry sectors are nevertheless subject to taxation, in particular petrochemical extraction companies and branches of foreign banks. In addition, tax is payable on certain forms of catering and on the sale of alcohol.

No transfer fee or stamp duty is levied on the acquisition of shares or transfer of assets, and no specific rules under UAE law specifically address duties on mergers and acquisitions. However, certain required steps in formalising a transfer of shares, particularly before the notary public, do attract a fee. Notary public fees are generally calculated on the value of a given transaction, subject to an upper limit – in the case of the Dubai Notary Public, Dh10,000.

(b) Regulatory considerations

The three main securities exchanges in the United Arab Emirates are the Dubai Financial Market (DFM), the Abu Dhabi Securities Exchange (ADX) and NASDAQDubai in the DIFC. Each of these has its own regulatory rules. The first two are also closely supervised by the Emirates Securities and Commodities Authority (SCA) and NASDAQDubai is supervised by the Dubai Financial Services Authority. The regulations pertaining to these exchanges set out listing rules, settlement procedures and rules on the filing of notifications and timings relating to these in connection with business combinations.

These regulators may also have internal guidelines or circulars that are not made public and which may influence, or even restrict, completion of an M&A transaction.

A number of laws affect an acquisition process in the United Arab Emirates. Those that primarily influence the majority of acquisition transactions include the following:

- The Commercial Companies Law (8/1984, as amended) – public joint stock companies, private joint stock companies and limited liability companies in the UAE are all subject to the Commercial Companies Law.
- The Law Governing the Emirates Securities and Commodities Authority and Market (4/ 2000, as amended) – transactions in shares of companies listed on the ADX or DFM are subject to regulation by the SCA. The SCA is an independent legal entity with broad authority to protect investors and ensure stability of the financial system in the United Arab Emirates. Additionally, the DFM and the ADX are self-regulating organisations with listing rules, settlement procedures and other rules that serve to supplement the primary regulations imposed by the SCA.
- SCA Resolution 3/2000 on Regulations on Disclosure and Transparency – particular emphasis is given to promoting transparency and fairness to encourage investment and stability. This particular resolution sets forth acquisition thresholds for providing notice to the markets. In addition to a number of requirements for post-transaction notification in respect of incremental changes in substantial shareholdings, every individual or entity that seeks to purchase 20% or more of the shares in any listed company in the United Arab Emirates must notify the relevant market (DFM or ADX) before it places the purchase order. The markets, in consultation with the SCA, may refuse to allow the purchase to proceed where they determine it to be prejudicial to the interests of the economy.

- The Central Bank Law (10/1980, as amended) – for financial institutions regulated by the UAE Central Bank, prior approval of the Central Bank must be sought in respect of any acquisition of 5% or more of a public joint stock company.
- The Labour Relations Law (8/1980, as amended) – the Labour Relations Law does not provide for the transfer of employees unless the company is changing its status (eg, a branch office changing to a limited liability company). Generally, if the transaction at issue is an asset purchase, not a share purchase, and the employees need to be transferred from the employment of one company to that of another, the employment with the first company will need to be terminated and the employees re-hired by the second company.
- The Civil Code (Law 2/1987, as amended) – the foundation and jurisprudence of UAE law is guided by the Civil Code, which has broad influence on practice and custom.

(c) Special considerations

In the case of the acquisition of a listed entity (a public joint stock company), there is no established set of takeover rules under UAE law. However, as discussed above, a number of regulatory influences can affect the timing and flow of an acquisition.

The lack of a comprehensive takeover code means that there is no concept of mandatory offer in the United Arab Emirates, so there is no requirement that an offer be extended to all shareholders. Additionally, there is no settled law as to available defensive measures to takeovers. Rather, actions constituting defensive measures will be viewed in accordance with the laws of the land and directors' duties as set forth pursuant to the Commercial Companies Law. Likewise, the minority squeeze-out is not a recognised manoeuvre under UAE law, so a minority shareholder's remedy is essentially to accept the reality of takeover or sell its shares.

It is foreseeable that a takeover code may be developed in future, but until such guidance is provided, compliance with market regulations and SCA approval on a case-by-case basis are the main regulatory hurdles to securing a takeover.

(d) Other considerations

Directors of commercial companies incorporated under the Commercial Companies Law are regulated by the law insofar as their duties to shareholders are concerned. Directors will be directly liable to shareholders for mismanagement or wrongful or abusive use of their powers. Non-compliance with the standards required of directors may also be subject to penal sanctions.

Each of the laws of the numerous free trade zones includes provisions dealing with the standards of behaviour and performance required of company officers in the performance of their duties, including in relation to the planning and implementation of business restructurings, acquisitions and disposals.

Generally, shareholders (whether they hold a controlling interest or not) will not be considered to have a duty towards other shareholders in relation to how they exercise their powers in a general shareholders' meeting. That said, various provisions of the Commercial Companies Law provide that if action is taken by majority shareholders so as to favour a particular group of shareholders to the disadvantage of another group of shareholders, those disadvantaged can seek a remedy before the courts.

Another factor that should be kept in mind while reviewing the structure of a target and planning an acquisition structure is that the Commercial Companies Law does not allow for different classes of shares with different rights attaching thereto (ie, preferred shares are not permissible under UAE law). All issued shares must have the same rights and liabilities. Likewise, UAE law does not permit any attempt to limit voting rights (eg, by amendment to the articles of association).

Recent amendments to UAE law, such as removing minimum capital restrictions, aim to encourage investments in the local economy.

(e) *Antitrust laws*

There is very little UAE law in terms of developed competition or antitrust law. Particularly when contrasted against the two largest and most influential systems of commercial competition regulation (in the United States and the European Union), it cannot be said that any form of independent competition review applies to mergers and acquisitions. The extent to which the SCA takeover approval requirements (discussed above) may contemplate components of competition regulation is a matter of speculation only.

However, the United Arab Emirates implemented a single-purpose Consumer Protection Law (24/2006) in late 2006. This law and its accompanying regulations contain the competition legislation that is to be found in the United Arab Emirates. With regard to competition law principle, the law simply states that the regulations implementing the law shall set out the basis of determining when there has been an abnormal increase in the price of goods and what constitutes an unlawful monopoly. The Consumer Protection Law could give effect to a UAE competition policy in its establishment of a single-purpose Consumer Protection Department within the Ministry of Economy to promote fair competition, eradicate monopolies and act as a consumer representative, among other things. However, the implementation of that statute is in its early stages, and to read in an intention to move beyond its business-to-consumer mandate would be highly speculative and beyond current UAE M&A practice.

(f) *Foreign investment laws and foreign ownership restrictions*

Foreign investors are subject to no foreign exchange or investment control in the United Arab Emirates, but this should not be confused with any idea that foreign ownership of UAE companies is entirely free of challenge. Article 22 of the Commercial Companies Law obliges companies incorporated in the United Arab Emirates to have a minimum UAE national shareholder participation of 51%. This is of general application and therefore affects any entity incorporated within the United Arab Emirates (not including free zones, a number of which permit foreigners to own up to 100% of the shares in companies domiciled there).

Consequently, a direct purchase which results in less than 51% of the shares in a public joint stock company being owned by UAE national shareholders is not legally permissible. In the event that there is an attempt to undertake such a transaction, the result will be automatically reversed by the trading monitors on the relevant market.

Where a non-UAE national investor seeks to acquire an interest exceeding 49% of the shares of a public joint stock company, it may be able to do so through nominee agreements. For example, the investor may establish a special purpose vehicle in order to enter the sale and purchase agreement to purchase more than 49% of the target's shares. This would allow the investor effectively to control more than 49% of the shares of the public joint stock company through the special purpose vehicle.

Likewise with respect to private entities, it is common practice for UAE nationals or national-owned companies to lend their patronage to a particular business or to act as nominee shareholders where a particular level of UAE national participation is required by law, where a foreign investor requires a particular level of control or financial participation.

Similarly, where non-UAE national individuals or entities are seeking to participate in activities otherwise restricted to UAE nationals, parties may plan a post-transaction structure whereby UAE national interests may subcontract essentially all of the management function of the relevant business entity in return for a fee, such that the foreign manager will be in *de facto* control and will retain the lion's share of the profits generated by the enterprise.

In addition to foreign ownership restrictions, the Commercial Companies Law provides that UAE or GCC nationals must represent the majority of the board of directors in any joint stock company incorporated in the United Arab Emirates.

These key pre-transaction structuring issues should be taken into consideration in respect of acquisitions that may otherwise put a controlling stake of a shareholding in a foreign shareholder's hands.

3. Merger agreement

Absent other material factors specific to a given acquisition, an acquirer from outside the United Arab Emirates may typically be inclined to structure the transaction as an asset purchase rather than a share purchase. In theory, this permits the acquirer to acquire the benefit of only those assets that are central to the operation of the business, while avoiding any liabilities that the target may have accrued. This can be particularly significant where foreseeable liabilities may include un-quantified contingencies in the form of litigation or similar. However, where the acquisition relates to a going concern, this dynamic is influenced by the non-transferability of trading licences in the case of an asset purchase.

Trading licences and related approvals and issuance procedures can involve different governmental bodies and more administrative time than foreign purchasers may be accustomed to. An acquisition by way of share purchase will greatly increase the likelihood that an acquired entity will be able to maintain its operating licences and remain operational.

These factors are by no means definitive in respect of the transaction documentation, as each deal will have its own features. Nonetheless, they are key points that require strategic consideration at an early stage of the transaction.

3.1 Pre-merger agreements

(a) *Non-disclosure agreements*

Confidentiality and non-disclosure agreements are generally acceptable and enforceable under UAE law, and are implemented as standard practice in connection with mergers and acquisitions. As a matter of practice, non-disclosure agreements are generally executed between parties to a merger or acquisition of private businesses (and at times also between parties and their advisers). However, in the event of a breach of the agreement, the aggrieved party will be entitled to recover only any direct and actual loss arising from that breach. Specific performance in the form of injunctive relief against a threatened breach is unlikely to be granted by the UAE courts.

(b) *Exclusivity agreement*

Exclusivity agreements (entered into either separately or, for convenience, as a provision within the non-disclosure agreement) which seek to prevent one or both parties from negotiating with a third party pending conclusion of discussions between the parties in relation to a merger or acquisition are typically used and enforceable under UAE law, with the same caveat as applies to non-disclosure agreements: damages rather than specific performance will be the standard remedy for breach.

(c) *Letters of intent, memoranda of understanding, heads of terms*

Non-binding comfort instruments setting forth the core aspects of an intended merger or acquisition (again, drafted either independently or in a single document with binding non-disclosure agreement provisions and/or exclusivity provisions) are the rule rather than the exception in UAE practice.

3.2 Scope

(a) *Parties*

There should be certainty as to the parties to a legal agreement. Issues of authority, capacity and informed consent should always be observed as best practice. Where multiple shareholders are involved, all shareholders should be made parties to the relevant agreement, unless valid powers of attorney with appropriate scope have been executed in favour of a representative.

(b) *Description*

Certainty as to the subject-matter of a sale and purchase agreement should always be clearly established. While there are arguably corollaries of equitable remedies in the application of UAE civil law, there can be no substitute for clarity in setting forth the terms and conditions of the operative agreement.

3.3 Important clauses

(a) *Merger, acquisition or purchase clause*

The merger agreement should clearly set forth the intention of the parties by recording the terms of the merger or acquisition, and the nature and procedure for transferring consideration. There are no restrictions on type of consideration in the United Arab Emirates, so cash, shares or any combination thereof may be tendered.

(b) *Representation and warranties*

A typical acquisition agreement in the United Arab Emirates will feature a lengthy schedule of general warranties covering most facets of the target, including shares, financial accounts, assets, contracts, material liabilities, intellectual property, litigation, regulatory matters and employment. These provisions will form the basis for seeking recourse should the acquirer subsequently find that matters were not as the vendor had disclosed. Representations and warranties should apply equally at signing and on closing (or completion, if completion is subsequent to closing).

The sale and purchase agreement should include clear and robust conditions precedent to provide for any steps that need to be taken by the vendor to structure or organise matters appropriately before closing. This point is of particular importance where a private entity was remiss in its record keeping and administration prior to the transaction. An acquirer should insist that any disclosure letter or disclosure schedule, which purports to release a target from liability, be specific and detailed.

(c) *Liabilities and limitation of liabilities*

In the event of breach of an obligation under the merger or acquisition agreement, the claiming party (typically the acquirer) would be entitled to damages for direct and actual losses suffered. Article 390 of the Civil Code allows for contractual agreement as to liabilities (ie, liquidated damages) where there is a genuine pre-estimate of costs, but the UAE courts hold ultimate discretion to vary such damages so that they equal the actual loss.

The standard limitation period for actions brought under contract law in the United Arab Emirates is three years, subject to certain exceptions. Depending on the nature of the business and assets at issue in a given acquisition, this limitation period can be shortened by agreement and is often reduced to two years.

(d) *Choice of law*

UAE law most often governs contracts regulating corporate acquisitions or reconstructions in the United Arab Emirates. However, given the significance of foreign investment in the United Arab Emirates, it is also frequently the case that parties decide, for the sake of familiarity or where foreign law may be more sophisticated in terms of its regulations pertaining to particular issues, that a foreign governing law – for example, the law of England and Wales or New York – should apply instead. The law of the United Arab Emirates is based on the French Napoleonic Civil Code and so, together with a reliable court system, the choice of

UAE law and jurisdiction is generally considered to be a sensible and cost-effective option if the target is located within the United Arab Emirates.

(e) ***Dispute resolution***

Recourse to the courts is often not the preferred option and parties may choose for disputes to be submitted to resolution by arbitration proceedings. The United Arab Emirates has a number of flourishing arbitration institutions, which are gaining recognition internationally. In particular, the Abu Dhabi Commercial Conciliation and Arbitration Centre and the Dubai Chamber of Commerce and Industry have taken significant strides in promoting alternative dispute resolution mechanisms that can be both reliable and enforceable if appropriate provisions are correctly included in transaction documents

There are some issues which, if submitted to the UAE courts for determination, will always be considered in light of applicable UAE law – for example, the rights of exclusive commercial agents. It is a significant feature of UAE law that exclusive commercial agents enjoy certain protections and rights irrespective of whether such rights are provided for or even expressively excluded from a contract to which they are a party. Accordingly, to ensure that these rights are safeguarded, UAE law will always be considered by the UAE courts to be the applicable law if such issues arise.

4. Employment law issues

Labour relations are governed principally by the Labour Relations Law. Most of the free zones provide that the Labour Relations Law will also apply within their respective territories with or without some modification. The DIFC is the exception, having enacted its own employment law, which shares some characteristics with the Labour Relations Law and imports a number of concepts from European law models.

Generally, in the United Arab Emirates the law relating to the employment of a workforce is particularly favourable to the employer in terms of determining precisely what the rights and obligations of employees and employers are in any given context and allowing a fair degree of flexibility for the employer to manage its workforce. To this end, it is relatively inexpensive to reduce the size of the workforce. Consultation and other time-prescriptive requirements placed on employers are also minimalistic. It is therefore relatively easy for employers to effect redundancies where employees are no longer required in connection with a business amalgamation.

5. Approval process

5.1 Internal approvals

(a) ***Limited liability companies***

In a private acquisition of shares or underlying assets of a target, the target's shareholders must pass a resolution at a duly convened meeting approving the sale and, in the case of a share purchase, stating that the shareholders waive their pre-emptive right upon receiving an offer of shares. The resolution must be passed in the manner prescribed in the memorandum of association. Once the transaction proceeds, the memorandum of association should be amended to reflect the new shareholding and commercial licences should also be amended as necessary.

(b) *Joint stock companies*

When acquiring a joint stock company in the United Arab Emirates, it is important to consider the memorandum and articles of association, as these may contain provisions restricting the transfer of shares or fixing a limit on the ownership of shares by an individual or single entity. Generally, the acquirer will approach one or more of the current shareholders and negotiate the purchase.

An alternative approach is for the acquirer to approach the target, seeking to purchase sufficient newly issued shares to satisfy its takeover goals. Article 137 of the Commercial Companies Law permits a rights issue subject to three-quarters of the shareholding being represented at an extraordinary general assembly.

5.2 Approval by regulators

(a) *Limited liability companies*

There is no general requirement to make information concerning business combinations publicly available in the United Arab Emirates. The law respects the rights of commercial enterprises to keep confidential acquisition and disposal plans. There are, however, publication requirements in relation to asset acquisitions and mergers where an entity will necessarily be dissolved. The intention behind this requirement is to give creditors the opportunity to protest.

Insofar as private company acquisitions are concerned, government filings and regulatory authority consents are of key significance. Procedures in relation to share transfers throughout the United Arab Emirates and in the free zone territories require in each case, as a preliminary step, the obtaining of initial approval from the relevant government or free zone authority.

Procedures for the transfer of shares are relatively closely supervised. The elaborate nature of documentary requirements and notarial and other stamps required to effect a transfer of shares or business interests may surprise those more familiar with less intensively controlled procedures in certain common law jurisdictions. Each of the stamps, certificates and submissions necessary in connection with a transfer necessarily attracts a fee. These are generally relatively nominal in value. The notary public in the United Arab Emirates is empowered to review and reject documentation that is not in compliance with public order guidelines.

(b) *Public companies*

As discussed above in respect of regulatory issues, there is a number of disclosure requirements in relation to substantial shareholders of companies listed on the national exchanges. For example, natural persons whose shareholding, or whose shareholding along with that of their minor children, has reached 5% or more of a listed company's shares must notify the relevant financial market of such holdings immediately.

Legal persons whose shareholding has reached 5% or more of a listed company's shares must notify the relevant financial market of such holdings immediately.

Natural persons whose shareholding, or whose shareholding along with that of their minor children, and legal persons whose shareholding has reached 10% or more of a listed company's parent, subsidiary, associated or affiliated company, must notify the relevant financial market of such holdings immediately. Any natural or legal person whose holding reaches 10% or more of a listed company's shares and that wishes to purchase 20% or more of that company's shares must notify the relevant financial market before it submits a purchase order for execution on the trading floor. The director general of the relevant financial market, in consultation with the SCA, may prohibit the deal if it determines that it may be harmful to the national economy.

6. Post-merger issues

6.1 Employees

Under UAE law there is no universal equivalent of the transfer of undertakings regulations pertinent to employer-employee relations, as in the European Union. Accordingly, for employees of a business to transfer with it when acquired by a third-party purchaser, the consent of each individual employee is required before he or she can transfer from the former employer. Under UAE law, an assignment of rights takes effect as a novation, such that it is not sufficient simply for an employer to give notice to an employee that its rights with respect to the employment relationship will simply be assigned to the acquirer. Instead, the employee's consent is also required (any employees who do not consent must be given notice of termination or payment in lieu).

However, given that the regulations generally facilitate the dismissal of employees who under-perform or are redundant or dissident, if any employee objects to a proposed transfer, he or she will be aware that there is a strong likelihood of dismissal. An employee's rights on dismissal will not entitle him or her to compensation of the same order of magnitude as in other more employee-oriented jurisdictions.

The rules relating to post-termination remuneration (also commonly known as 'gratuity') are also relevant to the transfer of employees. This mandatory benefit accrues to employees who work continuously with an employer for more than a minimum period, and is calculated on the basis of their last remuneration package and length of service.

If a business is sold, then the consequent break in the employment relationship between the employees and their employer or the owner of the business in which they work triggers payment of the gratuity. It is for the target and the acquirer to determine whether they wish to pay off employees at the time of the business transfer or defer the aggregate gratuity entitlement to a later date when employees actually leave their employment.

Often, the parties to a prospective business sale transaction will offer employees the right to continue to accrue gratuity as if there were no break in employment as a result of the sale of the business, with a view to inducing them to consent to the transfer of their employment. This benefits the employee in terms of the aggregate amount of gratuity to which he or she will ultimately be entitled.

In any event, while this issue is dealt with here as a 'post-merger' issue, it is clear that there may be significant financial implications in determining how best to deal with employees of an acquisition target (specifically if there is a large and/or long-serving workforce). Particularly in asset purchases rather than share purchases, there can also be significant visa considerations in respect of foreign workers. Thought should be given at an early stage as to whether employees will be paid gratuity upon acquisition or whether gratuities will be rolled over into continued employment, and how the costs will be apportioned between the parties.

6.2 Change of control provisions and third-party consents

Typically, an agreement for sale of shares or underlying assets in an acquisition will contain representations as to the non-existence of any change of control provision in relation to material agreements, and the clarification and resolution of requisite third-party consents will be included in the list of conditions precedent. This is an issue that should be noted in the red-flag due diligence report and brought to resolution during the negotiation period before closing.

In certain transactions (eg, an acquisition of a service industry target), there may be a greater emphasis on the value of material contracts than in other cases. To secure the buyer's interest, it is important to support the seller's representations with appropriate warranties and indemnifications. Depending on the sensitivity of certain contracts (eg, above a certain threshold percentage of annual revenue), it may be prudent to make provision for an 'earn-out' or a portion of hold-back in the payment of consideration.

(a) Assets

In general terms, certain standard requirements apply to a transfer of company property in the transfer of employees. These include the need to provide original transfer documentation to a notary public for review and recording. The notary public is empowered not only to review documentation, but also to reject it if he or she determines that it is not entirely in conformity with UAE legal requirements.

Real estate should receive special attention if a non-UAE national party is involved, as there are significant restrictions on foreign ownership of land. Where there is a transfer of ownership, transfer of title will be required in respect of each piece of land. Moveable equipment and similar must be conveyed by transfer of possession. Items such as property and cars will require change of registered ownership.

Any leased assets may require a change in the lessee's details, depending on the nature of the relevant lease agreement. Similarly, any insurance policies in place may require changes in the beneficiaries' details.

It is not uncommon for shareholders of family companies in the transfer of employees to acquire assets and immoveables in their own names and to use them for the target's activities. For this reason, particular emphasis should be given in the due diligence stage, to ensure that there is (or will be, as a condition precedent to closing) a detailed inventory of all assets and proper registration of the same in the name of the target rather than in the name of one of the shareholders.

About the authors

Nada Abdelsater-Abusamra

Managing partner, Abdelsater Abusamra & Associates
nada.abdelsater@asaslaw.com

Nada Abdelsater-Abusamra is managing partner of the firm. She is admitted to the courts of New York and is a member of the Beirut Bar. She advises on major M&A, corporate and financial transactions, oil and gas and public-private partnership projects. Her clients include major international, regional and national businesses. She is a member of the committee set up by the Presidency of the Council of Ministers to reform the legal investment climate in Lebanon.

Ms Abdelsater-Abusamra is cited as a leading lawyer by leading guides for leading law firms worldwide. She holds an LLM from Harvard Law School, a French and Lebanese master of laws degree from St Joseph University and a bachelor of science degree from the American University of Beirut. She has also completed coursework for a master of international affairs degree at the Lebanese American University. She is the 2009 recipient of the Corporate Governance Rising Star Award, issued by Yale University (School of Management).

Grace Alam

Associate in training, Badri & Salim El Meouchi, LLP
grace.alam@elmeouchi.com

Grace Alam is an associate in training at the firm; she joined the Qatar office in 2008. She mostly practises in corporate and labour law, and is highly knowledgeable of the internal workings of the Ministry of Business and Trade. Ms Alam has also published articles on arbitration law in Qatar. She graduated from the Lebanese University with a bachelor of law degree. She is fluent in Arabic, French and English.

Steven Bainbridge

Regional head, sports law and events management, Al Tamimi & Company
s.bainbridge@tamimi.com

After a three-year hiatus from private practice, during which time he was general counsel at the iconic Yas Marina Circuit, Steven Bainbridge recently returned to private practice to establish the sports law practice at Al Tamimi & Company, the largest Middle-East based law firm. Mr Bainbridge is based out of Al Tamimi's offices in the Qatar Financial Centre, but as regional head manages the practice across Al Tamimi's 13 offices in seven countries.

Prior to dedicating his primary efforts to sports law, Mr Bainbridge's practice focused on high-value corporate projects. He has considerable experience representing governmental, institutional and corporate clients in cross-border investment and transactional matters. As noted in the *Legal 500*, Mr Bainbridge is known for his knowledge of unique factors in the Middle East and his understanding of issues important to western buyers – skills which he has consistently applied in large-scale M&A deals involving an array of industry sectors across multiple jurisdictions.

Mohieddine El Amari
Managing partner, El Amari & Associés
mea@elamari.com

Mohieddine El Amari is the founding partner of El Amari & Associés, a Moroccan law firm which specialises in advising major Moroccan corporate clients. Mr El Amari advises on project finance, private equity funds, securities offerings and a range of corporate and corporate finance transactions. Mr El Amari has extensive experience representing corporations, financial institutions and other principals. His experience spans public and private mergers and acquisitions, credit, capital markets, fund formation and winding-up, and a variety of strategic and advisory corporate assignments.

Ramy El Demerdash
Associate, Al Tamimi & Company
r.eldemrdash@tamimi.com

Ramy El Demerdash is an associate in Al Tamimi & Company's Kuwait office. He earned his master's degree in international and comparative law from Indiana University School of Law. With seven years of professional experience, he has accumulated experience in the areas of banking and finance, corporate and commercial law as well as mergers and acquisitions.

In the corporate and finance arena, he has represented various companies in Egypt and Kuwait by handling their establishment procedures, corporate commercial relevant matters and finance transactions. He has also been involved in various due diligence projects, in addition to handling the procedures and legal documentation of numerous non-governmental organisations in Egypt.

Chadia El Meouchi
Managing partner, Badri & Salim El Meouchi, LLP
chadia.elmeouchi@elmeouchi.com

Chadia El Meouchi is the firm's managing partner and manages the Lebanon and Qatar offices. She has been a member of the New York Bar since 2000. She joined the firm in 2000 and became partner in 2005. She has practised law in North America and the Middle East (including Lebanon and Qatar) for over 12 years.

Ms El Meouchi has published a number of articles on corporate and financial law, privatisation, corporate governance and transparency, and is also frequently invited to speak at conferences on numerous topics. She is a visiting professor at University Panthéon – Assas Paris II.

Ms El Meouchi obtained a bachelor of commerce degree, majoring in international business, from Concordia University in Montreal. She then obtained a bachelor of civil law degree at the University of Montreal before obtaining an LLM from Georgetown University in Washington DC. She also holds numerous postgraduate qualifications.

Mohamed A Ghannam
Partner, Helmy, Hamza & Partners
mohamed.ghannam@bakermckenzie.com

Mohamed A Ghannam is an international partner in Helmy, Hamza & Partners, a member firm of Baker & McKenzie International. He received his law degree with high honours from Cairo University Law School in 1985 and graduated among the top 1%. He received a master of laws degree from Harvard Law School in 1987 and a second master of laws degree from Chicago-Kent Law School in 1993 (Dean's List). Mr Ghannam worked as a prosecutor in the Prosecutor's Office in Egypt. He also practised law in United States, Saudi Arabia and Egypt. He specialises in mergers and acquisitions, major projects and project finance and transactional and corporate work. Mr

Ghannam is regarded as one of Egypt's leading lawyers in project finance and M&A in legal publications such as *Chambers Global, IFLR, Euromoney Expert Guides, Legal 500* and *PLC*. He has also worked on several projects in the Middle East, including in Jordan, Lebanon, Sudan and Libya.

Marie-Anne Jabbour
Associate, Badri & Salim El Meouchi, LLP
marieanne.jabbour@elmeouchi.com

Marie-Anne Jabbour joined the firm in 2008 and moved to the Qatar office in 2010. She graduated from La Sagesse University with a bachelor of civil law degree in 2004 and with an advanced graduate degree in private law in 2007.

Ms Jabbour primarily works in corporate, commercial and banking and finance law, and works on conventional and *Sharia*-compliant transactions. She has extensive experience in Qatari financial regulation and has frequent dealings with the Qatar Central Bank, the Qatar Financial Markets Authority and the Qatar Exchange.

Ms Jabbour has published articles on anti-money laundering, anti-corruption legislation and corporate governance in Lebanon and Qatar. She is fluent in Arabic, English and French.

Bill Jefferies
Partner, Trowers & Hamlins
bjefferies@trowers.com

Bill Jefferies is a corporate partner based in the United Arab Emirates, following his arrival in Dubai in early 2013 from the firm's Bahrain office. He spent over seven years in Bahrain working mainly on regional and international M&A and private equity transactions. Prior to that, he was based in the London corporate team.

During his time in the Middle East and North Africa region, Mr Jeffries has led teams of lawyers working on numerous high-profile international deals, particularly in the infrastructure, shipping, real estate, media, manufacturing and financial services sectors. He has been at the forefront of developing the firm's reputation for advising Middle Eastern clients on the execution, management and exit of high-value, complex UK inward investments in the real estate and social infrastructure sectors, often on a *Sharia*-compliant basis.

He advises clients on corporate structuring and restructuring matters, rationalisations, capital markets, company law matters, joint ventures, commercial contracts and pre-litigation strategy.

Michael Kortbawi
Partner, Bin Shabib & Associates (BSA) LLP
michael.kortbawi@bsa.ae

Michael Kortbawi has gained hands-on experience in the Middle East and North Africa region, having practised in the United Arab Emirates for over 10 years and having supervised the organic growth of Bin Shabib and Associates (BSA) LLP into the five jurisdictions in which it now operates.

His specific areas of expertise include mergers and acquisitions in the insurance and energy sectors, directors' and officers' duties under UAE and DIFC laws, setting up insurance and reinsurance companies in the GCC, and deregistration of commercial agencies.

Mr Kortbawi heads a team of eight corporate lawyers who are involved in corporate and regulatory advice in relation to all aspects of corporate law, including cross-border business transactions and mergers and acquisitions in the United Arab Emirates, Iraq, Oman and Lebanon.

Philip H Kotsis
Partner, Al Tamimi & Company
p.kotsis@tamimi.com

Philip Kotsis is a partner at Al Tamimi & Company and is located in the Kuwait office. Prior to joining Al Tamimi in October 2009, he was a senior legal consultant with an international law firm where he focused primarily in the commercial, corporate, banking and finance sectors.

Mr Kotsis has accumulated a broad range of experience in the areas of local and transnational commercial and corporate transactions, mergers and acquisitions, corporate/joint venture organisations, finance and public-private partnership projects. He began his legal career in the United States, where he gained vast experience in complex commercial transactions, real estate acquisition, petroleum distribution and marketing, and has litigated complex commercial matters before the state and federal courts.

Sofia Layachi
In-house counsel, Fonds Marocain de Développement Touristique
slayachi@fmdt.gov.ma

Sofia Layachi is in-house counsel with Fonds Marocain de Développement Touristique, based in Rabat, Morocco. She specialises in corporate M&A activity in the context of real estate and tourism-related investments and transactions. Ms Layachi handles matters relating to the day-to-day corporate life of sovereign wealth funds, as well as a range of corporate, corporate finance and commercial issues. Ms Layachi is a former lawyer with the Paris Bar, with experience representing companies in the context of high-profile international transactions, acquisitions and divestments, and equity and capital increase operations. She also advised international groups on setting up new businesses and the restructuring of their activities in France through mergers, and supervised the legal follow-up of their companies. Her experience spans private equity, corporate M&A, commercial practice and a variety of strategic and advisory corporate assignments.

Taimur Malik
Counsel, Curtis, Mallet-Prevost, Colt & Mosle LLP
taimurm@gmail.com

Taimur Malik was called to the Bar by the Honourable Society of Lincoln's Inn and is admitted as an advocate of the High Court in Pakistan. He holds degrees and certificates in various fields of law from the University of London, the University of Heidelberg, the Hague Academy of International Law and Boston University School of Law.

He has been a research scholar (international commercial contracts) at UNIDROIT in Rome, and his articles on legal issues have appeared regularly in leading Omani, Pakistani and Indian publications.

He has worked on a number of M&A transactions in Oman and Pakistan. These include the sale of the majority shareholdings in four listed Omani companies, including a power company, and the acquisition of the largest government-owned sugar mill in Pakistan. He is currently working as a counsel at the Muscat office of a leading international law firm, Curtis, Mallet-Prevost, Colt & Mosle LLP. Previously, he was head of legal (Middle East) at Vale, the world's second-largest mining and metals group.

Khaled Moussa
Partner, Helmy, Hamza & Partners
khaled.moussa@bakermckenzie.com

Khaled Moussa is a local partner in Helmy, Hamza & Partners, a member firm of Baker & McKenzie International. He received his law degree with high honours from Cairo University Law School in 2000 and graduated among the top 1%. Prior to joining Baker & McKenzie in 2003, he worked with the administrative courts of the State Council of Egypt. Mr Moussa's practice focuses on mergers and acquisitions, corporate, civil and commercial law, as well as private law. He also advises on many other sectors, including real estate, construction, telecommunications, mining and petrochemical projects. He has also worked on projects in the Middle East.

Abdullah Mutawi
Partner, Trowers & Hamlins
amutawi@trowers.com

Abdullah Mutawi is a corporate partner at Trowers & Hamlins and is the head of practice in the United Arab Emirates.

Mr Mutawi has substantial experience in cross-border M&A, capital markets and securities transactions. In addition to advising both buyers and sellers on a number of the region's M&A deals, he advises on high-profile insolvency, administration and restructuring matters, specialising in the banking and financial services sector. Most recently, he has been advising a number of strategic shareholders in a number of regional financial institutions on restructuring and shareholder control issues. Mr Mutawi is the lead partner advising the Central Bank of Bahrain on its administration of The International Banking Corporation BSC, which is one of the financial institutions at the centre of the region's biggest financial collapse involving the Al Gosaibi and Saad Groups of Saudi Arabia.

In addition to his corporate practice, Mr Mutawi heads the firm's TMT practice.

Alastair Neale
Head of company/commercial department, Jihad Al Taie Law Office
info@jatlo.com

Alastair Neale qualified as an English solicitor in 1973 and has since worked in London, Rotterdam, Paris, Kuwait, Bahrain and Oman. In Bahrain he worked on two major acquisitions in South America and Hong Kong for an Arab bank. In Oman he has worked on a number of M&A transactions, including the merger of Bank Dhofar Al Omani Al Fransi with Majan International Bank and the successful defence of a takeover bid for National Bank of Oman. He is currently head of the corporate/commercial department at Jihad Al Taie Law Office in Oman.

Alia Nimry
Associate, Khalifeh & Partners
a.nimry@khalifehlaw.com

Alia Nimry joined Khalifeh & Partners in 2008 and is a key member of the projects and corporate group. Ms Nimry has advised on large mergers and acquisitions, including advising Aabar on a joint venture entailing an acquisition of property in Jordan and Electricity Distribution Company on the acquisition of publicly listed Irbid District Electricity Company by way of a complicated multi-tranche block trade. She also has significant experience in structuring and drafting documentation relating to public-private partnerships such as design, build, operate and transfer agreements and build, own and operate agreements.

Hala Raphael-Abillama
Raphael & Associes Law Firm
hala.raphael@rzara.com

Hala Raphael-Abillama is co-managing partner of the firm. She has more than 23 years of experience in law in France and Lebanon. She has led major M&A and privatisation transactions. She recently handled the sale and/or acquisition of several telecoms operations in various countries of the Middle East, Africa and other countries; Raphaël & Associés handled all legal aspects, from constitution of the companies to negotiation of licences, drafting of contracts and all legal operations and set-up. For several years Ms Raphael-Abillama led the firm's operations from Paris. Ms Raphael-Abillama is member of various boards. She has published on foreign investments in Lebanon and commercial transactions. She has an LLM from Georgetown University, Washington DC (1991) and a master of French and Lebanese laws degree from St Joseph University, Beirut (1989).

Muhammad Arif Saeed
Partner, Dhabaan and Partners (in association with Eversheds)
Arif@aldhabaan.eversheds.com

Muhammad Arif Saeed is a partner with Dhabaan and Partners (in association with Eversheds) in Saudi Arabia. He has experience of international cross-border transactions and joint venture transactions, corporate mergers and acquisitions, demergers, private acquisitions and disposals, restructurings and equity capital markets, among other things. He advises a range of corporate, investment bank and financial institutions.

Mr Saeed is a regular speaker at conferences on the specialist subjects of mergers and acquisitions, private equity and capital markets, both regionally and internationally. He also regularly features as a contributor to the press and leading trade publications on his areas of M&A expertise.

Mr Saeed received his LLB from the University of Punjab and studied for his LLM at The London School of Economics & Political Science. He has worked as a lawyer in Pakistan and Saudi Arabia with Hassan & Hassan (Advocates) and Al Tamimi & Company respectively, and has been a partner for 10 years.

Sonia A Salah
Associate, Al Tamimi & Company
s.salah@tamimi.com

Sonia Salah is an associate with Al Tamimi & Company at the Kuwait office. She has worked on a wide variety of matters, including transactional and advisory matters in the corporate/commercial advisory and finance departments. In her practice areas, she provides advice to local and international clients regarding commercial agencies, franchises, corporate structuring, dispute resolution, employment, taxation and settlements. She has also advised on due diligence inquiries, finance transactions and various Capital Markets Authority matters related to mergers and acquisitions, the offering of foreign securities and general regulatory compliance.

Prior to embarking on a career with Al Tamimi & Company, Ms Salah studied and practised law in the United States, where she was an associate editor and a note and comment editor for the *Wayne Law Review*.

Mohamed Zaanouni
Senior partner, Zaanouni Law Firm
zaanouni.mohamed@zaanounilawfirm.com

Mohamed Zaanouni has been a senior partner in Zaanouni Law Firm since 1996. He is one of the leading attorneys practising in Tunisia and at the international level. He was previously a foreign associate at Walter, Conston, Alexander and Green in New York and More, Fisher and Brown in London. He has extensive experience of representing international companies in corporate matters. His clients include developers, lessors, investors, corporations and creditors' committees.

Mr Zaanouni advises clients in Tunisia, the Maghreb region and other countries on the legal aspects of their business activities and compliance with Tunisian laws in connection with their activities.

In 2010, he was nominated as the chapter chair of the New York State Bar Association in Tunisia

In 2011, he become an attorney at the Supreme Court of Tunisia